TRICIA AND BOB HAYNE wrote the first edition of this guide and updated the next two editions.

From discovering the Buckinghamshire country-side, where they live, to navigating Hadrian's Wall and encircling the Isle of Wight, they enjoy exploring Britain the best way – on foot. Tricia was for many years editorial director of Bradt Travel Guides and is now a freelance travel writer. Along with researching and writing Bradt guides to the *Cayman Islands* and the *Turks and Caicos Islands*, she and Bob have co-authored their guide to *St Helena, Ascension and Tristan da Cunha*, and have helped to update several others in southern Africa.

BRYN THOMAS (right) rewalked and updat-ed this fifth edition. Born in Zimbabwe where he grew up on a farm, his travels have included a Saharan journey in a kit car he built himself, a solo 2500km cycle ride through the Andes as well as other cycle trips to Portugal and in Nepal, more than a dozen Himalayan treks and 50,000km of rail travel. He is the author of *Trans-Siberian Handbook* and *Trekking in the Annapurna Region*, and for several years worked for Lonely Planet on guides to India and Britain. In 1991 he set up Trailblazer to publish the series of route guides for independent travellers that has now grown to over 40 titles.

Authors

Cotswold Way First edition: 2009; this fifth edition: 2024

Publisher Trailblazer Publications
The Old Manse, Tower Rd, Hindhead, Surrey, GU26 6SU, UK ⬛ trailblazer-guides.com

British Library Cataloguing in Publication Data
A catalogue record for this book is available from the British Library

ISBN 978-1-912716-41-8

© **Trailblazer** 2009, 2012, 2016, 2019, 2024: Text and maps

Series Editor: Anna Jacomb-Hood
Editing and proofreading: Nicky Slade and Jane Thomas **Cartography**: Nick Hill
Layout: Bryn Thomas **Index**: Anna Jacomb-Hood
Photographs: © Bryn Thomas (unless otherwise indicated)

Dedication
In memory of Tricia's mum, Mollie

Acknowledgements
FROM BRYN: I'm grateful to everyone who helped with information and advice along the
way, in particular to hiking companions Hilary Bradt, Susanne Härtel, Lee Miller, (and for
photos), Kate and Richard Booth and Helga St Blaize for making a wonderful walk even
more enjoyable in their company. Thanks also to all those readers who've emailed with com-
ments and suggestions, in particular Mary Louise Adams, Kumi Anzalone, Michael Batty,
Stuart Blackburne, David Burgess, Ian Cairns, Julie Cocks, David Durrant, Hans & Liset
Frijters-Pollen, Tim Fuller, Marilyn Green & Larry Jones, Andrew Guppy, William Hardy,
Dave Howell, Jo Kelly, Pete Knox, Charlotte Langston, Brian Lynch, Doris McCormick,
Yuki Mikidorikawa, Ali Merifield, Justin Morgan, John Myerson, Patricia Pearl, Sarah
Peirce, Morten Planer, Mandy Pressland, John Schnake, Philip Scriver, Ian Solomon, Andy
Strickland, Ann Thomas, Linda Weatherley, Flemming & Mari-Ann Weigand, Marie
Williamson, Paul Woodland (for the photo of Tricia & Bob) and Andreas Wüthrich.

At Trailblazer, for additional research thanks to Nicky Slade and Anna Jacomb-Hood,
Nick Hill for the maps and Jane Thomas and Nicky Slade for editing and proofreading.

A request
The authors and publisher have tried to ensure that this guide is as accurate as possible.
Nevertheless, things change even on these well-worn routes. If you notice any changes or
omissions, please write to Trailblazer (address above) or email us at ⬛ info@trailblazer-
guides.com. A free copy of the next edition will be sent to persons making a significant con-
tribution.

Warning: long-distance walking can be dangerous

Please read the notes on when to go (pp13-16) and outdoor safety (p58). Every effort has
been made by the authors and publisher to ensure that the information contained herein is as
accurate and up to date as possible. However, they are unable to accept responsibility for any
inconvenience, loss or injury sustained by anyone as a result of the advice and information
given in this guide.

Photos – Front cover: Broadway Tower (see p84). **Previous page**: Crossing a field of oil-
seed rape (Map 2). **This page**: Fine views from Crickley Hill (Map16). **Overleaf**: A breezy
walk below Cleeve Hill on the path to Cheltenham (Map 11).

Updated information will be available on: ⬛ **trailblazer-guides.com**

Printed in China; print production by D'Print (☎ +65-6581 3832), Singapore

★ trailblazer

Cotswold Way

44 large-scale maps & guides to 48 towns and villages

PLANNING – PLACES TO STAY – PLACES TO EAT

CHIPPING CAMPDEN TO BATH

TRICIA & BOB HAYNE

FIFTH EDITION RESEARCHED AND UPDATED BY

BRYN THOMAS

TRAILBLAZER PUBLICATIONS

Contents

INTRODUCTION

Cotswold Way

PART 1: PLANNING YOUR WALK

Practical information for the walker

Budgeting 29

Itineraries

What to take

Getting to and from the Cotswold Way

PART 2: MINIMUM IMPACT & OUTDOOR SAFETY

Minimum-impact walking

Health and outdoor safety

PART 3: THE ENVIRONMENT & NATURE

Conserving the Cotswolds

Flora and fauna

PART 4: ROUTE GUIDE AND MAPS

Contents

ABOUT THIS BOOK

This guidebook contains all the information you need. The hard work has been done for you so you can plan your trip without having to consult numerous websites and other books and maps. When you're ready to go, there's comprehensive public transport information to get you to and from the trail and detailed maps (1:20,000) to help you find your way along it.

● Reviews of campsites, hostels, B&Bs, guesthouses and hotels
● Walking companies if you want an organised tour and baggage-transfer services if you just want your luggage carried
● Itineraries for all levels of walkers
● Answers to all your questions: when is the best time to walk, how hard is it, what to pack and the approximate cost of the trip
● Walking times in both directions; GPS waypoints as a back-up to navigation
● Cafés, pubs, tea-shops, restaurants, and shops/supermarkets along the route
● Rail, bus and taxi information for the towns and villages on or near the Way
● Street maps of the main towns and villages
● Historical, cultural and geographical background information

POST COVID NOTE

This edition of the guide was researched after the Covid pandemic but is liable to more change than usual. Some of the hotels, cafés, pubs, restaurants and tourist attractions may not survive the further hardships caused by rising fuel prices, inflation and staff shortages. Do forgive us where your experience on the ground contradicts what is written in the book; please email us – info@trailblazer-guides.com so we can add your information to the updates page on the website.

❑ MINIMUM IMPACT FOR MAXIMUM INSIGHT

Nature's peace will flow into you as the sunshine flows into trees. The winds will blow their freshness into you and storms their energy, while cares will drop off like autumn leaves. **John Muir** (one of the world's first and most influential environmentalists, born in 1838)

Why is walking in wild and solitary places so satisfying? Partly it is the sheer physical pleasure: sometimes pitting one's strength against the elements and the lie of the land. The beauty and wonder of the natural world and the fresh air restore our sense of proportion and the stresses and strains of everyday life slip away. Whatever the character of the countryside, walking in it benefits us mentally and physically, inducing a sense of well-being, an enrichment of life and an enhanced awareness of what lies around us. All this the countryside gives us and the least we can do is to safeguard it by supporting rural economies, local businesses, and low-impact methods of farming and land-management, and by using environmentally sensitive forms of transport – walking being pre-eminent.

INTRODUCTION

Asked to conjure up an image of a quintessential Cotswold scene, most people will come up with some combination of a village of honey-coloured houses set against a backdrop of sheep grazing in hillside fields, demarcated by seemingly endless dry-stone walls. For once, the reality and the picture-postcard image still coincide, at least in part. Nevertheless, to walk the Cotswold Way is to discover a far more complex – and arguably more rewarding – environment, where wide tracts of arable land unfold over the hills, and ancient beech woods line the Cotswold escarpment.

For once, the reality and the picture-postcard image still coincide...

With the Cotswold villages of tourist brochures along the early part of the route, and the architectural glories of Georgian Bath that await the walker in the south, it's soon clear that Cotswold limestone

There are numerous attractive pubs to delay you along the Way, such as this one in Broadway. Don't rush on! When planning your trip give yourself enough extra time to enjoy more than just the walking.

The northern end of the Cotswold Way, at Chipping Campden, is marked with a circular limestone plaque (see p80) beside Market Hall.

has been hugely influential in defining the landscape. As you head south, so the stone of the houses gradually fades, from Stanton's golden cottages to the palest ivory of Painswick's villas. Simple parish churches, towering follies and stately homes make their mark, too, all constructed of the same stone. Yet it's not just the stone that hints at the region's history. You won't get far without coming across any number of humps, lumps and bumps, relics of earlier inhabitants who left their mark in burial mounds, hill forts, monasteries and even villas right across the trail. Their chosen spots were often some of those most revered by today's walkers: wide-open expanses on windy hilltops with views west to the wide River Severn and the Malvern Hills.

Almost the entire trail runs through the Cotswolds Area of Outstanding Natural Beauty*

Almost the entire trail runs through the Cotswolds Area of Outstanding Natural Beauty (AONB*), crossing fields still bounded by hedges and walls, and hills where sheep have grazed for centuries. In the early years, merchants grew rich on the bounty that was sheep's wool, their fortunes invested in the foundation of towns from Chipping Campden to Dursley. Where grazing has ended, human intervention has ensured that at least some of the rich grassland can remain a haven for the wild flowers, birds and insects that previous generations took for granted.

Thoughtfully, the Cotswold Way crosses all these places – and perhaps that's the greatest advantage of a man-made trail. While earlier walkers must have taken a direct route on pilgrimage to the abbey at Hailes, today's hikers on the Cotswold Way find themselves twisting and turning along a trail that effectively showcases the very best that the region can offer. That that

* In late 2023 AONBs were renamed 'National Landscapes' but it will be some time before this new name is in widespread use.

Right: Broadway and the wide road that gave the village its name, is the quintessential Cotswold village of honey-coloured stone houses and cottages.

includes historic castles, more than a passing nod to the Arts and Crafts Movement, and some excellent pubs, is to the benefit of all.

History

HISTORY OF THE TRAIL

The Cotswold Way runs for 102 miles (163km) through the Cotswold Hills from Chipping Campden in the north to the Georgian city of Bath. The route was originally devised as a long-distance footpath by members of the Ramblers' Association (now called Ramblers) and was established in conjunction with the Cotswolds AONB in 1970.

At the southern end of the Way is a similar plaque, outside Bath Abbey. It can be hard to get that final photo with so many tourists here.

INTRODUCTION

Its development as a national trail was approved in 1998, but it was not until May 2007 that the trail was formally launched, one of just 15 in England and Wales at that time. During the transition, several changes were made to the route, and others are still in the offing, although for the most part the original paths remain open.

The path is the responsibility of the National Trail Officer, under the auspices of the Cotswold Way National Trail Office (see box p44).

GEOLOGY

Look at a geological map of England and it is immediately clear that the origins of the present-day Cotswolds lie in the Jurassic period. Such maps show a con-

Cotswold stone is an oolitic limestone ... formed in the shallow seas of the Jurassic

tinuous swathe of Jurassic-age rocks, formed between 199 and 145 million years ago, extending all the way from Dorset to the Yorkshire coast, with the most complete and impressive outcrop making up the Cotswold Hills. Cotswold stone is an oolitic limestone, a sedimentary rock that was formed primarily in the

© Tricia Hayne

❏ DRY-STONE WALLS

The dry-stone walls that are so evocative of the Cotswolds are created from irregularly shaped blocks of the local limestone. Deceptive in their simplicity, they require a considerable level of skill to build, with an expert able to complete around six or seven yards (6-7m) a day.

Some beds of Cotswold stone break down naturally into layers of around two or three inches (50-75mm) thick. Typically, the wall is created from two parallel lines of stone, gradually coming together as they near the top. Stones on each side of the wall are fitted together like a jigsaw, laid sloping outwards to draw water away from the centre. Smaller pieces of stone, and offcuts, are used to fill the central cavities, adding strength and durability to the whole wall.

warm shallow seas of the Jurassic. It is comprised of a large number of almost spherical granules, or oolites, packed closely together, and its origins explain the regular occurrence in the rock of fossils, such as sea urchins. Occasional falls in sea level, however, resulted in dry land where dinosaurs roamed, leaving behind both their footprints and their bones. While most walkers will see little difference between the rocks at various places along the trail, to the geologist there are marked distinctions according to the stages at which the sediments were deposited and compressed. In addition, while the surface rock of the Cotswold range is predominantly limestone, the underlying structure is more usually of clays, silts and sands. It is the precise structure of these rocks that both determines the wildlife that populates the hillside and influences the buildings you will see in each part of the region.

Gloucestershire Geology Trust (🖥 glosgeotrust.org.uk) is committed to studying and conserving the region's geological heritage, and to recording regionally important geological sites. The trust publishes a series of trail guides entitled *Gloucestershire Uncovered*, which include Cleeve Hill Common, Leckhampton Hill and Crickley Hill.

Finally, a layer of slats, or 'combers', is laid along the top at right angles to the wall. The whole is usually around 3ft (1m) high, and some 20in (50cm) at the base, tapering to around 16in (40cm) at the top.

It is estimated that there are some 4000 miles (6000km) of dry-stone walls across the whole of the Cotswolds AONB. Weather, vegetation and accidents take their toll, so regular maintenance is essential. As a result of a revival of interest in traditional crafts, it is possible to go on a course to learn the basics, or to take part as a volunteer to help preserve the region's existing walls. For more information, contact Cotswolds Conservation Board (who run Cotswolds AONB, see p60) or the Dry Stone Walling Association of Great Britain (🖥 www.dswa.org.uk).

© Henry Stedman

How difficult is the path?

Familiarity with the Cotswolds – or at least with the tourist areas in the north – might lead to a sense that the Cotswold Way is little more than a walk in the park. While it would be unreasonable to suggest that it is seriously challenging, it would be equally wrong to underestimate the quite literal ups and downs of a route that takes you from just above sea level to 1066ft (325m) and back over a distance of more than 100 miles.

If, as is often suggested, you plan to complete the route in seven days, you're looking at an average of nearly 15 miles, or 6-7 hours' actual walking, every day. Some of those hills are steeper than you might expect from a casual glance at the landscape and poor weather can exacerbate what would otherwise be fairly straightforward. It makes sense, then, to have a reasonable level of fitness before you set off, if only to make sure that what should be an enjoyable week or so's walking doesn't turn into a test of endurance.

Below: Approaching the (almost) halfway marker outside Painswick. The path is not difficult and the route is well signposted so you shouldn't get lost; look for the acorn logo.

INTRODUCTION

How long do you need?

This is the great imponderable. Is it reasonable – as many hikers do – to walk the path from end to end in a week? Well yes, but it's a qualified yes. If you have just seven days' holiday but need two of those to get to and from the trail, you'll be faced with walking 20 miles a day, which isn't for the faint hearted. If, on the other hand, you can spend most of those seven days on the trail, a week is realistic. That said, averaging almost 15 miles a day won't leave much time for exploring the villages on the route, taking time out for a cream tea in Broadway, or a pint of Donnington's at The Mount Inn in Stanton, or exploring

So while the world reckons that this is a week's walk, give it eight days and you'll be adding in time to breathe

Selsley Common for orchids. You might find yourself casting a wistful backward glance at old churches as you march purposefully past the lych gate, or promising yourself you'll come back to do justice to Hailes Abbey, or Dyrham Park, or even to Bath. So while the world reckons that this is a week's walk, give it eight days and you'll be adding in time to breathe.

If time is really short, you could reasonably leave out the last section, perhaps south of Cold Ashton and down Lansdown Hill into Bath (pp161-5). That isn't to say this isn't worthy of walking – far from it. But Bath is a destination in its own right, so the chances are that you could justify returning on another occasion.

See p33 for some suggested itineraries covering different walking speeds

Plenty of people can't spare the time to walk from end to end in one go, but still get that sense of achievement by building up the miles over a series of day or weekend walks until they've completed the route. Alternatively, you could simply sample the highlights (though lowlights are few); see pp36-7 for some recommendations.

When to go

SEASONS

Autumn that name of creeper falling and tea-time loving,
Was once for me the thought of High Cotswold noon-air   **Ivor Gurney**, *Old Thought*

While English weather is hardly predictable, at least some generalisations can be made. Statistically, the months when the weather is least likely to be inclement are May to September, but statistics – as we all know – can be very misleading. The air temperature at this time is generally at its warmest, with frosts unlikely from the end of May. Rain, though, is another factor. Some years can see contin-

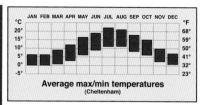

Average max/min temperatures
(Cheltenham)

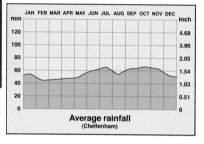

Average rainfall
(Cheltenham)

uous rain for several weeks and parts of the path will become impassable. While it's tempting to think that this is only likely to happen in winter, the last widespread flooding in Gloucestershire was in the summer of 2007, with 2008 running a close second. Conversely, April and October often bring days that are bright and breezy, when the walking and the surroundings are at their best.

Spring

The weather in spring is as unpredictable as the rest of the year. In **April**, it can be warm and sunny on odd days, but seldom for sustained periods. Conditions are more likely to be changeable, with blustery showers and cold spells reminding you that winter has only just passed. On the other hand, the days are long, and less rain falls on average in spring than at any other time of the year. This, coupled with the milder weather of **May** and **June**, and the proliferation of wild flowers early in the year, makes it one of the best times to tackle the trail.

Summer

July and **August** are the traditional holiday months and the conditions can be especially good for walking, with generally mild temperatures and still many hours of daylight. This, however, is also the time when the Cotswolds experience a surge in visitors, especially around the tourist honeypots of Broadway and Bath. Fortunately, most of the trippers won't be out in the fields and on the hills, so here at least you can leave the hordes behind.

Autumn

Many connoisseurs consider autumn, especially early autumn, the best time of year for walking. **September** and **October** can be lovely months to get out on the trail, especially when the leaves begin to turn. That said, although the air temperature usually remains relatively mild, October can see the first frosts and rain is an ever-present threat.

Winter

Only the very hardiest of souls will attempt the Cotswold Way in winter. There is less daylight; once the clocks have gone back at the end of October, until mid March, you will need to be at your destination by 4.30-5pm to avoid walking in the dark. Cold weather, wind and driving rain are not the best recipe for a day's walking, although a crisp winter morning takes a lot of beating.

DAYLIGHT HOURS

If you're planning to walk in autumn, winter or early spring, you'll need to take into account how far you can walk in the available daylight. It won't be possible to be out for as long as you would in the summer. The table gives the sunrise and sunset times for the middle of each month at latitude 52° North, which runs through the Cotswold Hills, giving a reasonably accurate picture for daylight

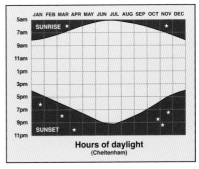

Hours of daylight
(Cheltenham)

along the Cotswold Way. Depending on the weather, you should get a further 30-45 minutes of usable light before sunrise and after sunset.

❏ FESTIVALS AND ANNUAL EVENTS

The following events may need to be considered when planning your walk since all will affect the availability and sometimes price of accommodation in their area. Two with a particularly strong impact locally are The Festival in Cheltenham in March, and Badminton Horse Trials in May.

In addition to the following annual fixtures, be aware that weekend events held by the **Prescott Speed Hill Climb** (🖥 prescotthillclimb.co.uk) outside Winchcombe between about April and October can put a lot of pressure on the town's resources.

March
● **The Cheltenham Festival** (🖥 thejockeyclub.co.uk) is the best known race meeting in the National Hunt racing calendar and is held over four days in mid March. It's also one of the racing calendar's highlights – both in racing terms and socially – culminating in every jump jockey's dream, the Cheltenham Gold Cup. Tickets are hard sought after and accommodation throughout the area is often booked a year ahead. If you have no choice but to walk in this week, make sure you plan well ahead.

April/May
● **Wotton-under-Edge Arts Festival** (🖥 utea.org.uk) This 2-week festival usually takes place around the end of April and early May.
● **Cheltenham Jazz Festival** (🖥 cheltenhamfestivals.com/jazz) A week of jazz is celebrated early May.
● **Annual Cheese Rolling** – Cooper's Hill There's still strong support for this wacky village event, traditionally held on the last May Bank Holiday Monday; see box p117.
● **Badminton Horse Trials** (🖥 badminton-horse.co.uk) Hugely important among the riding fraternity, this 5-day trial takes place east of the trail near Old Sodbury in early May. Accommodation is limited in this area, and guesthouses, pubs and hotels for miles around get prebooked months in advance: you've been warned!
● **The Bath Festival** (🖥 bathfestivals.org.uk/the-bath-festival) Taking place from the middle of May, this 10-day festival showcases music and literature.
● **Chipping Campden Music Festival** (🖥 campdenmayfestivals.co.uk) A 2-week festival of classical music, held in mid to late May and based in St James's Church.
(*cont'd overleaf*)

❏ FESTIVALS AND ANNUAL EVENTS

May (*cont'd from p15*)

● **Olimpick Games**, Dover's Hill, Chipping Campden (🖳 olimpickgames.co.uk) Friday after the last May Bank Holiday, followed the next day by the Scuttlebrook Wake; see box p80.

● **Winchcombe Walking Festival** (🖳 winchcombewelcomeswalkers.com) A series of graded walks and evening events taking place over a weekend in May.

June

● **Wotton Walking Festival** (🖳 wottonwalkingfestival.com) A three-day festival (held early in June) focusing on walks around the town.

● **Cheltenham Science Festival** (🖳 cheltenhamfestivals.com/science) Held over six days in early to mid June.

● **Cheltenham Food and Drink Festival** (🖳 cheltenhamfooddrinkfestivals) Three days of foodie heaven in Montpellier Gardens; mid June.

● **Cotswold Way Relay** (🖳 cotswoldwayrelay.co.uk) It might be best to avoid walking on the last Saturday in June, or first in July. For details, see box p31.

● **Winchcombe Festival of Music & Arts** (🖳 musicandartswinchcombe.co.uk) A week-long celebration of local talent held at the end of June.

July

● **Nibley Festival** (🖳 nibleyfestival.co.uk) Not-for-profit three-day festival held in early July with music, food and entertainment for all the family.

● **Cheltenham Music Festival** (🖳 cheltenhamfestivals.com/music) Popular eight-day festival in early July with international artists playing an eclectic mix of primarily classical music.

● **Cotswold Beer Festival** (🖳 postlip.camra.org.uk) One of CAMRA's national beer festivals, usually held at Postlip Hall outside Winchcombe over the penultimate or last weekend in July.

● **Cheltenham Cricket Festival** (🖳 gloscricket.co.uk/cheltenham-cricket-festival) Founded in 1872, the 2-week festival is held in the grounds of Cheltenham College around the end of July/early August.

August

● **Frocester Festival** (🖳 frocesterfestival.com) Two days of beer tasting, music and camaraderie, held near Stonehouse; August Bank Holiday weekend.

September

● **Painswick Feast** (🖳 visitstroud.uk/painswick-feast) A bizarre ancient festival that was incorporated into the church calendar and involves dancing round the church-yard, singing the 'clypping song' and then partaking of 'puppydog pie' (now made using beef, you'll be glad to hear); on a Sunday in late September.

October

● **Cheltenham Literature Festival** (🖳 cheltenhamfestivals.com/literature) This 10-day festival in mid October goes from strength to strength, showcasing a range of international authors.

● **Dursley Walking Festival** (🖳 dursleywelcomeswalkers.org.uk) A 4-day festival (held early in October) focusing on walks around the little town of Dursley.

(**Opposite**) The path is generally in good condition, with some sections such as this climb up Charlton Kings Common (Map 14) towards Leckhampton Hill having recently been improved and resurfaced. There are wide views from here across Cheltenham and beyond.

Bath's grand Royal Crescent (**above**) greets the walker on the final stretch of the Way. One of the best examples of Georgian architecture in Britain, it was completed in 1774. There are several other magnificent Georgian crescents in the city, including Lansdown Crescent (**below**) and The Circus (**below left**).

The Tyndale Monument (see p143) offers sweeping views across the Cotswolds landscape and it's well worth climbing the 121 steps to the top.

PLANNING YOUR WALK

1

Practical information for the walker

ROUTE FINDING

Established more than 50 years ago, it's no surprise that the Cotswold Way is clearly signposted along almost its entire length. Indeed, more than one website claims that the Cotswold Way is the most signposted of all the national trails. Be that as it may, there are a few occasions – usually in a field or a wood – where there may be some ambiguity, though in these instances the maps in this guide should quickly put you straight.

The waymark throughout the walk is the National Trails' acorn symbol, to be found on stiles, kissing gates, fingerposts and guideposts. Sometimes as an alternative you will find the standard yellow or blue footpath or bridlepath roundel overprinted with the words 'Cotswold Way', and the authorities in Bath have devised more discreet signs, sometimes a small metallic acorn on a black background, supplemented by stickers on lamp-posts and other street furniture.

GPS on your smart phone

These days individuals who don't routinely clutch a **smart phone** every waking hour are regarded as eccentric. But not all devoted users appreciate that a modern mobile can receive a **GPS** signal from space as well as estimate your position often as accurately using **mobile data** signals from hilltop masts. These signals are two different things: GPS comes free from American, Russian or European satellites and is everywhere all the time but works best outdoors. Much stronger 4- or 5G mobile signals beam off towers up to 40 miles away and are what you pay the phone company for.

Accessing an online map with mobile data (internet via your phone signal, not wi-fi), your position can be pinpointed with great accuracy. But with no signal – as is the case in Britain's remoter regions – your phone will use GPS to display your position as a dot on the screen. Except that, *unless you import a map into your phone's internal storage* (which may require an app and even a small financial outlay), without a signal the kilobit-sized 'tiles' which make up a **zoomable online map** cannot be downloaded. The internet browser's cache may retain a few tiles until the signal resumes or until you walk off that tile's coverage. Much will depend on your service provider.

The best way to use your mobile as an accurate navigation aid is to **download a mapping app plus maps covering the route** (see box p42). That will work with GPS where there is no phone signal. The online map which shows the Cotswold Way most accurately and consistently is the well-known OS 1:25k Explorer series. Pre-digital era hikers won't need persuading of OS maps' readability and reliability. On these maps, National Trails are marked as three green dashes then a green diamond, plus a 'Cotswold Way' every once in a while. Ideally, your on-screen location dot is pulsing right on that track. Currently, the **OS Maps app** (🖳 shop.ordnancesurvey.co.uk/apps) costs just £4.99 for a month – less than a single OS paper map. By the year it's much cheaper.

Although there are free online maps and mapping apps, they don't have the same reliability and might have adverts, or full functionality disabled until you cough up some money. On some of these apps the Cotswold Way is shown but not always identified alongside other adjacent paths and tracks, and so downloading a tracklog and our waypoints (see below) may clarify the way ahead.

When considering whether or not to use satellite navigation on your phone, one thing to note is that it may **drain battery power faster than usual**. Having the phone on standby and minimal other apps working will maximise your battery life, but obviously carrying a back-up power bank makes sense.

Tracklogs

A **tracklog** is a continuous winding line marking the walk from end to end, displayed on your screen; all you have to do is keep on that line. If you lose it on the screen you can zoom out until it reappears and walk towards it. A tracklog can be traced with a mouse off a digital map, or recorded live using a GPS enabled device. When recorded live, tracklogs are actually hundreds of waypoints separated by intervals of either time or more usefully distance (say, around 10 metres). Some smartphones or mapping apps can't display a tracklog with over 500 points so they get truncated into fewer straight lines, resulting in some loss in precision.

National Trails have a free tracklog at 🖳 nationaltrail.co.uk/en_GB/trails – look for 'GPX downloads'.

Waypoints and what3words

Besides those navigation options, this book offers an additional one. The maps in the book all feature at least one numbered **waypoint**, marked directly onto the map. Where a tracklog is a continuous line, waypoints are single points like cairns. These waypoints correlate to the list on pp183-4 which gives the grid reference and description. For these waypoints we've now also listed the three-word geocode used by **what3words** (🖳 what3words.com, p57 and pp183-4) which could be useful in an emergency.

You can either manually key the nearest presumed waypoint from the list at the back of this book into your phone/GPS (a process prone to user errors), or just download the list for free at 🖳 trailblazer-guides.com/gps-waypoints.

In summary

Stepping back a bit, we're on the Cotswold Way, not the Tibetan plateau, so in clear conditions you'll rarely need to refer to your phone for navigation. By and large the waymarking is crystal clear; often so is the track below your feet, and this book's hand-drawn maps show what lies ahead. It's worth repeating that the vast majority of people who tackle the Cotswold Way do so perfectly successfully without GPS.

Whatever your navigation method, it does pay to **regularly keep track of your position** so when you go wrong you can tell where you've veered off. You're most likely to make a mistake due to fallen or otherwise obscured posts or waymarkers, or while chatting away. Backtracking usually solves that.

ACCOMMODATION

The Cotswold Way is generally well served with bed-and-breakfast (B&B), guesthouse and pub accommodation, but there are one or two places, particularly between the Cheltenham area and Dursley, where the options are quite limited and you may be faced with up to a mile further at the end of the day's walk. That said, most places listed in this guide are either on or within easy reach of the trail. Campers, though, will find themselves with quite a challenge and may have to combine camping with the odd night at a B&B. A comprehensive selection of places to stay is given in each section of the route guide (Part 4), though do bear in mind that even the most long-standing establishments can change hands, or close, without warning.

Camping

There are few official campsites along the Cotswold Way and some sites are more for motorhomes. Rates for camping range from £5-15 per person per night.

Wild camping is not permitted anywhere, which is no help to those who prefer the great outdoors to a B&B. It may be worth asking at a farm along the route if you can pitch a tent in a field. Farmers used to be more amenable to the odd inconspicuous tent but attitudes have changed.

A few people 'stealth camp' though you won't spot them if they're doing it right! For ideas and a recent experience see 🖥 10milehike.com; Stephie's a professional at this.

Glamping

The craze for **glamping** continues – where you're provided with a posh tent (often a bell tent or yurt) fitted out with rugs, furniture and a proper bed to sleep in. There are also some **shepherd's huts** along the trail that can be used by walkers for accommodation. Smartly furnished and very cosy, these huts aren't cheap at around £40-60pp.

You'll also find a cheaper form of glamping: **camping pods**, which are basic but comfortable sleeping sheds, usually simply furnished with a table and sleeping platform, though you'll often have to have your own bedding/sleeping bag. Prices vary widely but the better ones are around the £30-40pp mark.

Hostels

Hostel accommodation along the Cotswold Way itself is available only in Bath, where there are three hostels; two independent and a YHA hostel. The latter, where accommodation discounts are available to members of the Youth Hostels Association (YHA; ☎ 01629-592700, or tollfree ☎ 0800 019 1700, 🖳 yha.org.uk) and **Hostelling International** (🖳 hihostels.com), is a good mile east of the centre, so a fair trek for walkers. For membership details see the YHA website.

B&B-style accommodation

Although historically there is a distinct difference between a guesthouse and the more personal B&B, the edges are becoming increasingly blurred. Traditionally, those staying in a B&B, where overnight visitors are limited to no more than six at any one time, will find themselves very much as guests in a private house. Establishments accommodating greater numbers have to be registered as a guesthouse.

Staying in **B&Bs** brings you into contact with local people in a way that guesthouses and hotels can't. For anyone unfamiliar with the concept, you get a bedroom in someone's home along with a cooked breakfast the following morning. The accommodation is invariably clean and comfortable, traditionally with the emphasis on floral patterns and chintz – although things are changing fast and rooms in many B&Bs along the Cotswold Way compete with the best for style and elegance. If one night you find yourself in a modern bungalow, the next could be in a picture-perfect cottage, or on a working farm.

Guesthouses, which effectively bridge the gap between B&Bs and hotels, may be more structured in approach – although in reality, especially in some of the towns along the trail, you may have no idea whether you're in a B&B or a guesthouse. What matters is a warm welcome, a comfortable room, and – ideally – someone who understands that walkers tend to have muddy boots and wet clothes.

Where visitor numbers are high, such as in Bath or Broadway, you may well find that a minimum two-night stay is imposed, which can cause problems for walkers. Others simply charge a higher rate for one-nighters. Such restrictions are most likely to be the case at weekends or in the height of the tourist season.

What to expect For most long-distance walkers, tourist-board star-rating systems have little meaning. At the end of a long day you'll simply be glad of a place with hot water and a smiling welcome. It is these criteria that have been used for places included in this guide, rather than whether a room has tea- and coffee-making facilities and a TV – though almost all do. In the trend towards making rooms **en suite**, many places have carved out a tiny area for a shower and a loo. Yet a larger room with a bathroom across the corridor, often for your own private use, could well be preferable – and the option of a hot bath has significant appeal if you're cold and wet; establishments with at least one bath in, or for, a room are indicated in this guide with a ▼ symbol.

Finding anywhere with a **single** room isn't easy and those there are tend to be pretty small. A **double** room is supposed to have one double bed, and a **twin** room two singles, but sometimes the two are interchangeable, allowing greater flexibility. Some places have rooms that can sleep three (**triple**), four (**quad**) or more – these rooms come in a variety of arrangements (see p74) but can also always sleep just two people.

Some B&Bs and guesthouses have a **sitting room** exclusively for guests' use, a real bonus at the end of a day when retiring to your room instead of relaxing in a comfy chair can seem something of an anti-climax. Others will welcome guests to sit out in the **garden** on a summer's evening.

An **evening meal** is sometimes on offer at the more isolated establishments, though you should always pre-book this or you could go hungry. If you're expecting a meal, but are delayed, do ring ahead. Nobody wants to serve (or eat) dried-up lasagne and limp salad. If meals are not available, many owners will offer you a lift to the nearest pub if it's too far to walk.

Rates The image of B&B as a cheap option is no longer valid; costs have soared in recent years. Expect to pay £45-75pp per night based on two sharing a room; for single occupancy you may need to pay £60-100, and often the full room rate. See box above and p30.

Transport Where places offering accommodation are not right on the Cotswold Way, B&B owners may offer to collect walkers at an agreed rendezvous point and deliver them back to the trail next day. It's a service that is usually provided free of charge, but do check first. It is important to agree lift arrangements at the time of booking and, if possible, to phone ahead to warn of your impending arrival at the pick-up point – or of any delays, of course. If the B&B doesn't offer an evening meal and is in a remote location, they may offer you a lift to a local pub or town for dinner.

Pubs Many pubs offer B&B accommodation and some supply every modern convenience – including luxuries such as four-poster beds. Obviously they tend to be less personal than B&Bs, but for some walkers that's a bonus – and you don't have far to go to the bar, either. Of greater concern for most people is that pubs can be quite noisy, especially at weekends, so bear this in mind if you fancy an early night. In general, pub prices along the Cotswold Way are similar to those at B&Bs (see p23).

Hotels

Hotels are usually less well equipped for walkers and the higher rates (from £100pp for two sharing) may put off the cash-conscious traveller. During festivals or at similar times rates can be extortionate. However, there are some good-value places to stay and you may well want to treat yourself in the course of your trip, particularly since there are some wonderful hostelries along the route.

Airbnb and holiday cottages

The rise and rise of **Airbnb** (🖳 airbnb.co.uk) has seen private homes and apartments opened up to overnight travellers on an informal basis. Because contact details and even locations are hidden and property details vague, we don't include them in this guide, though many of the lodgings we do list are also on Airbnb.

Airbnb was originally intended to offer 'unique stays and experiences' for guests to connect with locals and communities. While this is still the case for some listings, you might also find anything from luxury self-catering apartments, with no local host in sight, to rooms in a pub and rates may or may not include breakfast.

Remember that Airbnbs aren't all officially registered or accredited so standards (and prices) may vary widely. The best are indistinguishable from a regular B&B and will offer evening meals as well as packed lunches. The key to success is to read the listing details carefully so you are clear what is on offer and to message the property owner before booking if you need to clarify anything.

Likewise, the inclusion of **holiday cottages** is outside the scope of a guide dedicated to walkers on the move but they may be the perfect option for those who would prefer to stay at a fixed base, doing daily walks on the Cotswold Way. Try 🖳 holidaycottages.co.uk or 🖳 homeaway.co.uk. If you're after something more individual, you could try one of the properties owned by the Landmark Trust (see p62).

If you're travelling with a group of friends, one way of walking the Cotswold Way and saving money is to book a self-catering Airbnb or a holiday cottage for a few days at a time. You'll need two cars for this so you can park one at the end of the day's walk. If you rent one place at the beginning of the trail, one at the end and a couple strategically-placed along the way this will minimise the driving to get back each evening.

FOOD AND DRINK

In Bath you'll come across a few regional specialities (see box on p178), but elsewhere savvy travellers seek out the delights of Old Spot pork, Cotswold honey, or Double Gloucester cheese. Tea rooms do a fine trade in cream teas, too, though it would be stretching a point to suggest that this is typical of the region.

❏ REAL ALE ALONG THE TRAIL

Much of the beer found in pubs along the path is pasteurised and manufactured in millions of gallons for distribution throughout the UK. Known as 'keg beer', it has been reviled by real ale drinkers in its time but is invariably smooth and tastes the same wherever you are. However, traditional real ale, the product of small-scale local breweries, is always in demand. Real ale continues to ferment in the cask so can be drawn off by hand pump or a simple tap on the cask itself. Keg beer, on the other hand, has the fermentation process stopped by pasteurisation and needs the addition of gas to give it fizz and sparkle.

Keep an eye out for pubs displaying the CAMRA sticker, which shows they have been selected by the **Campaign for Real Ale** (🖳 camra.org.uk). This invaluable organisation, which publishes the annual *Good Beer Guide*, has been largely responsible for the revival of independent breweries in the UK. Their 'LocAle' initiative encourages pubs to stock at least one locally brewed ale and has been taken up by an increasing number of landlords along the trail. Many also have a selection of guest ales from surrounding counties to add variety. Some of the local brews you'll find along the Cotswold Way are those by: **Abbey Ales** (🖳 abbeyales.co.uk), **Bath Ales** (🖳 bathales.com), **Blindmans Brewery** (🖳 blindmansbrewery.co.uk), **Butcombe** (🖳 butcombe.com), **Donnington** (🖳 donnington-brewery.com), **North Cotswold Brewery** (🖳 northcotswoldbrewery.co.uk), **Purity** (🖳 puritybrewing.com), **Stanway** (🖳 stanwaybrewery.co.uk), **Stroud** (🖳 stroudbrewery.co.uk) and **Uley** (🖳 uleybrewery.com). You'll come across offerings from the Hereford-based **Wye Valley Brewery** (🖳 wyevalleybrewery.co.uk), too, while the Cornish contingent is represented by **Sharp's** (🖳 sharpsbrewery.co.uk). All create good pints, but try the brews above 4% ABV for better taste and flavour.

Whether you're after a quick half at lunch or putting your feet up in the evening, there's no shortage of pubs with good-quality beer. Scanning the pumps at the *Crown & Trumpet* (see p86) in **Broadway** you'll spot ales from the North Cotswold Brewery and the Stanway Brewery. Broadway comes up trumps at the *Horse & Hound* (p86) too, where you could strike lucky with a pint of Purity's Mad Goose.

An evening meal at *The Mount Inn* (see p90) at **Stanton** washed down with a pint of Donnington's is hard to beat. While wandering around **Painswick**, drop into the *Royal Oak* (see p126) for a selection from the Stroud (organic beer) brewery. If you time it right a lunch break at *The Edgemoor Inn* (see p128), at **Edge**, offers Uley's Old Spot amongst others, or their latest bottled ale – Cotswold Way. Well worth a short detour is *The Old Crown* (see p134) at **Uley** which, as well as supporting its own local brewery, offers an ever-changing choice of other beers including Wye Valley HPA; if it all gets too much you can stay overnight, too.

Further south you arrive at ale-seekers' heaven, *The Old Spot* (see p140) in **Dursley**, voted CAMRA Pub of the Year in 2007, and still maintaining high standards. It offers a wonderful array of bitters, including Old Ric from Uley Brewery (named after owner Ric Sainty, who died in 2008). *Beaufort Arms* (see p152) at **Hawkesbury Upton** serves Butcombe Original amongst others; continuing along the trail, *The Dog Inn* (see p154) at **Old Sodbury** has Wye Valley HPA and Sharp's Doom Bar.

Celebrations should be in order on reaching **Bath** (see p181), where you'll be spoiled for choice. Try *The Star Inn* for a pint of Bellringer (Abbey Ales), *The Old Green Tree* for Blindmans Green Tree Bitter or seek out a pint of Gem (Bath Ales) at *The Salamander*. The *Volunteer Rifleman's Arms* is another good choice, but the medal winner is arguably to be found at *The Raven*, where they have their very own brews from Blindmans Brewery: Raven Gold and Raven Ale. They won Branch Pub of the Year in 2023.

Breakfast and lunch

A **breakfast** fry-up of bacon, eggs and sausages is considered *de rigueur* by many walkers – and supplied by nearly all good B&B hosts. Most offer a buffet of cereals and fruit juice and toast as well, perhaps with the addition of yoghurt and fresh fruit, so if a 'full English' isn't for you, you'll always be able to fall back on something lighter.

Unless you're planning to stop at a pub or café en route, you will probably need a **packed lunch**. Many B&B owners – indicated in this guide by the (Ⓛ) symbol – will provide one and some will also fill your flask with coffee or tea. If you don't fancy breakfast, it's worth asking if you could have a packed lunch instead. Alternatively you could pick up the makings of a picnic lunch at village shops along the trail: rolls, cheese, apples and cereal bars survive well in a rucksack for a couple of days. Plan ahead, though, as there are sections of the walk when you won't come across any shops at all. In any event, you should always carry some form of high-energy food in case of an emergency (see p40).

Evening meals

Perhaps more than any other national trail, the Cotswold Way is abundantly supplied with **pubs** and **inns**, not to mention some pretty exclusive – and expensive – **restaurants**. Where B&Bs are off the beaten track, most owners will provide an evening meal by prior arrangement, or will drive you to the nearest pub. Occasionally, however, you'll have to fend for yourself, which could involve considerable extra mileage at the end of a long day.

Aside from the ubiquitous pub grub, the choice on menus is varied usually with several vegan or vegetarian options. If you're keeping a strict eye on costs, stick to pubs rather than restaurants, or look for fixed-price menus – often available early in the evening.

Alternatively, there are numerous **takeaways** in towns along the route, from fish & chips, pizza parlours and kebab joints to Indian and Chinese cuisine.

Self-catering

There are enough shops along the path to allow you to buy supplies reasonably frequently so, in general, you should not need to carry food for longer than a couple of days. Most supermarkets are open seven days a week, often from 8am to 8pm or even later, taking full advantage of casual trade and the sale of alcohol. Village shops and independent places such as bakeries are open more limited hours.

Though expensive, there's something to be said for carrying a couple of lightweight, high-calorie freeze-dried backpackers' meals along with the means to boil water or a flask filled up that morning. A flask may not be such a bad idea as fuel for camp stoves may not always be available though, and, while Camping Gaz and meths can usually be found in the towns, it makes sense not to let supplies run low.

Drinking water

Carry at least a litre of water and top it up at public toilets during the day: these are marked on the trail maps in Part 4. Alternatively, ask locally; most people are happy to fill a bottle of water, though it's only fair to buy something first in a pub or café. Drinking from streams is not advisable.

MONEY

The pandemic saw the old-guard – both vendor and customer – plunge headfirst into **cashless transactions** so that these days B&Bs – like shops, pubs and restaurants – can be paid by debit or credit cards or via PayPal on the spot. But there's still a place for cash, so bring about £100 and replenish from supermarket **ATMs** in towns. As elsewhere, banks are becoming harder to find but cash can also be drawn at **village post offices** with a debit card. For further details see 🖳 postoffice.co.uk (Products & Services; then Branch & banking services). To find a post office with an ATM look at postoffice.co.uk/atm-locator.

For more on money, see p41; for budgeting, see pp29-30.

OTHER SERVICES

Many of the villages and all the towns along the trail have a small **shop** and a **post office**, or a post office counter. Apart from getting cash, post offices are also handy for sending home unnecessary equipment that may be weighing you down. In Part 4 mention is given to other services that may be of use to the walker such as **outdoor equipment shops**, **surgeries** (medical centres) and **pharmacies**, and **tourist information centres**. Most pubs, cafés, hotels and B&Bs have **wi-fi** so you shouldn't have a problem getting connected.

TAKING DOGS ALONG THE COTSWOLD WAY

There is no reason why your dog shouldn't accompany you on the Cotswold Way, provided you act responsibly and keep it under control at all times. The deal with dog mess is the same on a national trail as it is in the local park: clear it up. In Part 4 of this guide, the symbol 🐕 indicates that dogs are usually welcome, though you should still always check ahead; some may accept only small dogs, for example. Also note that dogs may have to be on a lead especially at campsites and in pubs/cafés. Not all B&Bs charge for dogs but hotels often do, with rates varying from £5 a night to £20 per stay. Hostels generally don't accept dogs at all, with the exception of assistance dogs.

For more on planning a walk with man's best friend, see pp184-6.

DISABLED ACCESS

Many areas of the trail are inaccessible to the majority of wheelchair and scooter users, and those of limited mobility, either because the terrain is unsuitable or because of the not inconsiderable number of kissing gates to be negotiated. Some sections, however, are more forgiving – particularly near country parks which also have nearby parking.

For more on countryside access for the disabled, contact Disabled Ramblers (🖳 disabledramblers.co.uk).

WALKING COMPANIES

For walkers wanting to make their holiday as easy and trouble-free as possible there are several specialist companies offering a range of services, from baggage carrying to fully guided group tours.

Baggage transfer/accommodation booking

The thought of carrying a heavy pack puts a lot of people off walking long-distance trails, but on the Cotswold Way it need not be an issue.

❏ INFORMATION FOR FOREIGN VISITORS

● **Currency** The British pound (£) comes in notes of £50, £20, £10 and £5, and coins of £2 and £1. The pound is divided into 100 pence (usually referred to as 'p', pronounced 'pee') which come in silver coins of 50p, 20p 10p and 5p and copper coins of 2p and 1p.

● **Rates of exchange** Up-to-date rates can be found at 🖳 xe.com/currencyconverter and at some post offices, or at any bank or travel agent.

● **Business hours** Most **village shops** are open Monday to Friday 9am-5pm and Saturday 9am-12.30pm, though some open as early as 7.30/8am; many also open on Sundays but not usually for the whole day. Occasionally you'll come across a local shop that closes at lunchtime on one day during the week, usually a Wednesday or Thursday; this is a throwback to the days when all towns and villages had an 'early closing day'. **Supermarkets** are open Monday to Saturday 8am-8pm (often longer) and on Sunday from about 9am to 5 or 6pm, though main branches of supermarkets generally open 10am-4pm or 11am-5pm.

Main **post offices** generally open Monday to Friday 9am-5pm and Saturday 9am-12.30pm; **banks** typically open at 9.30/10am Monday to Friday and close at 3.30/4pm, though in some places both post offices and banks may open only two or three days a week and/or in the morning, or limited hours, only. **ATMs (cash machines)** located outside a bank, shop, post office or petrol station are open all the time, but any that are inside will be accessible only when that place is open. However, ones that charge, such as Link machines, may not accept foreign-issued cards.

Pub hours are less predictable as each pub may have different opening hours. However, most pubs on the Cotswold Way continue to follow the traditional hours (Monday to Saturday 11am to 11pm, Sunday to 10.30pm), but some still close in the afternoon especially during the week and in the winter months.

The last entry time to most **museums and galleries** is usually half an hour, or an hour, before the official closing time.

● **National (Bank) holidays** Most businesses are shut on 1 January, Good Friday (March/April), Easter Monday (March/April), the first and last Monday in May, the last Monday in August, 25 December and 26 December.

● **School holidays** School holiday periods in England are generally as follows: a one-week break late October, two weeks around Christmas, a week mid-February, two weeks around Easter, a week in late May and from late July to early September.

● **Documents** If you are a member of a National Trust organisation in your country bring your membership card as you should be entitled to free entry to National Trust properties and sites in the UK.

● **Travel/medical insurance** Although Britain's National Health Service (NHS) is free at the point of use, that is only the case for residents. All visitors to Britain should be properly insured, including comprehensive health coverage. Though Britain has left the EU, the **European Health Insurance Card (EHIC)** does still entitle EU nationals (on

Using a **baggage-transfer service** to deliver your luggage to your accommodation each night will leave you free to walk unencumbered (well, with just a day pack) during the day. Charges vary, but expect to pay from £8 for the first bag for each leg of the journey, with discounts usually offered for additional bags.

Alternatively, some of the **taxi** firms listed in Part 4 will provide a similar service on request, or you could make an arrangement with your B&B host, some of whom handle baggage transport themselves. Prices vary widely,

---

production of the EHIC, so ensure you bring it with you) to necessary medical treatment under the NHS while on a temporary visit here. To make sure this is still the case when you visit, however, contact your national social security institution. Also note that the EHIC is not a substitute for proper medical cover on your travel insurance for unforeseen bills and for getting you home should that be necessary. Also consider cover for loss and theft of personal belongings, especially if you are camping or staying in bunkhouses, as there may be times when you'll have to leave your luggage unattended.

● **Weights and measures** Britain's illogical mix of metric and imperial measures is undoubtedly a source of confusion for many visitors. For example, in Britain milk can be sold in pints (1 pint = 568ml), as can beer in pubs, though most other liquid including petrol (gasoline) and diesel is sold in litres. The population remains split, too, between those (mainly the older generation) who still use inches (1 inch = 2.5cm), feet (1ft = 0.3m) and yards and those who are happy with millimetres, centimetres and metres; you'll often be told that 'it's only a hundred yards or so' to somewhere, rather than a hundred metres or so. Distances on road and path signs are also given in miles (1 mile = 1.6km) rather than kilometres, and yards (1yd = 0.9m) rather than metres.

Most food is sold in metric weights (g and kg) but the imperial weights of pounds (lb: 1lb = 453g) and ounces (oz: 1oz = 28g) may be displayed too. The weather – a frequent topic of conversation – is also an issue: while most use centigrade (C), some continue to think in terms of fahrenheit (F; see temperature chart on p14 for conversions).

● **Time** During the winter the whole of Britain is on Greenwich Mean Time (GMT). The clocks move one hour forward on the last Sunday in March, remaining on British Summer Time (BST) until the last Sunday in October.

● **Smoking & vaping** Smoking in enclosed public places is banned. The ban relates not only to pubs and restaurants, but also to B&Bs, hostels and hotels. These latter have the right to designate one or more bedrooms where the occupants can smoke, but the ban is in force in all enclosed areas open to the public – even in a private home such as a B&B. Should you be foolhardy enough to light up in a no-smoking area, which includes pretty well any indoor public place, you could be fined £50, but it's the owners of the premises who suffer most if they fail to stop you, with a potential fine of £2500. Although the ban does not apply to vaping, premises can and do impose their own restrictions on the use of e-cigarettes indoors.

● **Telephones** The international access code for Britain is +44, followed by the area code minus the first 0, and then the number you require. **Mobile phone reception** is better than you might think. If you're using a mobile phone that is registered outside Europe, consider buying a local SIM card to keep costs down.

● **Wi-fi** See p25.

● **Emergency services** For police, ambulance, fire and mountain rescue dial ☏ 999 (or the EU standard number ☏ 112).

depending on the mileage involved and the individual concerned, but generally you can expect to pay at least £20 a day, which makes a specialised baggage carrier much better value.

● **Carryabag** (☎ 01242-250642, 🖳 carryabag.co.uk; Cheltenham) Linked to Compass Holidays (see below); can also arrange parking in Cheltenham for the duration of your walk and transfers to and from the trail.

● **Cotswold Luggage Transfers** (☎ 01386-840688, 🖳 luggage-transfers.co.uk; Volunteer Inn, Chipping Campden; see p77).

● **Sherpa Van** (☎ 01748-826917, 🖳 sherpavan.com; Richmond, N Yorks)

Self-guided walking holidays The following companies provide customised packages for walkers, which usually include detailed advice and notes on itineraries, maps, accommodation booking, daily baggage transfer and transport at the start and end of your walk.

● **Absolute Escapes** (☎ 0131-610 1210, 🖳 absoluteescapes.com; Edinburgh)
● **Celtic Trails** (☎ 01291-689774, 🖳 celtictrailswalkingholidays.co.uk; Chepstow)
● **Compass Holidays** (☎ 01242-250642, 🖳 compass-holidays.com; Glos)
● **Contours Walking Holidays** (☎ 01629-821900, 🖳 contours.co.uk; Derbyshire) Trail running itineraries also offered.
● **Cotswold Journeys** (☎ 01242-254353, 🖳 cotswoldjourneys.com; Cheltenham)
● **Cotswold Walks** (☎ 01386-833799, 🖳 cotswoldwalks.com; Chipping Campden)
● **Discovery Travel** (☎ 01983-301133, 🖳 discoverytravel.co.uk; Isle of Wight)
● **Embark Walking Holidays** (☎ 01873-379100, 🖳 embarkwalking holidays.com; Abergavenny)
● **Footpath Holidays** (☎ 01985-840049, 🖳 footpath-holidays.com; Wilts)
● **Freedom Walking Holidays** (☎ 07733-885390, 🖳 freedomwalkingholidays .co.uk; Goring-on-Thames)
● **Great British Walks** (☎ 01600-713008, 🖳 great-british-walks.com; Monmouth)
● **Hillwalk Tours** (☎ +353 91-763994, 🖳 hillwalktours.com; Ireland)
● **Let's Go Walking** (☎ 01837-880075 or ☎ 020-7193 1252, 🖳 letsgowalking .co.uk; Devon)
● **Macs Adventure** (☎ 0141-530 8886, 🖳 macsadventure.com; Glasgow)
● **Mickledore** (☎ 017687-72335, 🖳 mickledore.co.uk; Keswick)
● **The Carter Company** (☎ 01296-631671, 🖳 the-carter-company.com; Bucks)
● **Walk the Trail** (☎ 01326-567252, 🖳 walkthetrail.co.uk; Cornwall)

Group/guided walking tours Fully guided tours are ideal for individuals wanting to travel in the company of others and for groups of friends wanting the reassurance of a guide. The packages usually include meals, accommodation, transport arrangements, minibus back-up and baggage transfer, as well as a qualified guide. Companies' specialities differ widely, with varied sizes of group, standards of accommodation, age range of clients and professionalism of guides, so it's worth checking carefully before making a booking.

● **HF Holidays** (☎ 020 3974 8865, 🖥 hfholidays.co.uk; Herts) Offer the whole Way from their own HF Holidays property.

● **Ramblers Walking Holidays** (☎ 01707 537527, 🖥 ramblersholidays.co.uk; Herts). Offer the whole trail from one base.

For those who would like **to complete the trail in stages**, there is an annual series of guided walks run by the Cotswold Voluntary Wardens. The walks take place between May and March and each covers about 10 miles, building up over the 11 months to the full distance. One series of walks heads south to north over the 11 months, and another series heads in the opposite direction. For more information visit 🖥 cotswoldsaonb.org.uk (Walking & Exploring).

Budgeting

How you budget for your trip will depend largely on the type of accommodation you use and where you have your meals. If you camp and cook for yourself you will be able to keep costs to a minimum. These escalate as you go up the accommodation and dining scales and will also be affected by the extent to which you use the services offered to guests, such as transportation of luggage, packed lunches and other refinements.

With a group of friends you could save money by **self-catering in an Airbnb or a holiday cottage** (see p22) and driving yourselves to the next section of the walk each day.

The UK is currently going through a period of higher than normal inflation so you may find prices higher than those quoted in the text.

CAMPING

Camping along the Cotswold Way and staying in official sites isn't possible as there aren't enough of them. Where there are places you'll spend £5-15 per person (pp), sometimes plus an extra £1 or so for the use of a shower. To do the Way on a seriously tight budget you'll need to stealth camp part of the time as wild camping isn't allowed. Living frugally, you could get by on as little as £15-20pp per night, pitching your tent at official sites where you can and cooking your own food. See 🖥 10milehike.com/cotswold-way for how to do it right.

Most walkers, however, will indulge in the occasional cooked breakfast (£7-9), the odd pint of beer (around £5), or a pub meal after a long hard day (£12-15), so about £40pp per day would be better if your budget can run to that.

HOSTELS

The only hostel accommodation you're going to find along the route is in Bath; Bath has a YHA, two independent hostels and a YMCA. A dorm bed in either of the independent hostels in Bath costs from £18pp, from £20pp a night at the YHA with YHA membership – and from £22pp at the YMCA.

There are self-catering facilities on-site in Bath's YHA hostel which should help you reduce your overall expenditure, or they do offer meals there too. Realistically, therefore, you'll either have to camp/glamp or B&B it for most/all of your nights on the trail.

B&B-STYLE ACCOMMODATION

If you're sharing a room in a B&B, pub or guesthouse, allow around £50-70 per head for an overnight stay including breakfast, perhaps more in the tourist towns over a summer weekend and certainly more if you stay in a hotel. Add on the cost of an evening meal at around £20; for a meal with a drink or two expect to pay around £30. Buying a packed lunch will cost an extra £8 or so. It's therefore best to reckon on about £70-90pp per day. Those travelling alone can anticipate at least an additional £30-50 a day for a single room, or single occupancy of a room.

EXTRAS

Don't forget to set aside some money for the inevitable extras, such as buses and taxis, drinks, cream teas, snacks and entrance fees – or, rather more crucially, any changes of plan. Around £100-200 should be about right.

Itineraries

All walkers are individuals. Some like to cover large distances as quickly as possible. Others are happy to amble along, stopping whenever the whim takes them. You may want to walk the Cotswold Way in one go, tackle it in a series of days or weekends, or use it as the basis for individual linear walks; the choice is yours. To accommodate these different options, this guide has not been divided up into strict daily sections, which could impose too rigid a structure on how you should walk. Instead it has been designed to make it easy for you to plan the itinerary that suits you.

If you need an added spur, consider signing up for the Cotswold Way Hall of Fame, an online database that records those who have completed the entire walk. You can download a form from the activity website of the Cotswolds AONB (🖳 cotswoldsaonb.org.uk/visiting-and-exploring/walking).

The **planning map** opposite the inside back cover and the **table of facilities** on pp34-7 summarise the essential information for you to make a plan of your own, in conjunction with the **distance chart** on pp194-5. Alternatively, to make it even easier, see the **suggested itineraries** (see p32) and simply choose your preferred speed of walking. There are also suggestions on pp36-7 for those who want to experience the best of the trail over a day or a weekend. The **public transport map** (p49) may help at this stage.

Having made a rough plan, turn to **Part 4** where you will find summaries of the route, full descriptions of accommodation, places to eat and other services in each town and village, with detailed trail maps.

WHICH DIRECTION?

Most guidebooks to the Cotswold Way assume you will walk from north to south, which is the direction that has been followed in the layout of this book. There are some compelling reasons for this. To start with, although the prevailing wind is from the west, the Cotswolds frequently experience some vicious north-easterlies, and walking into the teeth of these can be decidedly unpleasant. Then there's the fact that the north Cotswolds have more than their fair share of attractive villages and towns with plenty of places to stay and eat – so that distances can be kept shorter in the initial stages, and there's a good choice of restaurants and B&Bs at the end of a walking day. And for those in need of an incentive, what better way to celebrate the end of the walk than by relaxing in Bath's spa?

Of course, starting from Bath has its advantages, too. Some walkers prefer not to have the sun in their eyes, which can be a deciding factor (although less so than you might think, since the route takes a considerable number of twists and turns). Others may wish to explore one of the quintessential Cotswold villages at leisure once the walk is over. The maps in Part 4 give timings for both directions and, as route-finding instructions are on the maps rather than in the text, it is perfectly straightforward to walk from south to north using this guide.

PLANNING YOUR WALK

❏ COTSWOLD WAY RELAY

It's been over 30 years since the first Cotswold Way Relay (🖳 cotswoldwayrelay.co .uk) and the event continues to attract a considerable number of teams each year. Today, though, improved waymarking along the trail means fewer runners take the 'scenic' route – something that gains considerably in significance when you realise there are no marshals to guide the way.

The record for the fastest women's team is held by Bristol & West Athletic Club, who in 2022 knocked 17 minutes off the previous time to clock up an impressive 13 hours, 48 minutes and 31 seconds. The senior men's record has stood since 2016 at 11 hours and 48 minutes and 37 seconds, set by Cheltenham & County Harriers.

The race starts in Chipping Campden at 7am on the last Saturday in June or first Saturday in July, finishing at Bath Abbey as evening draws in. It follows the official route of the Cotswold Way, which is divided into 10 stages of varying lengths and difficulty. The shortest, between Dursley and Wotton-under-Edge, covers just 7¼ miles (11.5km), but some runners contend with distances of 12 miles (19km) or more, and one group faces an ascent of 513m into the bargain.

Each stage sees a mass start, triggered by the expected arrival time of the first runner from the previous leg. With up to 65 teams tackling the course, you might just want to step off the path and let them pass! You'll then have the one-upmanship of taking the time to savour the trail's attractions while others steam past with eyes only on the clock.

❏ **SUGGESTED ITINERARIES**

B&B-style accommodation is available at all the places listed below. Few places have a **campsite**; those that do have been asterisked* below.

● **Itinerary for slower walkers and those who want to linger**
(**10 days**; shorter route via Middleyard)
Walking 10-11 miles (16-17.5km) a day over 10 days, with one longer day of 13 miles (21km) and two shorter days of 7 miles (11km)

Day	Daily schedule	Miles	km	B&Bs & Hotels
1	Chipping Campden* to Stanton	10½	17	Stanton
2	Stanton to Winchcombe	7	11	Winchcombe*
3	Winchcombe to Charlton Kings	10	16	Charlton Kings
4	Charlton Kings to Birdlip	11½	18.5	Birdlip
5	Birdlip to Painswick	7	11	Painswick*
6	Painswick to Middleyard	10	16	Middleyard
7	Middleyard to Wotton-under-Edge	11	17.5	Wotton-under-Edge
8	Wotton-under-Edge to Old Sodbury	13	21	Old Sodbury
9	Old Sodbury to Cold Ashton	8½	13.5	Cold Ashton
10	Cold Ashton to Bath	10	16	Bath

● **Itinerary for steady walkers**
(**8 days**; longer route via Selsley Common and Stinchcombe Hill)
Walking 10-14 miles (16-22.5km) a day, with 2 longer days of 15-17 miles (24-27km)

Day	Daily schedule	Miles	km	B&Bs & Hotels
1	Chipping Campden* to Wood Stanway	12½	20	Wood Stanway, Hailes*
2	Wood Stanway to Cleeve Hill	11½	18.5	Cleeve Hill
3	Cleeve Hill Reserve to Birdlip	15½	25.5	Birdlip
4	Birdlip to Selsley	17	27	Selsley
5	Selsley to North Nibley	13½	21.5	North Nibley*
6	North Nibley to Old Sodbury	15	24	Old Sodbury
7	Old Sodbury to Cold Ashton	8½	13.5	Cold Ashton
8	Cold Ashton to Bath	10	16	Bath

● **Itinerary for faster walkers**
(**7 days**; longer route via Selsley Common and Stinchcombe Hill)
Walking 13-17½ miles (21-28km) a day, with one shorter day of 11 miles (17.5km)

Day	Daily schedule	Miles	km	B&Bs & Hotels
1	Chipping Campden* to Hailes	15½	25	Hailes*, North Farmcote
2	Hailes to Charlton Kings	12	19.5	Charlton Kings
3	Charlton Kings to Painswick	18½	29.5	Painswick*
4	Painswick to Penn Wood	11	17.5	Middleyard
5	Penn Wood to Wotton-under-Edge	14½	23	Wotton-under-Edge
6	Wotton-under-Edge to Tormarton	15	24	Tormarton*
7	Tormarton to Bath	16½	26.5	Bath

* campsite/camping facilities also available here

SUGGESTED ITINERARIES

The itineraries in the box opposite are suggestions only, based on the location of places to stay as well as the attendant distances. How you plan your walk will depend on several factors, from the availability of accommodation to personal interests, as well as the distance you choose to walk each day.

Don't forget to add travelling time before and after the walk, and to allow additional time for photography and breaks – or simply to stop and stare.

SIDE TRIPS

Most people embarking on the Cotswold Way do so with the express aim of completing the walk from A to B, and there's certainly enough of interest to justify spending at least a week along the trail. Yet it's always tempting to take off the blinkers occasionally and consider what happens to left and right.

With over 3000 miles (4800km) of footpaths in the Cotswolds AONB alone, and several long-distance trails crossing the region, there's a tantalising number of **side routes** you could follow.

Winchcombe is a great place to get sidetracked, for as well as the Cotswold Way, the town is a junction for several trails. Prime among these is **Winchcombe Way**, a 42-mile (67km) figure-of-eight route with the focus firmly on the town. Offering the option of an interesting 2-day loop are **Warden's Way** and **Windrush Way**, which run over different routes between Winchcombe and Bourton-on-the-Water, covering 13 and 14 miles (21km and 22.5km) respectively. Others include **Gloucestershire Way**, which meanders for 100 miles (160km) between Chepstow and Tewkesbury, taking in the Forest of Dean and the River Severn.

If the idea of joining up the dots appeals, you could hardly do better than look at the 55-mile (88km) **Wysis Way**. As it crosses the Cotswold Way north of Painswick, it forms a link with two other national trails: Offa's Dyke Path and the Thames Path.

Further south, around Lower Kilcott, **Monarch's Way** runs alongside the Cotswold Way for a short distance before continuing along its 615-mile (984km) journey between Worcester and Shoreham in West Sussex. The route mirrors that taken by Charles II during his escape to France after the Battle of Worcester in 1651. The journey took the king six weeks to complete – with Parliamentary forces in hot pursuit. It's certainly food for thought.

❏ **Important note – walking times**
Unless otherwise specified, **all times in this book refer only to the time spent walking**. You will need to add 20-30% to allow for rests, photography, checking the map, drinking water etc, not to mention time simply to stop and stare.

When planning the day's hike count on 5-7 hours' actual walking.

VILLAGE & TOWN FACILITIES & DISTANCES

Walking SOUTH from Chipping Campden to Bath

PLACE* & DISTANCE* APPROX MILES / *KM* FROM PLACE ABOVE	ATM (BANK)	POST OFFICE	INFO	EATING PLACE	FOOD SHOP	CAMP-SITE	HOSTEL	B&B HOTEL
WALKING TO BATH								
Chipping Campden	ATM	✔	TIC	✔✔✔	✔✔	✔		✔✔✔
Broadway Tower 4¼ / *7*				✔				
Broadway 1½ / *2.5*	ATM	✔	TIC	✔✔✔	✔			✔✔✔
Stanton 4½ / *7.5*				✔				✔✔
Stanway 1½ / *2.5*								
Wood Stanway ¾ / *1.3*								✔
t/o (North Farmcote) **2½ / *4*** (+500m)								✔
Hailes ¾ / *1.3*				✔		✔		✔
Winchcombe 2 / *3*	ATM	✔	TIC	✔✔✔	✔✔	✔		✔✔✔
Postlip 4 / *6.5*				(✔)				✔
Cleeve Hill 2 / *3*				✔✔				✔✔✔
(Cheltenham +5/*8*)	ATM + ✔	✔	TIP	✔✔✔	✔✔✔			✔✔✔
Prestbury Hill Reserve 1½ / *2.5*								
Ham Hill 2½ / *4*						✔		
t/o (Charltn Kings) **¼ / *0.4*** (+1) ATM				✔✔	✔			✔✔✔
Dowdeswell A40 crossing 1 / *1.6*				✔				
Seven Springs 3 / *5*				✔✔				
Ullenwood 3½ / *5.5*				✔		✔(camping pods)		
Crickley Hill 1½ / *2.5*				✔				
Birdlip 2½ / *4*				✔				✔
(Little Witcombe +1¼ /2)				✔				✔
Cranham Corner 4¼ / *7*				✔✔				
Painswick 2½ / *4*	ATM	✔	TIC	✔✔✔	✔	✔		✔✔✔
Edge 1½ / *2.5*				✔				
t/o (Randwick) **5 / *8*** (+ ¼ /*0.4*)				✔				
t/o (Westrip) **1½ / *2.5*** (+ ¼ /*0.4*)				✔				
Stonehouse (river/canal crossing) 1 / *1.6* – scenic route / short route junction								
Ebley (scenic route) 1 / *1.5*				✔	✔(½ mile)			
Selsley (scenic route) 1½ / *2.5*				✔				✔
KS (short rte) ¾/*1.2* (from canal)	ATM ✔			✔✔	✔			✔
Middleyard (short route) ½ / *0.8* from KS (King's Stanley)								✔✔
Penn Wood – scenic route/short route junction ¼ / *0.4* then **2 / *3*** to Nympsfield								
Penn Wood – scenic route/short route junction 1½ / *2.5*								
Nympsfield Long Barrow Car Park 2 / *3*								
t/o (Uley) **1½ / *2.5*** (+ ½ /*1*)		✔		✔✔	✔			✔
Dursley 2¼ / *4*	ATM	✔	TIP	✔✔✔	✔✔			✔✔

cont'd on p36

NOTES ***PLACE & DISTANCE*** Places in **bold** are on the path; places in brackets and not in bold – eg (Little Witcombe) – are a short walk off the path. **DISTANCE** is given from the place above. Distances are between **places on the route** or to the **main turnoff (t/o)** to places in brackets. For example the distance from Wood Stanway to the **turnoff** for North Farmcote is 2½ miles. Bracketed distances eg (+1) show the additional distance off the route – eg North Farmcote is 500m off the Way.

PLANNING YOUR WALK

VILLAGE & TOWN FACILITIES & DISTANCES
Walking NORTH from Bath to Chipping Campden

PLACE* & DISTANCE* APPROX MILES / *KM* FROM PLACE ABOVE	ATM (BANK)	POST OFFICE	INFO	EATING PLACE	FOOD SHOP	CAMP-SITE	HOSTEL	B&B HOTEL
WALKING TO CHIPPING CAMPDEN								
Bath (Abbey)	ATM + ✔	✔	TIP	✔✔✔	✔✔		YHA✔	✔✔✔
Prospect Stile 4½/*7.5* (by Bath Racecourse)								
Freezing Hill 3¼/*5.2* (Battle of Lansdown display board by stile)								
Cold Ashton 2½/*4*				✔				✔✔
Pennsylvania ¾/*1.3*				✔(snacks)				
Badminton Plantation 2¾/*4.2*				✔ (+½/*0.8*)				(+½/*0.8*) ✔
Tormarton 3¼/*5.1*				✔✔		✔		✔✔
Old Sodbury 2¼/*3.6*				✔✔	✔(snacks)			✔✔
Little Sodbury 1½/*2.5*								
Horton 1¼/*2.2*								
t/o (Hawkesbury Upton) 2½/*4* (+½)		✔		✔✔	✔			✔
t/o (Hillesley) 2¼/*3.7* (+½)					✔			
Wotton-under-Edge 5/*8*	ATM	✔	TIP	✔✔	✔			✔✔
North Nibley 2¾/*4.5*				✔		✔		
Dursley 4/*6.5*	ATM	✔	TIP	✔✔✔	✔✔			✔✔
t/o (Uley) 2¼/*4* (+ ½/*1*)		✔		✔✔	✔			✔
Nympsfield Long Barrow Car Park 1½/*2.5*								
Penn Wood – scenic route/short route junction 2/*3*								
Selsley (scenic route) 1½/*2.5*				✔				
Ebley (scenic route) 1½/*2.5*				✔	✔(½ mile)			
Middleyard (short route) ¼/*0.4* from scenic route/short route junction above								✔✔
King's Stanley (short rte) ½/*0.8*	ATM ✔			✔✔	✔			✔
Stonehouse (river/canal crossing) ¾/*1.2* then 1/*1.6 to* t/o (Westrip)								
Stonehouse (river/canal crossing) 1/*1.5* – scenic route / short route junction								
t/o (Westrip) 1/*1.6* (+ ¼/*0.4*)				✔				
t/o (Randwick) 1½/*2.5* (+ ¼/*0.4*)				✔				
Edge 5/*8*				✔				
Painswick 1½/*2.5*	ATM	✔	TIC	✔✔✔	✔	✔		✔✔✔
Cranham Corner 2½/*4*				✔✔				
(Little Witcombe +1¼/*2*)				✔				✔
Birdlip 4¼/*7*				✔				✔
Crickley Hill 2½/*4*				✔				
Ullenwood 1½/*2.5*				✔		✔(camping pods)		
Seven Springs 3½/*5.5*				✔✔				
Dowdeswell A40 crossing 3/*5*				✔				
t/o (Charltn Kings) 1/*1.6* (+1)	ATM			✔✔	✔			✔✔✔

cont'd on p37

PLANNING YOUR WALK

B&B/HOTEL/CAMPSITE/EATING PLACE ✔ = one place ✔✔ = two ✔✔✔ = three or more
EATING PLACE (✔) = seasonal or open daytime only POST OFFICE (✔) = limited hours
HOSTEL YHA = YHA hostel H = independent hostel (but no dorm rooms)
CAMPSITE Bracketed distance eg (½) shows mileage from Path
INFO TIC/P = Tourist or Visitor Info Centre/Point
BANK/ATM ATM = ATM only; ATM + ✔ = ATM+bank

(cont'd from p34)

VILLAGE & TOWN FACILITIES & DISTANCES

Walking SOUTH from Chipping Campden to Bath

PLACE* & DISTANCE* APPROX MILES / *KM* FROM PLACE ABOVE	ATM (BANK)	POST OFFICE	INFO	EATING PLACE	FOOD SHOP	CAMP-SITE	HOSTEL	B&B HOTEL
WALKING TO BATH								
North Nibley 4 / *6.5*				✓		✓		✓
Wotton-under-Edge 2¾ / *4.5*	ATM	✓	TIP	✓✓✓	✓			✓✓
t/o (Hillesley) **5 / *8*** (+½)				✓				
t/o (Hawkesbury Upton) **2¼ / *3.7*** (+½)		✓		✓✓	✓			✓
Horton 2½ / *4*								
Little Sodbury 1¼ / 2.2								
Old Sodbury 1½ / *2.5*				✓✓	✓(snacks)			✓✓✓
Tormarton 2¼ / 3.6				✓✓		✓		✓✓✓
Badminton Plantation 3¼ / 5.1				✓ (+½ / *0.8*)				(+½ / *0.8*) ✓
Pennsylvania 2¾ / *4.2*					✓(snacks)			
Cold Ashton ¾ / *1.3*				✓				✓✓
Freezing Hill 2½ / *4* (Battle of Lansdown display board by stile)								
Prospect Stile 3¼ / *5.2* (by Bath Racecourse)								
Bath 4½ / *7.5* (Abbey)	ATM + ✓	✓	TIP	✓✓✓	✓✓✓		YHA✓✓	✓✓✓

(for key and notes see previous page)

HIGHLIGHTS: THE BEST DAY AND WEEKEND WALKS

Day walks

The suggestions below take in various stretches of the Cotswold Way. In addition, the trail authorities have implemented a series of **circular walks**, ranging from 1½ to 6½ miles and varying in difficulty.

Although these walks are in part waymarked with a green roundel stating 'Cotswold Way Circular Walk', these signs are designed merely to complement the detailed and regularly updated route directions that can be downloaded from 💻 nationaltrail.co.uk/cotswold-way/additional-walks.

- **Chipping Campden to Broadway** (see pp80-3) A good **6-mile (9.5km)** introduction to the Cotswold Way, taking in two of the trail's most attractive towns as well as some superb views from Dover's Hill and Broadway Tower. If you don't want to retrace your steps, there are buses between the two towns.
- **Broadway to Winchcombe** (see pp88-95) From one of the Cotswolds' most popular villages, this **12-mile (19.6km)** stretch leads to one of the prettiest at Stanton – where there's an excellent pub to break up the day. The route drops down alongside the ruins of Hailes Abbey before continuing to the attractive wool town of Winchcombe. Marchants No 606 bus service links the two towns.
- **Dowdeswell Reservoir to Crickley Hill** (see pp111-116) This **7½-mile (11.5km)** walk is ideal for nature lovers, taking in both ancient beechwoods and areas of unimproved limestone grassland, as well as the Devil's Chimney at Leckhampton and some prehistoric sites. Finish at the Crickley Hill Country Park car park.

(cont'd from p34)

VILLAGE & TOWN FACILITIES & DISTANCES
Walking NORTH from Bath to Chipping Campden

PLACE* & DISTANCE* APPROX MILES / KM FROM PLACE ABOVE	ATM (BANK)	POST OFFICE	INFO	EATING PLACE	FOOD SHOP	CAMP- SITE	HOSTEL	B&B HOTEL
WALKING TO CHIPPING CAMPDEN								
Ham Hill ¼ /0.4						✔		
Prestbury Hill Reserve 2½ / 4								
Cleeve Hill 1½ /2.5				✔				✔✔
(Cheltenham +5/8)	ATM + ✔	✔	TIP	✔✔	✔✔			✔✔
Postlip 2 /3				(✔)				✔
Winchcombe 4 /6.5	ATM	✔	TIC	✔✔	✔	✔		✔✔
Hailes 2 /3				✔		✔		✔
t/o (North Farmcote) ¾ /1.3 (+500m)								✔
Wood Stanway 2½ /4								✔
Stanway ¾ /1.3								
Stanton 1½ /2.5				✔				✔✔
Broadway 4½ /7.5	ATM	✔	TIC	✔✔	✔			✔✔
Broadway Tower 1½ /2.5				✔				
Chipping Campden 4¼ /7	ATM	✔	TIC	✔✔	✔✔	✔		✔✔

(for key and notes see previous page)

● **Crickley Hill to Painswick** (see pp116-23) More woods characterise this lovely 9-mile (14.5km) walk along the Cotswold escarpment, broken up by Cooper's Hill and Painswick Beacon, and finishing in the attractive town of Painswick. Buses serve both ends of the route and can be connected via Gloucester and Cheltenham.

● **Circular walk around Selsley Common** (see pp131-3) Start in King's Stanley and link up with the Cotswold Way as it runs along the Stroudwater (Ebley) Canal, and thence to Selsley Common and Middleyard. It's a **5-mile (8km)** round trip that takes in some spectacular views, a fascinating Arts and Crafts church, and the two alternative routes along this stretch of the Cotswold Way. Stagecoach's 62 between Gloucester and Stroud is the most frequent bus service to King's Stanley.

● **Bath to Dyrham Park** (see pp158-67: ie reverse of the route description) Climb out of Bath towards the racecourse and the battlefields near Freezing Hill, then continue on to Dyrham Park. It's about **12½ miles (20km)**, so you might have enough time to explore the house or grounds before getting a taxi back to Bath (there are no buses to Dyrham Park).

Weekend walks
● **Chipping Campden to Cleeve Hill** (see pp80-103) If there's one walk along the trail that showcases the quintessential Cotswolds, this is it. Villages of Cotswold stone, rolling hills, woodland and some excellent views: they're all in this **24-mile (38.5km)** route. Stagecoach's No 606 bus serves both ends of the walk.

● **Dursley to Tormarton** (see pp141-56) Most of this **22-mile (35km)** walk follows the edge of the Cotswold escarpment, sometimes wooded, at others more open, with numerous small villages and the final stretch through Dodington Park. Stagecoach and Cotswold Green operate bus services to Dursley and Coachstyle (No 41) to Tormarton.

What to take

How much you take with you is a very personal decision which takes experience to get right. For those new to long-distance walking the suggestions below will help you strike a sensible balance between comfort, safety and minimal weight.

KEEP YOUR LUGGAGE LIGHT

If there's one maxim that is crucial to long-distance walking, it's 'keep it light'. It is all too easy to take things along 'just in case' but such items can soon mount up. If you are in any doubt about anything on your packing list, be ruthless and leave it at home. You're rarely far from a shop on the Cotswold Way, so if you find you've left out something that turns out to be essential, the chances are you'll be able to pick up an equivalent easily enough.

HOW TO CARRY IT

The size of your rucksack depends on how you plan to walk. If you are staying in B&B-style accommodation, you should be able to get all you need into a 40- to 50-litre pack: large enough for a change of clothes, waterproofs, essential toiletries and first-aid kit, a water bottle, a packed lunch, and ideally a change of shoes. Pack similar things in different-coloured stuff sacks or plastic bags so they are easier to pull out of the dark recesses of your pack, then put these inside a waterproof rucksack liner, or tough plastic sack, to protect everything if it rains. Those camping will also need space for a tent, sleeping bag, cooking equipment, towel and food: 65-75 litres' capacity should be about right.

Whatever its size, make sure before you set off that your rucksack is comfortable. Ideally it should have a stiffened back system and either be fully adjustable or exactly the right size for your back. Carrying the main part of the load high and close to your body with a large proportion of the weight on your hips (rather than on your shoulders) by means of the padded waist belt should allow you to walk in comfort for days on end. Play around with different ways of packing your gear and adjust all those straps until you get it just right. A useful extra is a bum/waist bag or a very light daypack to carry a camera, wallet and other essentials if you go off sightseeing.

Of course, if you decide to use a baggage-transfer service (see pp27-8) you can pack most of your things separately and simply carry a daypack with the essentials for a day's walking.

FOOTWEAR

A comfortable, well-fitting pair of leather or Gore-Tex-lined **boots** is the best footwear you can take and essential if you're carrying a heavy rucksack. In addition to offering proper ankle support, which is particularly important on rough ground, they are most likely to keep your feet dry. Make sure they are properly waxed or waterproofed, both before you set out and during your walk.

Traditionally walkers wear two pairs of **socks**, one thin pair, with a thicker pair on top. Aside from adding warmth, this is a good blister-avoidance strategy, though modern walking socks with two inbuilt layers can do the job just as well. Taking three pairs of socks should be ample.

In summer you could get by with a light pair of trail **shoes** if you're carrying only a small pack, though it's not generally advisable. A second pair of shoes to wear in the evening is well worth taking – they can be useful in case of injury, too. Lightweight trainers are best for the cooler months; in summer sports sandals are equally suitable.

CLOTHES

Wet and cold weather can catch you out even in summer, so go prepared for the unexpected. Most walkers pick their clothes according to the versatile layering system, which consists of: a base layer to transport sweat away from your skin; a mid layer or two to keep you warm; and an outer layer or 'shell' to protect you from the wind and rain.

Thermal material is ideal for **base layers** as it draws moisture away from skin, keeping you drier (and thus warmer when you stop for a break) than a conventional cotton T-shirt. A **mid layer** of micro-fleece is ideal, being both warm and light, with an additional sweater or fleece useful for colder days or when you stop as you can get cold very quickly. Both thermal tops and fleeces have the added advantage that they dry relatively quickly.

All this pales into insignificance when it comes to **waterproofs**. A waterproof jacket is essential year-round and will be much more comfortable (but also more expensive) if it's also 'breathable' to prevent the build-up of condensation on the inside. It can also be worn to protect you against the wind. Waterproof trousers are important most of the year but in summer could be left behind if your main pair of trousers is reasonably windproof and quick-drying. Gaiters are rarely necessary, though they come into their own if you're walking through wet crops.

Trousers and **shorts** should be light and quick-drying: trousers with zipped legs that convert into shorts can be ideal, especially in summer when the weather can change rapidly. Never wear denim jeans for walking: if they get wet they become heavy, cold and very uncomfortable. In winter, or if you're camping, consider a pair of thermal **longjohns** or thick tights.

What you take in the way of **underwear** is very much a personal preference, but if you want to change every day, you'll need three sets to ensure you always have one dry. Women may find a **sports bra** more comfortable because pack straps can cause bra straps to dig into your shoulders. A **warm hat** is important at any time of the year, and **gloves**, too, except perhaps in the height of summer. It's surprising how quickly you can get cold if it's raining. In summer a **sunhat** will help to keep you cool and prevent sunburn; **swimming gear** would be useful if you plan to take advantage of one of the pools en route or in the hot waters of Bath spa. Finally, don't forget a **change of clothes** for the evenings. While wearing the same kit all week suits some, putting on clean clothes after a shower is a great morale boost – and will probably make you feel more comfortable if you're eating out.

TOILETRIES

Take only the minimum. In addition to **toothpaste** and a **toothbrush**, **sunscreen** is invaluable; you'll need a small bar of **soap** if you're camping. Also take a suitable supply of any **medication** and, for women **tampons/sanitary towels**. A roll of **loo paper** in a plastic bag is handy, as is a lightweight **trowel** if you get caught out far from a toilet (see p53). What you pack in the line of deodorants, razors, hairbrushes etc is a matter of personal preference.

FIRST-AID KIT

Medical facilities in Britain are good so you only need the essentials to cover basic problems and emergencies. Ideally, take a waterproof bag containing the following: **plasters/Band Aids** for minor cuts; **Compeed**, **Moleskin** or **Second Skin** for blisters; a selection of different-sized **sterile dressings** for wounds; **porous adhesive tape**; a **stretch bandage** for holding dressings or splints in place and for supporting a sprained ankle; a **triangular bandage** to make a sling for a broken or sprained arm; **elastic knee support** for a weak knee; **antiseptic wipes**; **antiseptic cream**; **safety pins**, **tweezers** and **scissors**; and **aspirin** or **paracetamol** for mild to moderate pain and fever.

Most importantly, do make sure you have a modicum of first-aid knowledge, or much of your kit will be rendered useless.

GENERAL ITEMS

Essential

Essential items you should carry are a **whistle** to attract attention if you get lost or find yourself in trouble; a **torch** (flashlight) in case you end up walking after dark; a one- or two-litre **water bottle/pouch**; **emergency food** such as chocolate, cereal bars, or dried fruit; a **penknife** and a **watch**. If you're not carrying a sleeping bag or tent you could also consider carrying an emergency plastic **bivvy-bag** – although at no stage on the route are you far from civilisation. A **compass** can be invaluable, but do make sure you know how to use it.

Useful

Many would list a **mobile phone** as essential and some also a **camera** (with a **spare memory card** and **batteries/charger**) but a **notebook** or **sketchbook** are other good ways of recording your impressions, and **binoculars** mean you can observe wildlife more easily. A pair of **sunglasses** is useful, as is a **vacuum flask** for hot drinks. A **walking stick** or **pole** helps to take the shock off your knees (some walkers use two poles but this leaves no free hand).

A **GPS** (see pp17-18) device could also be useful in an emergency, but not as an alternative to a compass: batteries could just fail when most needed.

CAMPING GEAR

If you're camping you will need a decent **tent** able to withstand wet and windy weather; a two- or three-season **sleeping bag**; a **sleeping mat**; a **stove** and **fuel**; **cooking equipment** (a pan with frying pan that can double as a lid/plate is fine for two people); a **bowl**, **mug** and **cutlery** (don't forget a can/bottle opener); and a **scourer** for washing up.

MONEY

There are ATMs and/or post offices in most of the towns along the path so withdrawing money along the route with a **debit (or credit) card** is fairly straightforward. Cards are the easiest way to pay in restaurants, hotels and supermarkets, many of which offer a cash-back facility. For most B&Bs, if you haven't already paid in advance, you'll need to pay in cash, bank transfer or, if you still have a cheque book, by cheque. For more details, see p25.

TRAVEL INSURANCE

Do consider insurance cover for loss or theft of personal belongings, especially if you are camping or staying in hostels, as there may be times when you'll have to leave your belongings unattended. Many British walkers will be covered under their home insurance policy, but it's worth checking this.

For health insurance for visitors from overseas, see box pp26-7.

MAPS

The hand-drawn maps in this book cover the trail at a scale of just under 1:20,000, with plenty of detail and information to keep you on the right track. The **Ordnance Survey** (⊞ ordnancesurvey.co.uk) covers the whole route at a scale of 1:25,000 on four maps within their Explorer series: Nos 179, 168, 167, 155 and 45, each costing £9.99, or £15.99 for the 'weatherproof active' version. Fortunately, none of these is strictly necessary if you pay careful attention to the maps in this guide, which should help to lighten your load somewhat. That said, it's a good idea for safety's sake to carry the map covering the highest point of the walk, Cleeve Hill Common (Explorer 179). Although the area is not particularly isolated, visibility up there can be seriously compromised when the mist comes down, making it easy to become disorientated and wander dangerously close to the edge of the escarpment. In such conditions a map from which you can take compass bearings is essential.

❏ **DIGITAL MAPPING** see also pp17-18

There are numerous software packages now available that provide Ordnance Survey (OS) maps for a smartphone, tablet, PC, or GPS unit. Maps are downloaded into an app from where you can view, print and create routes on them.

For a subscription of £4.99 for one month or £28.99 for a year (on their current offer) **Ordnance Survey** (🖥 ordnance survey.co.uk) allows you to download and use their UK maps (1:25,000 scale) on a mobile or tablet without a data connection for a specific period. Their app works well.

Memory Map (🖥 memory-map.co.uk) currently sell OS Explorer 1:25,000 and Landranger 1:50,000 mapping covering the whole of Britain with prices from £21.66/13.33 (1:25k/1:50k) for a one year subscription. **Anquet** (🖥 anquet.com) has the full range of OS 1:25,000 maps covering all of the UK from £28 per year annual subscription.

Maps.me is free and you can download any of its digital mapping to use offline. You can install the Trailblazer waypoints for this walk on its mapping but you'll need to convert the .gpx format file to .kml format before loading it into maps.me. Use an online website such as 🖥 gpx2kml.com to do this then email the kml file to your phone and open it in maps.me.

Harvey (🖥 store.avenza.com/collections/harvey-maps) currently use the US Avenza maps app for their *Cotswold Way* map (1:40,000, $14.99).

It is important to ensure any digital mapping software on your smartphone uses pre-downloaded maps, stored on your device, and doesn't need to download them on-the-fly, as this may be expensive and will be impossible without a signal. Remember that battery life will be significantly reduced, compared to normal usage, when you are using the built-in GPS and running the screen for long periods.

Also worth considering is **AZ**'s (🖥 az.co.uk) *Cotswold Way A-Z Adventure Atlas* (£9.95); this contains OS maps at a scale of 1:25,000 as well as an index, though it does arrange the maps as if walking from Bath to Chipping Campden.

Another useful option is the **Harvey** map (🖥 harveymaps.co.uk) which covers the whole route at 1:40,000 on a single, waterproof sheet and costs £14.95. It's also available as a digital download (see above).

RECOMMENDED READING

Flora and fauna field guides

There are plenty of good field guides on the market, though deciding which, if any, will justify space in a rucksack is a tough decision.

The series published by Collins is unfailingly practical, if a little dated, though for visual appeal – and particularly bird identification – the RSPB's guides come out ahead.

● *Collins Bird Guide, 3rd edition* by Lars Svensson et al (Collins, 2023)
● *Collins Complete Guide to British Wild Flowers* by Paul Sterry (Collins, 2008) or *Collins Wild Flower Guide* by David Streeter et al (Collins 2016)
● *The Mammals of Britain and Europe* by David Macdonald and Priscilla Barrett (Collins, 2005)
● *Collins British Tree Guide* by Owen Johnson (Collins 2015) or the much more

user friendly *What's that Tree?* by Tony Russell with the RSPB (DK, 2013) which is available in Kindle format.
● *Collins Complete Guide to British Insects* by Michael Chinery (Collins, 2009)
● *RSPB Pocket Birds of Britain and Europe* (Dorling Kindersley, 2017)
● Also in the RSPB's series of *What's that* pocket guides for beginners are *What's That Bird?* (2012); *What's That Flower?* (2013) and *What's That Butterfly?* (2014) with useful visual comparisons.

There are also several **field guide apps** for smartphones, including those that can identify birds by their song and appearance. One to consider is ⌨ merlin.allaboutbirds.org. A similar app for identifying trees is at ⌨ woodlandtrust.org.

General reading
● *The Hidden Landscape: A Journey into the Geological Past* by Richard Fortey (Bodley Head, 2010) brings vividly and clearly to life the evolution of a landscape which most of us take for granted.
● *The Arts and Crafts Movement* by Elizabeth Cumming and Wendy Kaplan (Thames & Hudson, 1991) is an accessible introduction to the complexities of the movement (see box p76), from its roots in Britain to continental Europe and the United States. A more recent book on the subject, *The Arts and Crafts Movement in Britain* by Mary Greensted (Shire History, 2010) is also worth looking at.

Biography
No journey through the Cotswolds is complete without Laurie Lee's classic childhood autobiography, *Cider with Rosie* (Vintage Classics, 2002).

Fiction
The novelist Jane Austen lived in Bath for five years and set two of her novels, *Northanger Abbey* and *Persuasion*, in the city. Both can be found in several editions, including Penguin Classics, and afford a rather different perspective on the city and society to that seen by today's visitors.

More recently, JK Rowling of *Harry Potter* fame hails from the Cotswolds; indeed, the town of Dursley is evoked in the surname of Harry's unpleasant uncle and aunt – though there the connection ends.

If you're into crime fiction, the Cotswold Mysteries by Rebecca Tope, with titles such as *A Grave in the Cotswolds* (Allison and Busby, 2011), should give you something to ponder as you walk along the trail.

Poetry
Most prolific among the poets whose work has been influenced by the Cotswolds is the war poet Ivor Gurney (1890-1937), who was born in Gloucester and served in World War I, before suffering severe mental problems and being confined to an institution.

Others include James Elroy Flecker (1884-1915), who was buried in Cheltenham; and WH Davies (1871-1940), known the world over for his poem, *Leisure* (see p53), who made his home in Gloucestershire. Their work can be found in numerous poetry anthologies.

PLANNING YOUR WALK

❏ SOURCES OF FURTHER INFORMATION

Trail information

● **Cotswold Way National Trail Office** (🖥 nationaltrail.co.uk/cotswold-way) The website includes news of diversions and the occasional route change as well as details of events and other trail information.

● **Cotswold Way Association** (CWA, 🖥 cotswoldwayassociation.org.uk) Formed in 2016, its aim is to regularly check the condition of the path and support the continued improvement of the national trail and other walks in the area.

Tourist information offices

Tourist information offices provide all manner of locally specific information for visitors. A few have paid staff but others along the Cotswold Way are staffed by volunteers who usually have information on accommodation but may not be able to book it for you.

There are tourist information offices on or near the Way in **Chipping Campden** (see pp75-6), **Broadway** (see p85), **Winchcombe** (see p97), **Cheltenham** (see p106), **Painswick** (see p124) and **Bath** (see p171, although the main office here has closed).

Tourist boards

The Cotswolds (🖥 www.cotswolds.com) has responsibility for all matters touristic throughout the region. Bath, though, is covered by its own authority, **Visit Bath** (🖥 visitbath.co.uk). Another excellent source of information is **The Cotswolds Conservation Board** (see p60).

Organisations for walkers

● **Backpackers' Club** (🖥 backpackersclub.co.uk) A club aimed at people who are involved or interested in lightweight camping through walking, cycling, skiing and canoeing. Members receive a quarterly magazine, access to a comprehensive information service (including a library) as well as long-distance path and farm-pitch directories. Membership costs £20 per year, family £30.

● **The Long Distance Walkers' Association** (LDWA; 🖥 ldwa.org.uk) An association of people with the common interest of long-distance walking; their website has lots of information about long-distance paths. Membership includes a journal, *Strider*, three times per year. Membership is offered on a calendar year basis (individuals £18, family £25.50, less by direct debit); if you join in October the cost will include the following calendar year.

● **Ramblers** (formerly Ramblers' Association; 🖥 ramblers.org.uk) Looks after the interests of walkers throughout Britain. They publish a large amount of useful information including their quarterly *Walk* magazine and monthly e-newsletters. Membership costs £38.50/51.75 individual/joint. Members also receive discounts at various stores and have access to the Ramblers Routes online library (short routes only for non members), and an app as well as group walks.

Getting to and from the Cotswold Way

While Bath at the southern end of the trail is easily reached by train, bus, coach or car, getting to and from Chipping Campden is a bit more of a challenge. The nearest railway station is at Moreton-in-Marsh, from where there is a bus to Chipping Campden, though taking a train to Stratford-upon-Avon, followed by a bus or taxi, is a viable alternative. For details see box p46, p75 in Part 4 under Chipping Campden and the bus services table and map on pp48-50.

Although there are no other railway stations on the trail itself, trains do service Stonehouse, about half a mile (1km) west of the trail where it meets the Stroudwater (Ebley) Canal. There is also Cam & Dursley station, almost three miles (4.8km) north of Dursley, with a limited bus service to the town centre. Connections to Cheltenham, about 2½ miles (4km) west of the trail, are excellent. It is also possible to take the train to Stroud or Gloucester, then transfer by bus to the path from there. A network of local buses links many of the villages along the Cotswold Way, making it possible – with a bit of planning – to create a series of linear walks without having to retrace your steps.

NATIONAL TRANSPORT

By rail
The rail services of most relevance to walkers along the Cotswold Way are GWR's (London Paddington–Worcester) to Moreton-in-Marsh (1hr 40mins,

---

❑ **GETTING TO BRITAIN**

● **By air** Most international airlines serve London Heathrow and London Gatwick. In addition a number of budget airlines fly from many of Europe's major cities to the other London terminals at Stansted and Luton as well as London City Airport. There are a few flights from mainland Europe to Bristol and Birmingham which are closer to the Cotswold Way than London.

● **From Europe by train (with or without a car)** Eurostar (🖳 eurostar.com) operate a high-speed passenger service via the Channel Tunnel between Paris/Brussels/Amsterdam and London. Trains arrive at and depart from St Pancras International Terminal, which also has good underground links to other railway stations. For more information about rail services between Europe and Britain contact your national rail operator or Railteam (🖳 railteam.eu). **Eurotunnel** (🖳 www.eurotunnel.com) operates 'le shuttle', a train service for vehicles via the Channel Tunnel between Calais and Folkestone taking 35 minutes to cross between the two.

● **From Europe by ferry (with or without a car)** Numerous ferry companies operate routes between the major North Sea and Channel ports of mainland Europe and the ports on Britain's eastern and southern coasts as well as from Ireland to ports both in Wales and England. For further information see websites such as 🖳 directferries.co.uk.

● **From Europe by coach (bus) Eurolines** (🖳 eurolines.com) have a huge network of services connecting over 500 cities in 25 European countries to London.

though to get to Chipping Campden is about 3hrs in total) and from Paddington to Bath (about 1½hrs). For Chipping Campden you could also take Chiltern Railways' service to Stratford-upon-Avon (from London Marylebone via Leamington Spa; approx 2hrs 20mins) and catch Stagecoach's No 1/1A/2/2A buses from there (approx 40 mins). GWR also operates trains to Cheltenham Spa from Paddington (around 2hrs), with connections from there to Cam & Dursley (30 mins).

See box below for details of the operators and an outline of the services. For the latest on train times, fares and rail information, contact **National Rail** (☎ 03457-484950, 🖥 nationalrail.co.uk). Fares vary very widely, but significant savings can be made by booking well in advance and by travelling at off-peak times. You can buy tickets through the relevant rail operator, in person at a railway station, or online at 🖥 thetrainline.com. It helps to be as flexible as

---

❑ RAIL SERVICES   (Note: not all stops are listed)

Chiltern Railways (☎ 0345-600 5165, 🖥 chilternrailways.co.uk)
● London Marylebone to Birmingham Moor Street via Leamington Spa, daily 1/hr. Some services continue to Birmingham Snow Hill and a few to Kidderminster.
● Leamington Spa to Stratford-upon-Avon via Warwick, Mon-Fri 8/day, Sat 7/day, Sun 5/day.

Cross Country (☎ 0844-811 0124, 🖥 crosscountrytrains.co.uk)
● Edinburgh to Bristol via Newcastle-upon-Tyne, York, Leeds, Birmingham New Street & **Cheltenham Spa**, daily approx 1/hr
  Note: some services start from, or continue/link to, destinations that include Aberdeen, Glasgow, Manchester Piccadilly, Exeter, Plymouth and Penzance.
● Nottingham to Cardiff via Derby, Birmingham New Street, **Cheltenham Spa** & Bristol Temple Meads, daily 1/hr
  Note: from Birmingham New Street there are services to Cambridge and Stansted Airport.

GWR (Great Western Railway; ☎ 0345-7000 125, 🖥 gwr.com)
● London Paddington to Bristol Temple Meads via Reading, Didcot Parkway, Swindon, Chippenham & **Bath Spa**, daily 1-2/hr (11/day continue to Weston-super-Mare)
● London Paddington to Cheltenham Spa via Reading, Didcot Parkway, Swindon, Stroud, **Stonehouse** & Gloucester, daily approx 1/hr
● London Paddington to Worcester via Reading, Oxford, Moreton-in-Marsh & Evesham, daily approx 1/hr (several services continue to Great Malvern and some to Hereford)
● Bristol Temple Meads to Cheltenham Spa via Yate, **Cam & Dursley** & Gloucester, Mon-Sat approx 1/hr, Sun 4/day
● Worcester to Gloucester via Cheltenham Spa, daily approx 1/hr
● Cardiff to Portsmouth via Bristol Temple Meads, **Bath Spa**, Westbury, Salisbury & Southampton, daily 1/hr
● Gloucester to Westbury via **Bath Spa**, Mon-Sat 1/hr some services continue to Frome & Weymouth
● Bristol Temple Meads to Chippenham via **Bath Spa**, daily 1-2/hr

possible and don't forget that most discounted tickets carry some restrictions; check what they are before you buy your ticket. Travel on a Friday and Sunday may be more expensive than on other days of the week.

If you think you may need to book a taxi when you arrive, check the relevant place in the route guide; ☐ traintaxi.co.uk *may* also be able to help. It is also possible to book train tickets that include bus travel to your ultimate destination: enquire when you book your train ticket, or look at ☐ plusbus.info.

No discussion of the railways serving the Cotswold Way would be complete without mention of the scenic **Gloucestershire Warwickshire Steam Railway (GWSR)** which, although it operates a limited service, does link Broadway, Toddington and Winchcombe with Cheltenham; see p84 for more details.

By coach
National Express is the principal coach (long-distance bus) operator in Britain. Travel by coach is usually cheaper than by train but takes rather longer. Advance bookings can carry significant discounts so it makes sense to book at least a week ahead. The service of greatest use to Cotswold Way walkers is that to Bath, but coaches also run regularly to Cheltenham. Local buses connect Cheltenham to several points along the trail. See coach services box below.

By car
Chipping Campden lies west of Oxford, so the best access is via the M40 from London or Birmingham, leaving at junction 8 (northbound) or 9 (southbound) to link up with the A44 towards Evesham. The turning to Chipping Campden is the B4081 beyond Moreton-in-Marsh. Getting to **Bath** is infinitely more straightforward: leave the M4 at junction 18, then take the A46. Check that your car is compliant with Bath's Clean Air Zone (☐ gov.uk/clean-air-zones).or pay the charge.

The greater problem is what to do with your car while you are tramping along the trail – and how to get back to it when you reach the end. **Parking** on the road in Bath is not an option, while the maximum stay in the city's multi-storey car parks is seven days. In Chipping Campden, the occasional B&B may allow you to park for a week or so, provided you stay with them for a night or two. On the JustPark app (☐ justpark.com) you could rent a private parking space in any of the larger towns (Cheltenham, Bath, Cirencester, Chipping Campden and Broadway). Alternatively, at least one of the baggage-transfer companies can (for a fee) store your vehicle and organise transport to, or from, the start/end of the trail (see pp27-8). But given the logistics of returning to their starting point, many walkers choose to leave their car at home.

❏ **COACH SERVICES**   (**Note**: not all stops are listed)

National Express (☎ 0871 781 8181, ☐ nationalexpress.com)
403 London Victoria Coach Station (VCS) to **Bath** via Chippenham, 11-14/day
    (services also call at Heathrow Airport or Reading)
444 London VCS to Gloucester via **Cheltenham**, 11/day
445 London VCS to Hereford via **Cheltenham** & Gloucester, 3-4/day

LOCAL TRANSPORT

The public transport map opposite gives an overview of the most useful bus and train routes for walkers.

For contact details and the approximate frequency of rail services see the box on p46, for coach services the box on p47 and for local bus services the box below and on p50. **Timetables** are available from the operators; all timetables for bus services operating in, or through, Gloucestershire can be found on ⌨ easytraveling.org.uk/gcc. In addition to the companies listed service details can be obtained from the national public transport information line, **traveline** (⌨ traveline.info). **Rome2Rio** (⌨ rome2rio.com) is another useful travel resource.

Although much of the trail is well served by local bus services, there is little in the way of an integrated service, particularly between the northern and southern parts of the route. Most operators issue timetables twice a year; while these vary less than in some areas, it is important to check ahead to make sure the service you want is still running.

❑ LOCAL BUS SERVICES

Note that most local bus companies have no service on a Sunday. However, if there is a Sunday service it almost always operates on a Bank Holiday Monday as well.
     Also, not all stops are listed. Places in **bold type** are close to or on the trail.

● **Coachstyle** (☎ 01249-782224, ⌨ www.coachstyle.uk)
41   Malmesbury to Yate via Badminton, **Tormarton**, **Old Sodbury** & Chipping
       Sodbury, Mon-Sat 4/day

● **Community Connexions** (☎ 0345 680 5029, ⌨ communityconnexions.org.uk)
21   Brimpsfield to Gloucester via **Birdlip** & **Little Witcombe**, Wed & Fri 1/day

● **Cotswold Green** (☎ 01453-835153)
40   Stroud to **Wotton-under-Edge** via Nailsworth, Mon-Sat 4/day
65A Stroud to Coaley via **Selsley**, Nympsfield, **Uley**, Dursley & Upper Cam,
       Sat 2/day (see also Stagecoach)
230 Stroud circular route via **Ebley** & **Randwick**, Tue 2/day

● **First** (⌨ firstgroup.com/bristol-bath-and-west)
4/4a **Weston** to **Bath** bus station via Upper Weston, daily 3-4/hr

● **Hedgehog Community Bus** (☎ 01386-841849, ⌨ hedgehogbus.org)
H3A Mickleton to Stratford via **Chipping Campden**, Tue 1/day
H3B, H3C & H3E Mickleton to **Chipping Campden**, Wed, Fri & Sat 1/day
H5A & H5B Mickleton to Evesham via **Chipping Campden**, Tue & Thur 1/day

● **Marchants Coaches** (☎ 01242-257714, ⌨ marchants-coaches.com)
L   Cheltenham to **Leckhampton**, daily 8-10/day

● **NN Cresswell** (☎ 01386-48655, ⌨ nncresswell.co.uk)
R4 (Rural 4) Willersey to Evesham via **Broadway**, Mon-Fri 4-5/day

(cont'd on p50)

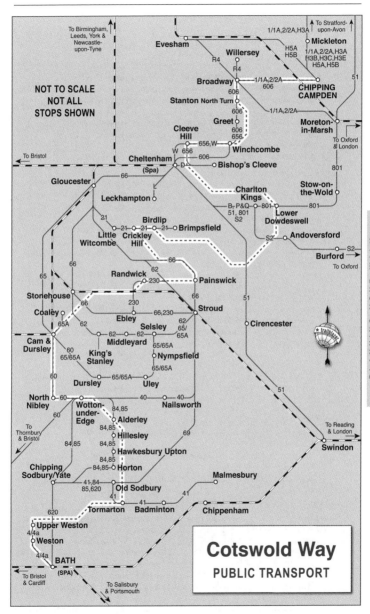

Cotswold Way
PUBLIC TRANSPORT

PLANNING YOUR WALK

(cont'd from p48)

❑ **LOCAL BUS SERVICES**

● **Pulhams Coaches** – now part of the Go Ahead group
(☎ 01451-820369, 🖳 pulhamscoaches.com)

51   Stratford-upon-Avon to Moreton-in-Marsh, Mon-Sat 5/day

606   **Cheltenham** to **Chipping Campden** via **Winchcombe**, Greet,
         Stanton North Turn & **Broadway**, Mon-Sat 2-3/day

656   Dumbleton to Bishop's Cleeve via Greet, **Winchcombe** & **Cleeve Hill**,
         Mon & Fri 2/day

801   **Cheltenham** to Moreton-in-Marsh via **Charlton Kings**, **Lower Dowdeswell**
         & Stow-on-the-Wold, Mon-Sat 8-9/day plus Sun & bank holidays
         early May to end Sep 2/day

P & Q   **Cheltenham** circular route to **Charlton Kings**, Mon-Sat 4/day

● **Stagecoach** (🖳 www.stagecoachbus.com/timetables)

1/1A   Stratford-upon-Avon to Moreton-in-Marsh via Mickleton,
         Chipping Campden & **Broadway**, Mon-Sat 2-3/day

2/2A   Stratford-upon-Avon to Moreton-in-Marsh via Mickleton &
         Chipping Campden, Mon-Sat 3/day

51   Swindon to **Cheltenham** via Cirencester, Mon-Sat approx 1/hr,
         Sun 5/day to Cirencester

60   **Dursley** to Thornbury via Upper Cam, **North Nibley** & **Wotton-under-Edge**,
         Mon-Sat 6/day

62   Gloucester to **Stonehouse** via Stroud, **Selsley**, Middleyard, **King's Stanley** &
         Leonard Stanley, Mon-Sat 10/day plus 2/day Stroud to Stonehouse
         Sun 4/day pus 1/day Stroud to Stonehouse

65   Stroud to Gloucester via **Selsley**, Nympsfield (5/day), Uley, **Dursley**,
         Lower Cam, **Cam & Dursley** station (2-3/day early morning and late
         afternoon only) & **Stonehouse**, Mon-Sat 9/day, Sun Dursley to Gloucester
         4/day (see also Cotswold Green)

66   Stroud to Cheltenham via **Painswick** & Gloucester, Mon-Sat 11/day, Sun 5/day

69   Stroud to **Old Sodbury**, Mon-Sat 4/day (connects with the 620)

166   Stroud to Brockworth via **Painswick** & **Cranham Corner**, Mon-Sat 2-3/day,
         Cheltenham to Stroud via **Painswick** & **Cranham Corner**, Sun 5/day

620   **Old Sodbury** to **Bath** via Chipping Sodbury & Yate, Mon-Sat 5/day
         (connects with the 69)

B   Cheltenham to **Charlton Kings**, Mon-Fri 2-3/hr, Sun 1/hr

D   Cheltenham Spa station to Bishops Cleeve via Cheltenham &
         Cheltenham Racecourse, daily 3/hr

S2   Cheltenham to Oxford via **Charlton Kings**, **Andoversford**, **Northleach**
         Burford & Witney, 7/day

W   Cheltenham circular route to **Winchcombe** via Prestbury & **Cleeve Hill**,
         Mon-Sat 11-12/day

● **The Big Lemon** (☎ 0117-244 7337, 🖳 thebiglemon.com/Bristol)
Community-run bus services with funding supplied each year by the council – which
means that you should check in advance that the service is still running.

84   Yate clockwise circular route: Chipping Sodbury, **Wotton-under-Edge**,
         Alderley, **Hillesley**, **Hawkesbury Upton**, **Horton**, Chipping Sodbury,
         Mon-Sat 3/day

85   Yate anti-clockwise circular route via Chipping Sodbury, **Horton**,
         Hawkesbury Upton, **Hillesley**, **Alderley** & **Wotton-under-Edge**,
         Mon-Sat 3/day

PLANNING YOUR WALK

MINIMUM IMPACT & OUTDOOR SAFETY

2

Minimum-impact walking

Walk as if you are kissing the Earth with your feet
Thich Nhat Hanh, *Peace is every step*

Simply by visiting the Cotswolds you are making a positive impact on the local community – as well as on your well-being. Your presence brings money into the local economy and creates jobs for local people. It ensures that the area maintains a high profile and helps to strengthen the value of local crafts such as dry-stone walling (see box p10) that could otherwise be left to die out. So much for the positives.

On the other side, there is the risk that large numbers of tourists can unwittingly destroy the very place they have come to enjoy. If such tourists adopt a blinkered approach, damage – both environmental and social – is inevitable. But if visitors make the effort to work with local communities to protect the environment, everyone will benefit.

The following guidelines are designed to help you reduce your impact on the environment where you are a visitor, to encourage conservation and to promote sustainable tourism in the area.

ECONOMIC IMPACT

Communities along the Cotswold Way are no strangers to crises, from foot-and-mouth disease to widespread flooding. More generally, political and economic expediency threaten the closure of rural post offices and local hospitals. Yet walkers can play their part in helping to keep such communities economically viable. The watchword is 'local': buy local, support local businesses, encourage local skills, all of which bring significant social, environmental and psychological benefits.

Support local businesses

Rural businesses and communities in Britain have been hit hard in recent years by a seemingly endless series of problems. Most people are aware of the Countryside Code – not dropping litter and closing the gate behind you are still as pertinent as ever – but in light of the economic pressures there is something else you can do: **buy local**.

It's a fact of life that money spent at local level – perhaps in a market, or at the greengrocer, or in an independent pub – has a far greater impact for good on that community than the equivalent spent in a branch of a national chain store or restaurant. While no-one would advocate that walkers should boycott the larger supermarkets, which after all do provide local employment, it's worth remembering that businesses in rural communities rely heavily on visitors for their very existence.

Look and ask for local produce to buy and eat; not only does this cut down on the amount of pollution and congestion that the transportation of food creates (the so-called 'food miles'), but also ensures that you are supporting local farmers and producers; the very people who have moulded the countryside you have come to see and who are in the best position to protect it. If you can find local food which is also organic so much the better.

ENVIRONMENTAL IMPACT

By choosing to walk you have already made a positive step towards minimising your impact on the wider environment. By following these suggestions you can also tread lightly through the Cotswolds.

Use public transport whenever possible
Using public transport rather than private cars benefits both visitors and locals, as well as the environment. Local buses (see pp48-50) service many of the villages through which you'll pass and it's often possible to use them at the end of a day or several days on the trail to get back to a convenient point. Also of use are local taxi firms – only too happy to ferry walkers or their luggage around.

Never leave litter
Leaving litter shows a total disrespect for the natural world and others coming after you. As well as being unsightly and unhygienic, litter kills wildlife, pollutes the environment and can be dangerous to farm animals. **Please** remove your rubbish and dispose of it in a bin in the next village. It would be helpful if you were to pick up litter left by other people, too.
● **The lasting impact of litter** A piece of silver foil left on the ground takes 18 months to decompose; a plastic bag 10 years; clothes 15 years; and an aluminium can 85 years. Would you want your great-grandchildren to find your discarded drink can next to their picnic?
● **Is it OK if it's biodegradable?** Not really. Apple cores, banana skins and the like are unsightly, encourage flies, ants and wasps, and can ruin a picnic spot for others. Orange peel left on the ground takes six months to decompose.

Erosion
● **Stay on the waymarked trail** Please. The effect of your footsteps may seem minuscule but when they are multiplied by several thousand walkers each year they become rather more significant. Avoid taking shortcuts, widening the trail or creating more than one path; your boots will be followed by many others.
● **Consider walking out of season** As the weather warms up, so plants start to grow and walkers appear on the hillsides. Thus areas of the trail subject to the greatest pressure are often prevented from recovering. Walking at less busy times eases this pressure on the environment. It can also be more rewarding,

with fewer people on the trail and a more relaxed atmosphere prevalent among local communities.

Respect all wildlife

Care for all wildlife you come across on the path; it has just as much of a right to be there as you. Tempting as it may be to pick wild flowers, leave them so the next person who passes can enjoy them too. Don't break branches off or damage trees in any way.

> *What is this life if, full of care,*
> *We have no time to stand and stare.*
> *No time to stand beneath the boughs*
> *And stare as long as sheep or cows.*
> *No time to see, when woods we pass,*
> *Where squirrels hide their nuts in grass.*
> *No time to see, in broad daylight,*
> *Streams full of stars, like skies at night.*
> *No time to turn at Beauty's glance,*
> *And watch her feet, how they can dance.*
> *No time to wait till her mouth can*
> *Enrich that smile her eyes began.*
> *A poor life this if, full of care,*
> *We have no time to stand and stare.*
> **William Henry Davies**, *Leisure*

If you come across wildlife, keep your distance and don't watch for too long. Your presence can cause considerable stress, particularly if the adults are with young or in winter when the weather is harsh and food scarce. Young animals are rarely abandoned. Never interfere if you find young deer or fledgling birds that are apparently alone; their mother will almost certainly return as soon as you have moved on.

The code of the outdoor loo

As more and more people discover the joys of the outdoors, sorting the toilet issue is of increasing importance. Even the least sensitive of people are offended by loo paper strewn across a path, or by the ill-disguised sight of human excrement. Not only is it offensive to our senses but, more importantly, it can infect water sources.

● **Where to go** Wherever possible wait until you come to a **public toilet**. These are marked on the trail maps in this guide. If you do have to go outdoors, choose a site at least **30m away from running water**. Use a strong stick to **dig a small hole** about 15cm (6") deep in which to bury your excrement. It decomposes quicker when in contact with the top layer of soil or leaf mould; using a stick to stir loose soil into your deposit will speed up decomposition even more. Do not squash it under rocks as this slows down the composting process. If you have to use rocks to hide it make sure they are not in contact with your faeces.

● **Toilet paper and tampons/sanitary towels** Toilet paper takes a long time to decompose, whether buried or not. Like tampons and sanitary towels, it is easily dug up by animals and could end up in water sources or on the trail. The best method for dealing with such items is to **pack them out**. Put them inside a paper bag, then inside another bag (or two). Then simply empty the contents of the bag at the next toilet you come across and throw it away.

ACCESS

Rights of way

As a designated national trail, the Cotswold Way is a public right of way, a path that anyone has the right to use on foot provided they stay on the path and do

MINIMUM IMPACT & OUTDOOR SAFETY

not cause damage or obstruct it in any way. The trail takes in several public rights of way which fall largely into one of three categories:

● A **footpath** (marked with a yellow arrow) is open to walkers only, not to cyclists, horse-riders or vehicles.

● A **bridleway** (blue arrow) is open to walkers, horse-riders and cyclists but on bridleways cyclists have to give way to other users.

❏ THE COUNTRYSIDE CODE

The Countryside Code, originally described in the 1950s as the Country Code, was revised and relaunched in 2004, in part because of the changes brought about by the CRoW Act (see opposite); it has been updated several times since, the last time in 2022. The Code seems like common sense but sadly some people still appear to have no understanding of how to treat the countryside they walk in. A summary of the latest Code (🖳 gov.uk/government/publications/the-countryside-code), launched under the banner 'Respect. Protect. Enjoy.', is given below.

Respect other people
● Be considerate to those living in, working in and enjoying the countryside
● Leave gates as you find them or follow instructions on signs. A farmer normally closes gates to keep farm animals in, but may sometimes leave them open so the animals can reach food and water. When in a group, make sure the last person knows how to leave the gate. Follow paths unless wider access is available, such as on open country or registered common land (known as 'open access land'). Leave machinery and farm animals alone – if you think an animal is in distress try to alert the farmer instead. Use gates, stiles or gaps in field boundaries if you can – climbing over walls, hedges and fences can damage them and increase the risk of farm animals escaping. If you have to climb over a gate because you can't open it always do so at the hinged end. Also be careful not to disturb ruins and historic sites.
● Do not block access to gateways or driveways when parking
● Be nice, say hello, share the space
● Follow local signs and keep to marked paths unless wider access is available

Protect the natural environment
● Take your litter home – leave no trace of your visit
● Do not light fires and only have BBQs where signs say you can
● Always keep dogs under control and in sight. Across farmland dogs should always be kept on a short lead. During lambing time they should not be taken with you at all.
● Dog poo – always clean up after your dog and get rid of the mess responsibly – 'bag it and bin it'. (See also box opposite and pp184-6)
● Care for nature – do not cause damage or disturbance

Enjoy the outdoors
● Check your route and local conditions. In some areas there may be temporary diversions in place. There are currently a couple of major diversions on the Cotswold Way – **Map 16** near Birdlip where roadworks on the A417 'Missing Link' project will continue until 2026-7 and **Maps 36-7**, on the Tormarton to Dyrham section.
● Plan your adventure – know what to expect and what you can do
● Enjoy your visit, have fun, make a memory

● A **restricted byway** (purple arrow) is open to walkers, horse-riders and cyclists, but not to motorised vehicles.

That said, not all footpaths are necessarily rights of way. Sometimes a landowner will allow a path across his land to be used for the convenience of walkers, although it may not be recognised as a right of way. This is known as a **permissive path**.

The maintenance of rights of way is down to the landowner in conjunction with the county council through whose area it passes, and sometimes the local authority. Farmers and land managers must ensure that: paths are not blocked by crops or other vegetation, or otherwise obstructed; the route is identifiable; and that the surface is restored soon after cultivation. If crops are growing over the path you have every right to walk through them, following the line of the right of way as closely as possible.

Should you find a path blocked or impassable, report it to the appropriate highway authority.

Right to roam

Following a concerted effort by groups such as the Ramblers (see box p44) and the British Mountaineering Council, the principle of access to open countryside and registered common land was finally allowed under the **Countryside and Rights of Way Act 2000**, affectionately known as CroW. In England, the act came into effect in full in 2005, creating a new right of access to the English countryside for recreation on foot.

There are restrictions, of course, some land (such as gardens, parks and cultivated land) is excluded, and high-impact activities such as driving a vehicle, cycling, and horse-riding may not be permitted. The act also: gives greater protection to SSSIs (see p61) and AONBs (see p60); lists habitats and species important to biological diversity in England; and covers the conduct of those walking with dogs (see p184-6). Land over which access has been granted may be marked with a circular brown-and-white waymark, depicting a Morph-like creature walking across a hill.

❏ **WALKING THROUGH FIELDS OF CATTLE**

It is rare that cows will attack walkers but it does happen. Cows get particularly nervous when dogs are about and cows with calves can be even more twitchy. Most of the time they will just watch you pass but very occasionally they will wander over out of curiosity. The following guidelines may prove helpful:
● Try not to get between cows and their calves.
● Be prepared for cattle to react to your presence, especially if you have a dog.
● Move quickly and quietly, and if possible walk around them.
● Keep your dog close and under proper control.
● Don't hang onto your dog if you are threatened by animals; let it go.
● Don't put yourself at risk. Find another way round the cows and rejoin the footpath.
● Don't panic! Most cows will stop before they reach you. If they follow just walk on quietly.
● Report any problems to the highway authority.

Health and outdoor safety

HEALTH

Prevention

Water and dehydration You need to drink lots of water while walking – probably more than you think. Many health specialists recommend 2-4 litres a day, depending on the weather and your physique. If you're feeling drained, lethargic or just out of sorts it may well be that you haven't drunk enough. Thirst is not always a reliable indicator of how much you should drink. The frequency and colour of your urine is a more useful guide: the clearer the better.

Sunburn Even on overcast days the sun still has the power to burn. Sunburn can be avoided by regularly applying sunscreen, remembering your lips and ears, and by wearing a hat to protect your face and the back of your neck. Those with fair skin should consider wearing a light, long-sleeved top and long trousers rather than T-shirt and shorts.

Blisters Worn-in, comfortable boots are a must, as are good, well-fitting socks. How many people set out on a long walk in new boots and live to regret it!

Look after your feet, too: air them at lunchtime, keep them clean and change your socks daily. If you feel any 'hot spots' on your feet while you are walking, stop immediately and apply a few strips of zinc oxide tape or one of the commercially available 'blister plasters', and leave on until the area is pain free or the tape/plaster starts to come off.

If you have left it too late and a blister has developed, you can still protect it from further abrasion with one of the 'blister kit' plasters. Popping it can lead to infection. If the skin is broken, keep the area clean with antiseptic and cover with a non-adhesive dressing material held in place with tape.

Joints and muscles If you're susceptible to joint problems – in particular your knees and ankles – do invest in a pair of walking poles and use one or both of them, especially during steep ascents or descents. Properly used, they can lessen the impact of long-distance walking on your joints and thus can help to prevent injury. Even the fittest athlete warms up before exercise and stretches afterwards – and it's good practice for walkers. It's surprising how much easier it is to set off in the morning without aching muscles; this, too, lessens the risk of injury.

Hypothermia and hyperthermia

Hypothermia, or **exposure**, occurs when the body can't generate enough heat to maintain its core temperature. Since it is usually as a result of being wet, cold, unprotected from the wind, tired and hungry, it is easily avoided by wearing suitable clothing (see pp39-40), carrying and consuming enough food and drink, being aware of the weather conditions, and checking on the morale of your companions. Early signs to watch for include feeling cold and tired with involuntary shivering. If in doubt, find shelter as soon as possible and warm the person up with a hot drink and chocolate or other high-energy food. If possible, give them another warm layer of clothing and allow them to rest.

If the condition is allowed to worsen, strange behaviour, slurring of speech and poor co-ordination will become apparent and the victim can quickly progress into unconsciousness, followed by coma and death. Quickly get the victim out of the wind and rain, improvising a shelter if necessary. Rapid restoration of body warmth is essential and best achieved by bare-skin contact: someone should get into the same sleeping bag as the patient, both having stripped to their underwear, with any spare clothing laid under and over them to build up heat. This is an emergency: send for help.

At the other end of the scale, **hyperthermia** occurs when the body is allowed to overheat. **Heat exhaustion** is often caused by water depletion and is a serious condition that could eventually lead to death. Symptoms include thirst, fatigue, giddiness, a rapid pulse, raised body temperature, low urine output and, later on, delirium and coma. The only remedy is to re-establish the balance of water. If the victim is suffering severe muscle cramps it may be due to salt depletion. **Heat stroke** is caused by the failure of the body's temperature-regulating system and is extremely serious. It is associated with a very high body temperature and an absence of sweating. Early symptoms can be similar to those of hypothermia, such as aggressive behaviour, lack of co-ordination and so on. Later the victim goes into a coma or convulsions; death will follow if effective treatment is not given. Sponge the victim down or cover with wet towels, then vigorously fan them. Get help immediately.

Dealing with an accident

● Ensure both you and the casualty are out of further risk of danger, but otherwise do not move someone who may be seriously injured.

● Use basic first aid to treat the injury to the best of your ability.

● Try to attract the attention of anybody else who may be in the area: the **emergency signal** is six blasts on a whistle, or six flashes with a torch (flashlight).

● If you have to go for help, ideally leave someone with the casualty. If there is nobody else, make sure the casualty is warm, sheltered and as comfortable as possible: leave spare clothing, water and food within easy reach, as well as a whistle and/or torch for attracting attention.

● Telephone ☎ 999 (or ☎ 112) and ask for the police or other rescue service. Be sure you know exactly where you are before you call.

● Report the exact position of the casualty and his or her condition.

❏ WHAT3WORDS

On the app **What3words** (🖳 what3words.com) the world is divided into three-metre squares and each has its own three-word geocode so it makes it easy to tell people where you are.

See pp183-4 for the what3words references for the waypoints in this book.

❏ **LYME DISEASE**

Ticks are small blood-sucking creatures that live on cattle, sheep and deer and cannot fly. When you are walking with bare arms or legs through long grass or bracken, small ticks can brush off and attach themselves to you, painlessly burying their heads under your skin to feed on your blood. After a couple of days of feasting they will have grown to about 10mm and will drop off. To avoid this, wear boots, socks and trousers when walking through, or sitting on, long grass, heather and bracken.

There is a very small risk that ticks can infect you with Lyme disease, although one would normally have to be attached to you for 24-36 hours before you were affected. Check your body after a walk and remove any ticks by pinching the head as close to your skin as possible and pulling steadily away from your body, without twisting. Keep the area clean with disinfectant. If you suffer flu-like symptoms, or lasting irritation at the site of the bite for a week or more, see a doctor.

For more information see ▣ lymediseaseaction.org.uk.

OUTDOOR SAFETY

The Cotswold Way is not a hazardous undertaking and presents no greater risk than you would encounter on an average day's walk in the countryside. Nevertheless, there are some sensible precautions that can help to prevent problems.

Check the weather forecast (see below) before you set out and go properly equipped. Be sure to carry plenty of food to last you through the day and at least a litre of water. Drinking from streams is not recommended since they are likely to contain traces of pesticides and other chemicals used on the land. Should the weather close in, take particular care to stay on the route, especially if you are on Cleeve Hill, or one of the other stretches of the Cotswold Way that run along the escarpment. If in doubt, stop and check your position on the map and GPS.

Weather information

Anyone familiar with the British weather will know that it can change quickly. What started out as a warm sunny day can be chilly and wet by lunchtime, so don't be fooled. Newspapers, television and radio stations all give the forecast for the day ahead and local people will have plenty of advice on the subject. Weather forecasts can be found online at ▣ metoffice.gov.uk and ▣ bbc.co .uk/weather.

Walking alone

If you enjoy walking alone you must appreciate and be prepared for the increased risk. Try to tell someone where you are going. One way of doing this is to telephone your booked accommodation and let them know you are walking alone and what time you expect to arrive. If you leave word with someone else, don't forget to let them know you have arrived safely. Carry a mobile phone, though there's no guarantee of good reception.

THE ENVIRONMENT & NATURE

Given its route within the relatively narrow range of the Cotswold Hills, the Cotswold Way runs through an unexpectedly broad range of habitats. Among these, grasslands and beechwoods stand out from the dominant farmland, where grazing land and arable farming have created their own habitats. Open moorland contrasts with long-established towns and villages; there's even a river and a canal across the trail. To do justice to the flora and fauna of such an area would take a book several times the size of this one. What follows, then, is a brief description of the animals, birds and plants you may come across – and a few that are there, but which you're unlikely to spot. To find out more, look at one of the field guides listed on pp42-3.

While it's interesting in itself to be able to identify individual plants and creatures, far more valuable is to understand their place within their environment and how we, as walkers, can help to protect that fragile relationship. Conservation is part of that relationship, which is why these issues are explored here.

Conserving the Cotswolds

It's the business of government to see that the countryside is preserved for the pleasure and sanity of all of us. The fatal mistake has been to imagine that the interests of the countryside are in some way different from the interests of farmers. The countryside can only be maintained by a healthy agriculture. If farming dies, a most precious part of Britain dies with it. **John Mortimer**

Perhaps John Mortimer had the Cotswolds in mind when he penned these words. He certainly could have done, for farming has been an intrinsic part of these hills for many centuries, shaping the countryside – and the towns and villages – that are seen today.

Yet for all that the Cotswolds draw tourists in their droves, the pressure for development, the economic reality of maintaining small communities, and the red tape imposed on Britain's farmers all conspire against maintaining an equable balance with nature. If it has taken just over 70 years for over 96% of the region's unimproved limestone grassland (that's permanent grassland which has not been regularly cultivated) to disappear, how long will it be before there's nothing left?

There are plenty of organisations that are determined not to let the unthinkable happen; some are listed opposite and on p62. Environmental issues are of growing interest on the political field and thanks to the efforts of these groups, many of them voluntary, the fight-back is gaining ground. Their work relies on the active participation of everyone who cares.

GOVERNMENT AGENCIES AND SCHEMES

Primary responsibility for countryside affairs in England rests with **Natural England** (⌨ gov.uk/government/organisations/natural-england). The organisation is responsible for: enhancing biodiversity, landscape and wildlife in rural, urban, coastal and marine areas; promoting access, recreation and public well-being; and contributing to the way natural resources are managed.

One of Natural England's roles is to designate: national trails; national parks; national landscapes (the new name for AONBs – areas of outstanding natural beauty), which afford the second level of protection after a national park; sites of special scientific interest (SSSIs); and national nature reserves (NNRs), and to enforce regulations relating to these sites.

Cotswolds AONB (National Landscape)

Now for some statistics. Some 95% of the Cotswold Way national trail falls within the **Cotswolds Area of Outstanding Natural Beauty** (⌨ cotswolds aonb.org.uk), the largest of the 46 AONBs in England, Wales and Northern Ireland. Established in 1966, and extended in 1990, it runs from north to south for 78 miles (126km) and covers a total of 790 square miles (2038sq km).

The area has been inhabited for around 6000 years; today over 150,000 people live within its boundaries. Despite that, around 86% of the land is still farmland, its fields demarcated by an estimated 4000 miles of dry-stone walls. A further 10% or so is woodland, especially beech, though the walker on the Cotswold Way could be forgiven for thinking that the woods accounted for a significantly higher proportion than this!

Significantly, in terms of the area's natural history, over half of the UK's total Jurassic limestone grassland is to be found here, much of it protected within SSSIs (see opposite). That figure, though, tells only a part of the story. While the region's flower-rich limestone grasslands as a whole covered 40% of the AONB in 1935, that area has shrunk to just 1.5% today. Given that such habitats can harbour almost 400 species of plants and 25 species of butterfly, it's hardly any wonder that conservation of what little remains is such a vital issue.

The **Cotswolds Conservation Board** (and a team of Cotswold Voluntary Wardens) is responsible for much of the work involved in running the AONB, including the Cotswold Way, from footpath maintenance and hedge-laying to publicity and fundraising. Others lead walks, including an annual series along the Cotswold Way (see p29). A bi-annual newspaper, *Cotswold Lion*, ensures that both local people and visitors are kept informed of what's going on across the region. (Editions can be downloaded from the AONB website).

Sites of special scientific interest (SSSIs) and national nature reserves (NNRs)

The designation **SSSI** affords protection to specific areas against anything that threatens their unique habitat or environment. There are currently 89 SSSIs across the Cotswolds, including parts of Cleeve Hill & Cleeve Common (🖥 cleevecommon.org.uk), Leckhampton Hill, Crickley Hill and Painswick Beacon along the Cotswold Way. 'Triple SIs' are managed in partnership with the owners and occupiers of the land who must give written notice of any operations likely to damage the site and who cannot proceed until consent is given. Many SSSIs are also designated as **national nature reserves** (NNRs), including several that combine to make up the Cotswolds Commons and Beechwoods NNR.

Geoparks

The European Geoparks initiative was originally set up to help the development and management of deprived areas which nevertheless benefit from a rich geological heritage. The concept has since moved on, with today's geoparks designed to raise awareness of an area and to educate the general public.

The Cotswold Way runs through **Cotswold Hills Geopark** (🖥 cotswoldhills geopark.net); it was established by Gloucestershire Geology Trust (see p10), in partnership with the Cotswolds AONB and Natural England, and reaches as far south as Wotton-under-Edge.

VOLUNTARY CAMPAIGNING & CONSERVATION ORGANISATIONS

Voluntary organisations started the conservation movement back in the mid 1800s and are still at the forefront of developments. Independent of government but reliant on public support, they can concentrate their resources either on acquiring land which can then be managed purely for conservation purposes, or on influencing political decision-makers by lobbying and campaigning.

The **National Trust** (NT; 🖥 nationaltrust.org.uk) with its four million members protects about 248,000 hectares in the United Kingdom. NT properties on or close to the trail include Snowshill Manor (box p88), Horton Court (p152), Newark Park (p144) and Dyrham Park (p160), as well as significant tracts of land. Of these, some of the most interesting are Dover's Hill just outside Chipping Campden, and Haresfield Beacon, as well as several areas of woodland.

Separated in 2015 from the governmental body responsible for listed buildings and heritage research (now Historic England), **English Heritage** (🖥 english-heritage.org.uk) has gained independent charitable status. It is responsible for the care and preservation of ancient monuments in England, including Hailes Abbey (box p93), several of the long barrows along the Cotswold Way, and Sudeley Castle (box p96).

The **Royal Society for the Protection of Birds** (RSPB; 🖥 rspb.org.uk) has more than a million members and 200 nature reserves, but the nearest to the trail is at Highnam Woods, some 3¾ miles (6km) west of Gloucester.

Rather smaller in scale is the work of **Butterfly Conservation** (🖥 butterfly-conservation.org), which owns and manages the 31-hectare Prestbury Hill Reserve, to the south of Cleeve Hill. The two-part reserve, incorporating both Masts Field and Bill Smyllie Reserve, features a diversity of habitat and is home to some 30 species of butterfly. In 2012 they also acquired the 18-hectare Rough Bank Reserve, south of Birdlip.

The **Woodland Trust** (🖥 woodlandtrust.org.uk) aims to conserve, restore and re-establish trees, particularly broadleaved species. Their properties along the Cotswold Way include Lineover Wood, Penn Wood, Stanley Wood and Coaley Wood.

In a different mould altogether is the **Landmark Trust** (booking enquiries ☎ 01628-825925, 🖥 landmarktrust.org.uk), which works to preserve historic, or architecturally interesting, buildings and to make them suitable for short-term holiday lets. The trust has accommodation options along the trail that include both the East and West Banqueting Houses that once flanked the grand Jacobean Old Campden House at Chipping Campden (see p75), Beckford's Tower (see box p164), and two very close to Bath Abbey.

Then there's the work of two other organisations, both important in environmental terms. Those keen on voluntary work may be interested in **The Conservation Volunteers** (TCV; 🖥 tcv.org.uk), which encourages people to value their environment and take practical action to improve it. And more broadly there's the **Campaign to Protect Rural England** (CPRE; 🖥 cpre.org.uk) – whose name speaks for itself.

Flora and fauna

TREES AND SHRUBS

While the Cotswold Hills are widely revered for their hills and steep cliffs, among their less-sung attractions are the magnificent woods of **beech** (*Fagus sylvatica*) that define the edge of the escarpment. Some veteran species are at least 250 years old, and one – in Lineover Wood south-east of Cheltenham – dates back over 600 years and is said to be the third biggest beech in England. They are seen at their best in spring, when the soft green of the new leaves adds texture rather than darkness to the woodland panorama. Time is inevitably taking its toll on these old timers, which are threatened by factors such as disease, wind damage and erosion, as well as the vigorous seedlings of other species such as **ash** (*Fraxinus excelsior*).

Also interspersed with the beech are **sycamore** or **sycamore maple** (*Acer pseudoplatanus*), and **oak** (*Quercus robur*), as well as **horse chestnut** (*Aesculus hippocastanum*), **lime** or **linden** (*Tilia vulgaris*) and **birch** (*Betula pubescens*). Another species, the **large-leaved lime** (*Tilia platyphyllos*), is one of the rarest trees in Britain, but there's a bank of them in Lineover Wood, whose name derives from the Anglo-Saxon word for 'lime bank'.

Amongst mixed woodland you will come across trees such as **rowan** or **mountain ash** (*Sorbus aucuparia*), popular with birds who seek out its bright orange berries around August, **silver birch** (*Betula pendula*), **aspen** (*Populus tremula*), **alder** (*Alnus glutinosa*), and **hazel** (*Corylus avellana*). While there are **conifers** to be found, most are incidental to the deciduous trees; there are none of the dark conifer plantations so prevalent in many woodland areas.

In the hedgerows, the white, star-like blossom of the **blackthorn** (*Prunus spinosa*) heralds the beginning of spring, giving way as the year progresses to dark-blue, almost dusty-looking sloes which make great sloe gin. Later, a mass of creamy flowers proclaims the **hawthorn** (*Crataegus monogyna*), whose fruit adds a splash of red in autumn. Then, in early summer, the glory goes to the **elder** (*Sambucus nigra*), with its sweet-smelling clusters of cream flowers which by September have formed into a purplish-black fruit, ripe for making jelly or wine.

WILD FLOWERS

Of speedwell and thistles there are indeed plenty, but Gurney – writing after World

> *On Cotswold Edge there is a field and that*
> *Grows thick with corn and speedwell and the mat*
> *Of thistles, of the tall kind*
> **Ivor Gurney**, *Up There*

War I – does little more than hint at the richness of the flora to be found in his native Cotswolds. While much has changed since then, and habitats have declined significantly, there are still wild flowers aplenty along the trail.

Limestone grassland

Until the 1950s, sheep grazed the limestone grasslands that are so characteristic of the Cotswolds (some say the name derived from the Saxon words *wold*, referring to high, open country, and *cod* meaning 'found', but others claim it came from the Cotswold sheep), encouraging a broad range of wild flowers and an attendant population of butterflies and other insects. With changes in agriculture, what was left of this 'unimproved' grassland became overgrown, but several areas are now managed to ensure that this unique habitat can continue to prosper. Over 200 species of wild flower have been identified at Crickley Hill alone, with other similar areas including Leckhampton Hill, Painswick Beacon, Coaley Peak, Selsley Common and Prestbury Hill Reserve, as well as a small patch of ground at Great Witcombe Roman Villa.

Many of the wild flowers that grow in this habitat, such as **cowslips** (*Primula veris*), are also to be found along hedgerows and in fields, but some are specific to this environment. In spring there's the **early purple orchid** (*Orchis mascula*), but it's in summer that the wild orchids really come into their own. Relatively easy to find among colourful patches of **birdsfoot trefoil** (*Lotus corniculatus*), purple **self-heal** (*Prunella vulgaris*) and red or white **clover** (*Trifolium* spp) are the bright pink **pyramidal orchid** (*Anacamptis pyramidalis*), and **common spotted orchids** (*Dactylorhiza fuchsii*), which can be pink, pale lilac or white. The **bee orchid** (*Ophrys apifera*), named for its close resemblance to a bee, is a rarity, and is carefully protected where it does grow.

Also present are the **fly orchid** (*Ophrys insectifera*) – which does look like a fly – and the rather inconspicuous **musk orchid** (*Herminium monorchis*).

Striking in their summer glory are the tall spikes of startlingly blue **viper's bugloss** (*Echium vulgare*), and the **thistles** (*Cirsium* spp) and **knapweeds** (*Centaurea scabiosa*), their colourful purple flowers a magnet for bees.

The delicate **harebell** (*Campanula rotundifolia*) is also at home here, as is the **scabious** (*Knautia arvensis*), their pale-blue flowers contrasting with bold **ox-eye daisies** (*Leucanthemum vulgare*) and the rather less flamboyant **yellow rattle** (*Rhinanthus minor*), named for the sound made by its seeds when they're ripe. Lower down is the **common rock rose** (*Helianthemum nummularium*), its bright-yellow, five-petalled flowers familiar to many gardeners. Look out, too, for the pinkish-purple flowers of wild herbs such as **basil** (*Clinopodium vulgare*), **marjoram** (*Origanum vulgare*) and the ground-hugging **thyme** (*Thymus serphyllum*).

Moorland

Up on the hills and on open spaces such as Cleeve Common you'll come across plenty of **bracken** (*Pteridium aquilinum*), its fronds turning to a crisp brown as the year progresses. Here, too, the bright-yellow flowers of **gorse** (*Ulex europaeus*) brighten up the hillside.

Hedgerows and field boundaries

As the days grow longer and the air begins to warm up, wild flowers start to appear along the hedgerows. Needing little introduction are the more common species which even the uninitiated will soon recognise, such as: **primrose** (*Primula vulgaris*); **common dog violet** (*Viola riviniana*); **common speedwell** (*Veronica officinalis*), which can cure indigestion, gout and liver complaints; **bugle** (*Ajuga repans*); **tufted vetch** (*Vicia cracca*); **lesser celandine** (*Ranunculus ficaria*), not unlike the related buttercup; and **red campion** (*Silene dioica*).

Here, too, you might find the occasional **green alkanet** (*Pentaglottis sempervirens*) which, with its bright-blue flowers and soft, hairy leaves, is often mistaken for borage, and the tall, deep-purple **honesty** (*Lunaria redivia*), whose flat, translucent seedpods are sought after by flower arrangers.

Later, from May to September, these will be joined by **buttercup** (*Ranunculus acris*), the flowers of which children will use to tell you if you like butter, and the small pink-flowered **herb robert** (*Geranium robertianum*).

The **dandelion** (*Taraxacum officinale*) grows almost everywhere, including on waste ground, as does the tall **rosebay willowherb** (*Epilobium angustifolium*). Equally tall is the purple **foxglove** (*Digitalis purpurea*). Its flowers are attractive to bees but the plant is poisonous to humans – although it's from the foxglove that the drug Digitalin is extracted to treat heart disease.

Unmistakable is the vivid red splash of the **field poppy** (*Papaver rhoeas*). Then there are the tall white-flowering heads of members of the carrot family such as **cow parsley** (*Anthrisus sylvestris*), **yarrow** (*Achillea millefolium*) and **hedge parsley** (*Torilis japonica*).

Early Purple Orchid
Orchis mascula

Common Spotted-Orchid
Dactylorhiza fuchsii

Pyramidal Orchid
Anacamptis pyramidalis

Bee Orchid
Ophrys apifera

Field Scabious
Knautia arvensis

Common/Spear Thistle
Cirsium vulgare

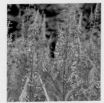

Rosebay Willowherb
Epilobium angustifolium

Herb-Robert
Geranium robertianum

Common Centaury
Centaurium erythraea

Red Campion
Silene dioica

Common Vetch
Vicia sativa

Common Dog Violet
Viola riviniana

Gorse
Ulex europaeus

Meadow Buttercup
Ranunculus acris

Marsh Marigold (Kingcup)
Caltha palustris

Bird's-foot trefoil
Lotus corniculatus

Water Avens
Geum rivale

Tormentil
Potentilla erecta

Primrose
Primula vulgaris

St John's Wort
Hypericum perforatum

Honeysuckle
Lonicera periclymemum

Common Ragwort
Senecio jacobaea

Hemp-nettle
Galeopsis speciosa

Cowslip
Primula veris

Harebell
Campanula rotundifolia

Dog Rose
Rosa canina

Forget-me-not
Myosotis arvensis

Yellow Rattle
Rhinanthus minor

Self-heal
Prunella vulgaris

Meadow Cranesbill
Geranium pratense

Wood Sorrel
Oxalis acetosella

Common Hawthorn
Crataegus monogyna

Germander Speedwell
Veronica chamaedrys

Common Knapweed
Centaurea nigra

Yarrow
Achillea millefolium

Hogweed
Heracleum sphondylium

Foxglove
Digitalis purpurea

Bluebell
Hyacinthoides non-scripta

Common Poppy
Papaver rhoeas

Green Alkanet
Pentaglottis sempervirens

Rowan (tree)
Sorbus aucuparia

Scarlet Pimpernel
Anagallis arvensis

Old Man's Beard
Clematis vitalba

© Jane Thomas

Red Admiral butterfly (*Vanessa atalanta*) on
Hemp Agrimony (*Eupatorium cannabinum*)

Ramsons (Wild garlic)
Allium ursinum

Opposite: Wild garlic is very common in many wooded areas, often competing with the bluebell for space and light.

Left: Chipping Campden lies at the northern end of the Cotswold Way and the trail begins by 400-year-old Market Hall (bottom left). Above: From the moment you leave Chipping Campden until you walk into Bath you'll see a lot of sheep on this trail. Below: The view from Cleeve Common.

Left: You can see as far as the Severn River and beyond to the Brecon Beacons from Frocester Hill and Coaley Peak. **Above**: The Devil's Chimney on Leckhampton Hill (see p115). **Lower left and below**: The Lychgate, Painswick (see p122) and the spectacle stocks by the churchyard.

Above: In early summer you'll see dazzling yellow fields of oil-seed rape, the crop used for vegetable oil, biodiesel and animal feed. **Below**: Dyrham Park (see p160). **Left**: Approaching Cam Long Down (Map 27).

Above: Site of the Battle of Lansdown. **Below**: Private sculpture garden with macabre works by David Michael Morse, by Lansdown Golf Course. **Left, top**: The folly near Little Sodbury. **Left, bottom**: On your walk you'll see many examples of ornate topiary. (Photo © Lee Miller).

THE PUMP ROOM

THE ROMAN BATHS

Above: Sampling Bath's thermal waters in The Pump Room (© Lee Miller).
Above and right: A visit to the Roman Baths and the museum is highly recommended. From the walkway above the ancient bathing pool there are also good views of Bath Abbey. **Below**: Pulteney Bridge and the weir.

Peacock
Inachis io

Small Tortoiseshell
Aglais urticae

Large Blue
Maculinea arion

Large Garden/Cabbage White
Pieris brassicae

Small Heath
*Coenonympha
pamphilus*

Red
Admiral
Vanessa atalanta

Small Garden/Cabbage White
Artogeia rapae

Painted Lady
Cynthia cadui

Small Copper
Lycaena phlaeus

Silver-washed Fritillary *Argynnis paphia*

Summer is when the climbers and ramblers come into their own. Almost everyone is familiar with the common **bramble** (*Rubus fruticosus*), sought out in autumn by blackberry pickers. **Honeysuckle** (*Lonicera periclymenum*), also known as woodbine, makes its appearance growing through hedges and in woodland from June to September, the fruits ripening to red in the autumn. **Hedge bindweed** (*Calystegia sepium*), with its white trumpet-shaped flowers, and the related pink **field bindweed** (*Convolvulus arvensis*) are a common sight during the summer months, as is the pale-pink **dog rose** (*Rosa canina*), which later produces rosehips, an excellent source of vitamin C and used to make a subtle-flavoured jelly. Then there's another autumn beauty, the almost translucent scarlet berries of the **white briony** (*Bryonia cretica*) that tumble in profusion down many a hedgerow. Beware, though: they're extremely poisonous.

Woodland

Spring has to be the best time to walk through the Cotswolds' beech woods. This is when the air is pungent with the smell of densely packed white **ramsons** (*Allium ursinum*), widely known as **wild garlic**. In some places, carpets of **bluebells** (*Hyacinthoides non-scripta*) appear, while others are favoured by **dog's mercury** (*Mercurialis perennis*) – no floral beauty, this, but its bright green leaves make a splendid floor covering. Beneath the still-open tree canopy, the woodland floor is liberally sprinkled with white **wood anemones** (*Anemone nemorosa*), whose petals close up at night and in bad weather. With a similar night-time habit but with more rounded leaves is the smaller **wood sorrel** (*Oxalis acetosella*). The plant with the red stem, dark green leaves and soft green bracts is the **wood spurge** (*Euphorbia amygdaloides*). A little later you might see the occasional patch of **lily-of-the-valley** (*Convallaria majalis*), or the much taller **Solomon's seal** (*Polygonatum multiflorum*).

In darker areas, especially along rocks and walls (look out for them in Penn Wood and Coaley Wood), are **hart's tongue ferns** (*Phyllitis* or *Asplenium scolopendrium*), their long narrow leaves slightly furled; this is the only British fern whose leaves are undivided.

In summer and autumn, there's often the opportunity to supplement a packed lunch with wild **alpine strawberries** (*Fragaria vesca*) and to a lesser extent **wild raspberries** (*Rubus idaeus*). Steer well clear, though, of the poisonous purple fruits of **bittersweet** or **woody nightshade** (*Solanum dulcamara*).

Riverbanks and wet areas

You won't have much opportunity to spot plants along riverbanks as you're walking the trail, but there is the occasional stream, and the alternative route along Stroudwater (Ebley) Canal offers a few water-loving specimens. In summer, the soft cream heads of **meadowsweet** (*Filipendula ulmaria*), which has similar medicinal properties to aspirin, contrast with tall **purple loosestrife** (*Lythrum salicaria*).

On the edge of water courses bright-yellow **marsh marigolds** (*Caltha palustris*) may be seen, while on the water itself (take a look on the canal) are large **yellow waterlilies** (*Nuphar lutea*). You might also see the pink **cuckoo**

THE ENVIRONMENT & NATURE

flower (*Cardamine pratensis*) and **ragged robin** (*Lychnis flos-cuculi*), as well as **watermint** (*Mentha aquatica*), easily identified by its smell, and **hemp agrimony** (*Eupatorium cannabinum*), with its large pink flowers.

BUTTERFLIES   [see colour plate opposite p65]

The existence of unimproved limestone grasslands is one of the major features that make butterflies so important to the Cotswolds region. Some 34 species are found in this environment, with the area significant for both the **small blue** (*Cupido minimus*), and the **Duke of Burgundy fritillary** (*Hamearis lucina*). Part of the Cotswolds AONB near Stroud has seen the reintroduction of the **large blue** (*Maculinea arion*), which, along with the **Adonis blue** (*Lysandra bellargus*), had been declared extinct in this area.

Those with a serious interest would be well advised to spend some time at the Prestbury Hill Reserve south of Cleeve Hill, where many species are protected within a reserve managed by Butterfly Conservation (see p62). Some, such as the **large whites** (*Pieris brassicae*) and **small whites** (*Artogeia rapae*), and the nettle feeders like **red admiral** (*Vanessa atalanta*) and **painted lady** (*Cynthia cadui*), are familiar to many of us from our gardens and parks and are easily spotted in many other places. Other, rarer species, such as the **large skipper** (*Ochlodes venata*), **brown argus** (*Aricia agestis*), **chalk-hill blue** (*Lysandra coridon*), **green hairstreak** (*Callophrys rubi*), **dark green fritillary** (*Argynnis aglaja*), **marbled white** (*Melanargia galathea*), **grayling** (*Hipparchia semele*), **small copper** (*Lycaena phlaeus*), **small heath** (*Coenonympha pamphilus*), **speckled wood** (*Pararge aegeria*), **comma** (*Polygonia c-album*), **peacock** (*Inachis io*), **tortoiseshell** (*Aglais urticae*), and **meadow brown** (*Maniola jurtina*), benefit significantly from this protection. Some of these are also found in other reserves including Leckhampton Hill, or at Painswick Beacon. Elsewhere, perhaps in Buckholt Wood (see Map 18), you may be lucky enough to spot the **silver-washed fritillary** (*Argynnis paphia*), the largest of the British fritillaries with a wingspan of almost 3" (70mm).

There may be considerable difference between the male and female of a species, which can be particularly frustrating for the novice attempting to identify a creature that scarcely holds still for a moment. Many of the blue butterflies, for example, take their name from the male; the female is often a rather insignificant brown.

BIRDS
High overhead ran frenzied larks, screaming, as though the sky were tearing apart
Laurie Lee, Cider with Rosie

To most of us, the song of a skylark overhead is decidedly more appealing than to Laurie Lee's childhood ears. And fortunately, there are still several places along the Cotswold Way where skylarks can be seen. Of the 86 species of bird that have been identified in the region as a whole, the skylark is considered to be one of 20 that are designated as 'nationally important' – along with the linnet, starling, house sparrow and yellowhammer.

Open farmland and upland areas

Out on the hills is where you'll find the **sky-lark** (*Alauda arvensis*), which is often heard long before it is seen, its clear song delivered as it soars overhead. Look out for them on Cleeve Hill Common and Selsley Common; they even do an impressive job of drowning out the traffic noise on fields near the M4 south of Tormarton. The same environment could throw up the similarly sized **meadow pipit** (*Anthus pratensis*), while two other birds that you're likely to see are the **wheatear** (*Oenanthe oenanthe*), the male of which has a steel-grey back and crown and often bows and flicks its tail and perches on walls or rocks, and the **stonechat** (*Saxicola torquata*), much smaller and darker in plumage and identifiable by its call, a single sharp 'teck'. In autumn, flocks of **redwings** (*Turdus iliatus*) and **fieldfares** (*Turdus pilaris*) arrive from their breeding grounds in northern Europe to feed on wild fruit and berries.

SKYLARK
L: 185MM/7.25"

THE ENVIRONMENT & NATURE

Most easily spotted on hedgerows alongside farmland is the **yellowham-mer** (*Emberiza citronella*), its familiar song widely translated as 'little-bit-of-bread-and-no-cheese'. This bright yellow bird with a reddish-brown back is regularly seen at Dover's Hill and Leckhampton Hill, too.

Out on the fields and across the hills is big crow country. You can't miss these gregarious birds, collectively known as corvids, whether the grey-headed **jackdaws** (*Corvus monedula*), the **rooks** (*Corvus frugilegus*), or the **carrion crows** (*Corvus corone corone*). If you doubted their community instincts, look out for jackdaws in particular at Wontley Farm, near Belas Knap, where they have taken over the derelict buildings en masse. In a similar environment you'll find **lapwings** (*Vanellus vanellus*), with their smart crests; during the breeding season the male performs a spectacular display, tumbling through the air to attract its mate.

LAPWING/PEEWIT
L: 320MM/12.5"

Increasingly seen near urban dumps, or anywhere that they can pick up scraps, are **lesser black-backed gulls** (*Larus fuscus*), usually in the company of the noisy and closely related **herring gulls** (*Larus argentatus*). Despite their prevalence, these two still seem entirely incongruous in a rural setting.

In an area where such a large proportion of land is given over to agriculture, the presence of game birds comes as no surprise. **Pheasants** (*Phasianus colchicus*) and **partridges** (*Perdix perdix*) are found practically everywhere, so don't be surprised if one suddenly flies up just in front of you, startled at your approach. You may also put up a **snipe** (*Gallinago*

gallinago), which has a zig-zag flight when flushed, or in wooded areas the nocturnal **woodcock** (*Scolopax rusticola*), easily distinguished from the snipe by its larger size and more rounded wings. Its camouflage makes it difficult to observe during the day.

Lording it over them all are the birds of prey. Both the **kestrel** (*Falco tinnunculus*) and the **sparrowhawk** (*Accipiter nisus*) can be seen, but it's the much larger **buzzard** (*Buteo buteo*), with its brown colouring and cruel yellow talons, that attracts most attention. Its mewing cry can send a shiver down the spine as it soars over fields, woods or moorland in search of its prey, anything from a beetle to a rabbit. The buzzard's fierce reputation won't stop other birds from defending their nests: rooks in particular will sometimes gang up to chase it away, although if sufficiently provoked the buzzard could well retaliate. The **red kite** (*Milvus milvus*) puts in a regular appearance, encroaching west following its successful re-introduction in the Chiltern Hills. It is easily distinguished in flight from other birds of prey by its forked tail.

Woodland

Many of the woodland residents such as the **chaffinch** (*Fringilla coelebs*), **greenfinch** (*Carduelis chloris*), **robin** (*Erithacus rubecula*), **song thrush** (*Turdus philomelos*), **blackbird** (*Turdus merula*), **blue tit** (*Parus caeruleus*) and **great tit** (*Parus major*), are familiar to us from our gardens, although less well known is the **long-tailed tit** (*Aegithalos caudatus*), which is distinguished from other tits by its very long tail: it tends to frequent woodland fringes and clearings.

Of the finches, the **goldfinch** (*Carduelis carduelis*) and **linnet** (*Acanthis cannabina*) are relatively common, too, but you might also spot the **siskin** (*Carduelis spinus*), which is smaller and more streaked than the greenfinch, and more yellow in colour. The **brambling** (*Fringilla montifringilla*), which often mixes with chaffinches in winter, is easily distinguished from them by its distinct white upper rump. The **bullfinch** (*Pyrrhula pyrrhula*) is notable for the male's brilliant red chest; the female is like a monochrome copy of her mate. They feed on berries, buds and seeds in the trees and bushes, their movements slow and deliberate. A much smaller bird is the **goldcrest** (*Regulus regulus*), which is the smallest European bird, recognised by its yellow crown with black edges.

The **willow warbler** (*Phylloscopus trochilus*) and **chiffchaff** (*Phylloscopus collybita*) will keep you guessing since distinguishing between them is quite difficult. The chiffchaff is generally rather browner than the willow warbler and its legs are blackish. More obviously, the willow warbler has the more melodic song.

Even if you're unfamiliar with the **treecreeper** (*Certhia familiaris*), it's not difficult to put a name to this small, brown bird with a curved bill that does exactly that: creeps up trees searching for insects. A similar location might also throw up the **nuthatch** (*Sitta europaea*), with its bluish-grey upper side and pinkish-cream chest, though this species tends to make its way down the trunk head first. Similar in size, although not in habit, is the **blackcap** (*Sylvia atricapilla*), quite easy to identify not just for the said black head (as well as brown back and lighter chest), but also for its pretty song. Usually a summer visitor, it nests in woods or dense shrubs. Another summer visitor is the inconspicuous **tree pipit** (*Anthus trivialis*); this one happiest on woodland fringes or any rough country, from where it delivers itself into the air, singing as it goes.

Larger and far more conspicuous are members of the woodpecker family. The **green woodpecker** (*Picus viridis*), a striking bird with a bright green body and red head, is also notable for its curious call, a kind of laughing cry that carries a long way. More often heard than seen are the **lesser spotted woodpecker** (*Dendrocopos minor*) and the much larger **great spotted woodpecker** (*Dendrocopos major*), distinctive for its striking black-and-white plumage, with a bright red patch under the tail and – in the male – similarly coloured crown. Both habitually drum on trees, usually to mark their territory and extract insects rather than to bore holes for a nest site.

It is highly likely that you'll see the **magpie** (*Pica pica*) in its handsome black, white and blue plumage, and the colourful **jay** (*Garrulus glandarius*) is becoming more common everywhere; both are highly efficient at cleaning eggs out of birds' nests and even taking young birds. Rarely seen, although its distinctive call is known even to children as the first harbinger of summer, the **cuckoo** (*Cuculus canorus*) is grey or occasionally brown in colour, not unlike a heavy male sparrowhawk. From the dove family, **wood pigeons** (*Columba palumbus*) and **collared doves** (*Streptopelia decaocto*) can be seen – and heard – everywhere.

GREEN WOODPECKER
L: 330mm/13"

Finally, there are the birds of the night, of which the one you're most likely to see – even occasionally in the daytime – is the **tawny owl** (*Strix aluco*). It can be quite unnerving to look up from a lunchtime picnic to find you're being observed from on high.

Streams, canals, rivers and reservoirs

Large tracts of open water are not something you'd associate with the Cotswolds, with the notable exceptions of the canal near Ebley, and the parallel River Frome, but reservoirs and the occasional stream or ornamental pond are enough to attract **swallows** (*Hirundo rustica*), **house martins** (*Delichon urbica*) and **swifts** (*Apus apus*). Watch their acrobatics in summer as they swoop low, picking up insects on the wing. You'll also spot these birds further afield, too. House martins often build their nests under the eaves of houses or churches, while swifts can often be seen rising on the currents; look out for them above Selsley Common. Distinctive in flight for its scimitar-shaped wings, the swift cannot perch like the swallow and martin, and spends almost its entire life aloft. The less-common **sand martin** (*Riparia riparia*) nests in colonies in holes in steep riverbanks and cliffs such as those in Witcombe Wood, near the reservoir.

THE ENVIRONMENT & NATURE

In evidence along the canal are the familiar **mute swans** (*Cygnus olor*), **mallards** (*Anas platyrhynchos*), **coots** (*Fulica atra*) and **moorhens** (*Gallinula chloropus*), but there are other birds around too. The **grey wagtail** (*Motacilla cinerea*) in particular, with a blue-grey head and a bright-yellow underside, can be seen year-round bobbing up and down by bridges over fast-flowing rivers.

MAMMALS

You might occasionally spot a **roe deer** (*Capreolus capreolus*) in the woods along the Cotswold escarpment. Small in stature, with an average height of 60-75cm at the shoulder, they are reddish brown in summer, but grey in winter, and have a distinctive white rear end which is conspicuous when the deer is alarmed. Males have short antlers with no more than three points. They are active at dawn and dusk and can sometimes be heard barking. If you come across a young kid apparently abandoned, leave it alone and go away; it's normal behaviour for the mother to leave her kid concealed while she goes off to feed.

An enclosure of **red deer** (*Cervus elaphus*) can be seen at Broadway Tower, but these animals are not found in the wild in the Cotswolds.

Far more visible is the **rabbit** (*Oryctolagus cuniculus*). While many town-ies consider them to be cute relatives of Peter Rabbit, to the farmer they're a pest, responsible each year for damage to crops that can be counted in the millions. Despite being prey to buzzards, foxes, feral cats, stoats and man, they breed rapidly, bucks mating at four months old and does at three-and-a-half months, so their numbers are on the increase.

The **brown hare** (*Lepus europaeus*) is larger than the rabbit with large powerful hind legs and very long, black-tipped ears. They are found on upland, such as Leckhampton Hill, and rely for escape on their great acceleration, capable of attaining speeds of up to 45mph (70km/h).

Badgers (*Meles meles*) are nocturnal animals and rarely seen during the day, lying up in their underground burrows, or setts. Litters of cubs are born in February. Like rabbits, they are responsible for considerable damage on farmland, but unlike rabbits they are a protected species and cannot be destroyed. There is also some suggestion that cattle can catch the TB virus through contact with badgers.

Red foxes (*Vulpes vulpes*) are common, in spite of occasional persecution by man and the British roads. Readily identifiable by their colour and bushy tail, foxes are shy animals that come out mainly at night to hunt for food. Their supposed habit of killing all the hens in a coop and taking only one is apparently not the result of vicious rage but done to take advantage of abundance while it is available to compensate for times when food is scarce. Although the issue remains controversial, a ban on fox hunting was implemented in 2005.

The ubiquitous **grey squirrel** (*Sciurus carolinensis*) needs no introduction, having driven the native red squirrel into just one or two strongholds since the former's arrival here from North America in the 19th century.

The **weasel** (*Mustela nivalis*), one of Britain's smaller carnivores, is found in a wide range of habitats and is not a protected species. In fact, it may be trapped and killed by gamekeepers out to protect their birds from its claws. Mainly nocturnal and preferring dry areas, the weasel is smaller than the **stoat** (*Mustela erminea*), the tip of whose tail is always black.

Other small creatures that hide away in hedgerows include the nocturnal **hedgehog** (*Erinaceus europaeus*), which curls into a tight prickly ball when startled, as well as **shrews** (*Sorex sp.*), **voles** (*Microtus arvalis*) and **harvest mice** (*Micromys minutus*).

Of the 18 species of **bat** in the UK, several are found in the Cotswolds. The most obvious place to spot them is at Woodchester Mansion (see box p132)

❏ FARM ANIMALS

Dotted across the hills, **sheep** seem to take on the colour of Cotswold stone, rather dirty in the rain, but a soft warm cream in the sun, their lambs improbably white. In the Middle Ages, Cotswold sheep, or 'Cotswold Lions' as they were known, were bred for their long, thick fleeces, which brought immense fortunes to local merchants, enabling them to build the splendid manor houses and imposing 'wool' churches that still grace the region's towns. The animal is distinctive to the layman both for its long coat and a rather unkempt fringe.

Today, because of the widespread crossing of breeds, most of the sheep seen in the fields are cross-breeds, reared primarily for their meat. Yet some of the old breeds are still used, particularly for grazing on Cleeve Hill, so don't be surprised to see the occasional flock of Cotswold sheep.

While the majority of grazing animals in the Cotswolds are sheep, there are still **cattle** to be found, particularly further south along the trail. Many are the familiar black-and-white Friesians, but more conspicuous are the occasional belted Galloways, almost entirely black but with a broad white belt around their girth. Near Stanley Wood you may spot a herd of English longhorn cows, their downward curved horns distinctly different from the norm. The 'local' breed, Gloucester cattle, are distinctive, too, though you'll be lucky to see them. Once bred for Double Gloucester cheese, they have smart, near-black coats (occasionally spotted) enlivened by a bold white streak running from the middle of their spine through to their tail. Other distinguishing features are a black head and legs, and black-tipped horns.

No summary of farm animals in Gloucestershire would be complete without a nod to the **Gloucestershire Old Spot pig**. Named for the large black spots that dot their otherwise pink skins, these pigs once thrived in the outdoors, foraging on scraps and windfall apples. In fact, the spots are said to be bruises from falling apples in the orchards. They're immortalised at The Old Spot in Dursley!

Finally, there are **horses**. Lots of them – though nowadays they scarcely fall into the bracket of farm animals. From children's ponies to thoroughbred racehorses, you'll find plenty that point to man's passion for equines. Riding stables are much in evidence, especially in the north of the region, and many's the day when you'll come across a rider or party of riders as you walk along the trail. With this obvious local involvement, it's no accident that two of the country's biggest events in the horsey calendar, the Cheltenham Gold Cup and Badminton Horse Trials, take place in the Cotswolds.

If you want a closer look at many of these animals and more rare breeds, pay a visit to **Cotswold Farm Park** (☎ 01451-850307, 🖳 cotswoldfarmpark.co.uk; mid Feb-Dec daily 9.30am-4pm; £14.95, or £13.95 online), east of Winchcombe, about four miles (6.4km) from the trail at Stumps Cross, off the B4077.

THE ENVIRONMENT & NATURE

❏ THE SMALLER THINGS IN LIFE

While you're looking out for things at ground level, perhaps you'll spot two other grassland natives that are both now rare, but can still be found in this habitat.

© Tricia & Bob Hayne

The **glow worm** (*Lampyris noctiluca*) was once so common that people could read by the light of several found together.

And **Roman snails** (*Helix pomatia*, right) were considered a delicacy by the Romans, which is presumably how they acquired their name. Look out for them around Leckhampton and Crickley Hill; their cream-coloured shells can be up to two inches wide.

where six different species roost in the house and grounds. These include the endangered **greater horseshoe bat** (*Rhinolophus ferrumequinum*), with a wingspan of around 14" (35cm), and its cousin, the **lesser horseshoe bat** (*Rhinolophus hipposideros*), as well as the tiny **pipistrelle** (*Pipistrellus pipistrellus*), which is Britain's most common species of bat – and the smallest, with a wingspan of just 8" (20cm).

REPTILES

The **adder** (*Vipera berus*) is the only venomous snake in Britain but poses very little risk to walkers and will not bite unless provoked or unwittingly disturbed; if you're lucky enough to see one, leave it in peace. Their venom is designed to kill small mammals such as mice and shrews; human deaths are rare.

You are most likely to encounter an adder in spring when they come out of hibernation, and during the summer when pregnant females warm themselves on open ground in the sun. They are easily identified by the striking zig-zag pattern on their back and a 'V' on the top of their head behind their eyes.

Grass snakes (*Natrix natrix*) are Britain's largest reptile, growing up to a metre in length. They prefer rough ground with plentiful long grass in which to conceal themselves, laying their eggs in warm, rotting vegetation such as garden compost heaps, the young hatching in August. Its body has vertical black bars and spots running along the sides and usually has a prominent yellow collar round the neck. They are sometimes killed by people mistaking them for adders but are neither venomous nor aggressive.

The equally harmless **slow worm** (*Anguis fragilis*) looks like a snake but is actually a legless lizard. It has no identifying marks on its body, which varies in colour from coppery brown to lead grey and is usually quite shiny in appearance. Like lizards, they are able to blink; snakes have no eyelids. They love to sun themselves and are also found in old buildings under stones or discarded roofing sheets. Also present is the **common lizard** (*Lacerta vivipara*), which like other reptiles is partial to sunning itself during the day to warm up its body temperature.

Using this guide

The route guide has been divided into stages but these should not be seen as rigid daily itineraries; people walk at different speeds and have different interests. The **route summaries** describe the trail between significant places and are written as if walking the path from north to south, since this is by far the most popular direction for people tackling the trail. There's nothing to stop you, of course, from tackling the trail in the other direction.

To enable you to plan your own itinerary, **practical information** is presented clearly on each of the trail maps. This includes walking times in each direction, places to stay and eat, as well as shops where you can buy supplies. Further **service details** are given in the text; note that the hours stated for pubs relate, for the most part, to when food is served; most venues serve drinks outside these hours.

For **map profiles** see the colour pages at the end of the book. For an overview of this information see **itineraries** (p32) and the town & village **facilities table** (pp34-7). The cumulative **distance chart** is on pp194-5.

TRAIL MAPS [see key map inside cover; symbols key p186]

Scale and walking times

The trail maps are to a **scale** of just under 1:20,000 (1cm = 200m; $3^1/_8$ inches = one mile).

Walking times (**see box below**) are given along the side of each map and the arrow shows the direction to which the time refers. Black triangles indicate the points between which the times have been taken. The time-bars are a tool and are not there to judge your walking ability. There are so many variables that affect walking speed, from the weather conditions to how many beers you drank the previous evening. After the first hour or two of walking you will be able to see how your speed relates to the timings on the maps.

❏ **IMPORTANT NOTE – WALKING TIMES**

Unless otherwise specified, **all times in this book refer only to the time spent walking**. You should add 20-30% to allow for rests, photos, checking the map, drinking water etc, not to mention time simply to stop and stare. When planning the day's hike count on 5-7 hours' actual walking.

Up or down?

The trail is shown as a dotted line – – –. An arrow across the trail indicates the slope; two arrows show that it is steep. Note that the arrow points towards the higher part of the trail. If, for example, you are walking from A (at 80m) to B (at 200m) and the trail between the two is short and steep it would be shown thus: A– – –>>– – – B. Reversed arrow heads indicate a downward gradient.

Accommodation

Accommodation marked on the map is either on or within easy reach of the trail. Where accommodation is scarce, however, some of the places listed are a little further away. If that is the case, many B&B proprietors will collect walkers from the nearest point on the trail and deliver them back again the next morning, if requested in advance. Some may make a charge for this service. Details of each place are given in the accompanying text.

The number of **rooms** of each type is stated, ie: **S** = Single, **T** = Twin room, **D** = Double room, **Tr** = Triple room and **Qd** = Quad. Note that most of the triple/quad rooms have a double bed and one/two single beds (or bunk beds); thus for a group of three or four, two people would have to share the double bed, but it also means that the room can be used as a double or twin. See also p20.

Rates quoted for B&B-style accommodation are **per person (pp) based on two people sharing a room** for a one-night stay; rates may well be discounted for longer stays and for more than two people sharing a room. Where a **single room (sgl)** is available, the rate for that is quoted if different from the rate per person. The rate for **single occupancy (sgl occ)** of a double/twin may be higher. Unless specified, rates are for bed and breakfast. At some places the only option is a **room rate**; this will be the same whether one or two people (or more if permissible) use the room. In tourist towns, particularly, you can expect to pay extra at weekends (whereas in establishments catering for business people the rate is likely to be higher during the week). Note that several places only accept advance bookings for a two-night stay, particularly at weekends and in the main season, though nearer the time may accept a single-night stay.

Your room will either have **en suite** facilities, or a **private** or **shared** bathroom or shower room just outside the bedroom. The text indicates whether a bath (◗) is available for, or in, at least one room – for those who prefer a relaxed soak at the end of the day. It also indicates if a **packed lunch** (Ⓛ) can be prepared, subject to prior arrangement; and if **dogs** (🐾 – see also p25 and pp184-6) are welcome, again subject to prior arrangement.

Other features

The numbered **GPS waypoints** refer to the list on pp183-4. Generally, other features are marked on the maps when they are pertinent to navigation.

In order to avoid cluttering the maps and making them unusable, not all features have been marked each time they occur.

DIRECTION INDICATORS ON MAP SIDE BARS

Walking to the south from Chipping Campden to Bath

Route to Bath continues on Map 5

Walking to the north from Bath to Chipping Campden

Route to Chipping Campden continues on Map 8

ROUTE GUIDE AND MAPS

The route guide

CHIPPING CAMPDEN [MAP 1a, p79]

It feels fitting to start the trail in Chipping Campden, a beguiling town at the most northern point of the Cotswolds Area of Outstanding Natural Beauty, where the classic Cotswold images of warm honey-coloured stone and rolling green hills are so perfectly balanced.

Chipping Campden was founded on the wool industry in the 14th and 15th centuries, largely through the efforts of one of the country's most successful wool merchants, William Grevel. His home, **Grevel House**, still stands on the High St, and to him and other wealthy benefactors the town owes the outstanding, and revered, **St James's Church**.

Over two hundred years later, another local worthy, Sir Baptist Hicks, trumped Grevel House with his **Campden House** in 1612, most of which burned down in 1862. Some of the remaining parts are now used by the Landmark Trust (see p62). Hicks was also responsible for the **Market Hall**, today owned by the National Trust and still in regular use, and for the **almshouses** on Church St.

Fast forwarding through the centuries brings us to the **Arts and Crafts Movement** (see box on p76), which played an influential role in reversing the town's decline following years of agricultural doldrums. Now tourism is the key to the economy, with plenty of restaurants and a range of accommodation suited to walkers and sightseers alike.

For something original, have a look round the **Guild** on Sheep St in Silk Mill. Home to several artisans, it boasts a good art gallery (daily 10am-5pm), but the real draw is upstairs, where Hart's **silversmith** (🖳 hartsilversmiths.co.uk; Mon-Fri 9am-5pm, Sat 9am-noon) has operated for over 100 years. Commission your own family heirloom, or just watch the craftspeople at work. The designs of another silversmith,

Robert Welch (🖳 robertwelch.com; open daily), are displayed at the shop bearing his name on Lower High St.

Every year in May the town hosts a two-week music festival (🖳 campden mayfestivals.co.uk) and – on Dover's Hill – the Olimpick Games (see box on p80).

Getting here

Access to Chipping Campden is relatively straightforward by road, but by **public transport** is more challenging. GWR (see box on p46) operate train services to the nearest railway station at Moreton-in-Marsh; from there take Stagecoach's bus Nos 1/1A or 2/2A.

Alternatively it's possible to get a Chiltern Railways (see box on p46) train to Stratford-upon-Avon from Leamington Spa; Leamington Spa is a stop on Chiltern's London Marylebone to Birmingham line. From Stratford take Stagecoach's 1/1A/2/2A service to Chipping Campden (see box p48).

Getting around

Stagecoach's **bus** Nos 1/1A2/2A stop on the High St as do Pulhams' No 606 and Hedgehog Community Bus's various H3 & H5 buses; see pp48-50.

Taxi firms include: Red Lion Private Hire (mob ☎ 07565-226887, 🖳 redlionpri vatehire.co.uk) and Les Proctor (mob 07580-993492, see Cornerways, Where to stay).

Services

The good **tourist information centre** (☎ 01386-841206, 🖳 chippingcampdenon line.org; open daily year round in summer 9.30am-1pm Mon, Tue, Thur, Fri and until 4pm on Wed and at the weekend; winter hours reduced) has its base in the Old Police Station on the High St. In addition to plenty of maps, guides, brochures and leaflets, there is a town guide for £2.50 and you can buy Cotswold Way Trail commemorative T-shirts for £19. It's under threat of closure so please sign their petition to help keep it open as they do a worthwhile job.

The **post office** stands a couple of doors down from the tourist office off the High St behind Cambrook Court. There's an **ATM** in One Stop.

Nearby are two small **convenience stores**: Co-operative (daily 7am-10pm), and One Stop (daily 7am-10pm). More individ-

ual fare is to be found at **bakeries** and **delis** such as the delightfully old-fashioned **Maylam's Delicatessen** (Mon-Sat 9am-5pm, Sun 10am-4pm) where they'll make up good-value sandwiches and rolls to order; **Huxleys Bakery Shop** (🖥 cafehuxleys.co.uk, Mon-Sat open 'from 9.30am until I'm tired') with freshly baked bread, rolls, cakes and Italian coffee to go; **Victor's** (Tue-Fri 7.30am-2pm, Sat 7.30am-noon); the nearby **Fillet & Bone** (Mon-Sat 9am-6pm, Sun 10am-4pm); and

ROUTE GUIDE AND MAPS

❑ ARTS AND CRAFTS MOVEMENT

The Arts and Crafts Movement was founded in late Victorian Britain, born of a backlash against the uniformity which resulted from the Industrial Revolution. Its proponents – practical architects and designers as well as theorists – were largely concerned with restoring a sense of individuality and cohesion to an increasingly fragmented workplace. There was more than a touch of the romantic in their ideals, which included spiritual harmony and a oneness with nature. These aims were to be achieved in part through reuniting the fields of art, craft and design, so that the designer would be brought back in touch with the maker. Authenticity was a key principle, for example with houses to be constructed from naturally occurring materials and fitting into their environment. If buildings and furniture were relatively simple, ornamental pieces such as books and needlework were considerably more elaborate, often drawing on influences not only from the past but from external cultures. Ironically, high-minded intentions to improve the lot of the working man proved unrealistic, since individually crafted work was expensive to produce and out of the reach of all but a privileged few.

The major founders of the movement were the writer and critic John Ruskin, and William Morris, who trained as an architect and was variously a designer, Socialist and author. Although the movement was essentially urban, many of its practitioners moved to the country, and some to the Cotswolds. One of these, the architect CR Ashbee, was the founder in 1888 of the **Guild of Handicrafts**, which he moved from London to Chipping Campden's Silk Mill [33] in 1902. When Ashbee went bankrupt eight years later, his workshop was taken over by the silversmith George Hart. The work of Ashbee and eight other craftsmen is featured at **Court Barn Museum of Art & Design** [4] (🖥 courtbarn.org.uk; Apr-Sep Tue-Sun & bank hol Mon 10am-5pm, Oct-Mar Tue-Sun & bank hol Mon 10am-4pm; £7), in a converted barn near the church.

Other places along the trail that are linked to the movement include **Gordon Russell Design Museum** in Broadway (see p84), **The Wilson** in Cheltenham (see p107), inspired by William Morris, **Ashton Beer Collection** in Painswick (see p122), and **All Saints' Church** in Selsley (see p130).

Arts and Crafts visionaries had an impact on gardens, too, typically using topiary hedges to create a series of 'rooms'. Such influences were important at both **Owlpen Manor** (see box on p138) and **Hidcote** (off Map 1a; ☎ 01386-438333, 🖥 nationaltrust.org.uk; Easter-Sep daily 10am-6pm, Mar-Easter & Oct daily 10am-5pm, mid-end Feb & early Nov-mid Dec weekends only 11am-4pm; £16, NT members free), a few miles north of Chipping Campden.

Toke's (🖳 tokesfoodanddrink.co.uk, Mon-Fri 9am-6pm, Sat 10am-5pm, Sun in summer), where bread, cheese and pork pies are lined up alongside racks of wine.

Every second Saturday morning (Mar-Nov 10am-5pm) each month there's an **indoor market** (🖳 campdenmarket.co.uk) with food and craft stalls in the Town Hall. **Draycott Books** deals in secondhand books.

Campden Surgery (☎ 01386-841894, 🖳 chippingcampdensurgery.co.uk; Mon-Fri 8.30am-1.30pm & 2-6pm) is along Back Ends.

The **pharmacy** (Mon-Fri 9am-1pm & 2-6pm, Sat 9am-1pm) is on the corner of the High and Church streets.

There are public **toilets** behind the tourist office and opposite Silk Mill.

Where to stay

Many walkers starting at Chipping Campden will want to stay a night before setting off the following morning, if only to have a chance to see something of the town. There's less choice than there was as several of the smaller B&Bs closed during the pandemic and accommodation does get booked up quickly, especially in the summer and at weekends.

Campers should phone *Wolds End Farm* (☎ 01386-840853 or 841008; 🐾) on Aston Rd for details.

There is some **glamping** available on the edge of the town – but for a minimum of two nights midweek and three at weekends – at *Campden Yurts* (☎ 07792-624036, 🖳 campdenyurts.co.uk; **fb**; 2 yurts each sleeping up to 5 people, en suite; ➴; 🐾). It's a 15-minute walk north of the centre at Hillside Nursery, Kingcombe Lane. Prices are from around £100 per yurt per night with discounts if you book on their website. Campfires and the peace and quiet make this a place to linger. It would be a great start or end to a walk.

Bantam Tea Rooms (☎ 01386-840386, 🖳 bantamtea-rooms.co.uk; **fb**; 1S/2T/4D, all en suite; ➴; Ⓛ) charges from £57.50pp (sgl/sgl occ from £90). If you stay the night (and subject to arrangement) you can leave your car here for the duration of your walk for £5 per day.

Run by a friendly and helpful owner, *Badgers Hall* (☎ 01386-840839; **fb**; 2D/1T or D/1T, all en suite; Ⓛ) is centrally-located in one of the stone cottages of the High St. There's usually a minimum stay of two nights but the room with the low beams may be available to Cotswold Way walkers for a one-night stay. B&B costs from £85pp (sgl occ full room rate).

South of the main street on George Lane sits a modern option with footpath access to the High St: *Cornerways* (☎ 01386-841307, 🖳 cornerways.info; 1Tr/1Qd, both en suite). They only accept advance bookings for at least two nights; contact them for prices. They also offer station pick ups: contact Les Proctor (see Getting around).

If a pub is more your idea of a convivial place to spend the night, Chipping Campden comes up trumps. On Lower High St, almost opposite St Catharine's Church, the 17th-century *Volunteer Inn* (☎ 01386-840688, 🖳 thevolunteerinn.net; **fb**; 4D/3D or T/1T/1Qd, most en suite) has a couple of rooms where an extra bed can be added, but some rooms are over the bar so can be noisy. B&B costs from £45pp. They also offer a luggage-transfer service (end Mar to end Oct; see p28) under the name 'Cotswold Luggage Transfers'.

Further along the High St and not to be confused with its namesake in Broadway, is the *Lygon Arms* (☎ 01386-840318, 🖳 lygonarms.co.uk; **fb**; 7D or T/3Tr, all en suite; ➴; Ⓛ; 🐾), a 16th-century coaching inn. Featuring exposed beams and stone walls, there's accommodation from £65pp (sgl occ from £90).

Eight Bells Inn (☎ 01386-840371, 🖳 eightbellsinn.co.uk; **fb**; 6D, all en suite; 🐾 bar area), on Church St, is a 14th-century hostelry where the rooms are furnished in a contemporary yet sympathetic style. Note that from May to September and at weekends throughout the year there's a minimum two-night stay for advance bookings; rates per night are £50-90pp (sgl occ full room rate from May to Sep).

Smarter still are the **hotels**. *Noel Arms* (☎ 01386-840317, 🖳 bespokehotels.com/

noelarmshotel; **fb**; 17T or D/11D, all en suite; ▬; 🐾) charges £55-93.50pp (sgl occ £100-195).

In this rather elevated sphere, there's also *Cotswold House Hotel & Spa* (☎ 01386-840330, 🖳 cotswoldhouse.com; **fb**; 8D/20D or T, all en suite; ▬; (L); 🐾), which might justify a splurge at the end of a walk. Dynamic pricing makes B&B rates – £58 to £184pp for the smaller doubles (sgl occ £94-260), including use of the hydrotherapy pool and steam rooms – something of a lottery, but come in the winter months and you could strike lucky.

Right in the centre of town is the luxury boutique hotel, *Woolmarket House* (☎ 01386-840374, 🖳 woolmarkethouse.com, 2D / 4D or T, all en suite) with B&B for £105-125pp (sgl occ full room rate). Some rooms have a freestanding rolltop bath right in the bedroom and the bathrooms have underfloor heating. At weekends and other busy periods a minimum two-day stay is required. Run by the same family, Michael's Mediterranean (see Where to eat) is downstairs.

Where to eat and drink

Top-quality food with prices to match is done well along Chipping Campden's High St, but there's a good range of more accessible fare as well, especially at lunchtime.

For lingering over tea, coffee or a light lunch, several places fit neatly into the frame. For irresistible cakes, *Bantam Tea Rooms* (see Where to stay; daily 9.30am-5pm) has an enviable selection. Breakfast dishes are served through until 3.30pm; a full Bantam Breakfast is £13.50. Cream teas (from £8.50) are served from 9.30am. Light lunches include soups, salads, sandwiches, omelettes, toasties and panini.

Another good place for a coffee, breakfast or light lunch is *Victor's* (☎ 01386-840401, Tue-Fri 7.30am-2pm, Sat 7.30am-noon), beside One Stop. They also do breakfast baguettes and salad boxes.

Just off the High St in Cambrook Court is *Katie's Café & Coffee Shop* (☎ 01386-841248, **fb**; 🐾; daily 9.30am-5pm), with outdoor seating and very reasonably-priced snacks, soups and light lunches.

In **Silk Mill** on Sheep St there's coffee and cake at *Campden Coffee & Crystals*

CHIPPING CAMPDEN – MAP KEY

Where to stay
1 Campden Yurts
2 Wolds End Farm
6 Eight Bells Inn
11 Lygon Arms
12 Bantam Tea Rooms
14 Badgers Hall
18 Woolmarket House
20 Cotswold House
   Hotel & Spa
23 Noel Arms
24 Cornerways
34 Volunteer Inn

Where to eat & drink
6 Eight Bells Inn
11 Lygon Arms
12 Bantam Tea Rooms
13 Da Luigi

Where to eat & drink
(cont'd)
18 Michael's
   Mediterranean
21 Katie's
23 Noel Arms
26 Victor's
28 Red Lion Tavern
29 Huxley's
33 Campden Coffee &
   Crystals (in Silk Mill)
34 Maharaja &
   Volunteer Inn

What to see & do
3 Campden House
4 Court Barn Museum
5 Almshouses
8 Grevel House
17 Market Hall

What to see & do
(cont'd)
33 Silk Mill
35 Graham Greene's
   House

Other
7 Pharmacy
9 Toke's
10 Maylam's
15 Co-operative
16 Tourist Information
   Centre
19 Campden Surgery
21 Post office
22 Town Hall
25 Fillet & Bone
27 One Stop & ATM
30 Huxley's Bakery
31 Draycott Books
32 Robert Welch

(☎ 01386 849251; Tue-Sun 10am-4pm). Coffee beans are freshly ground and the cakes – including gluten free – are home-made. As well as selling crystals they also run holistic workshops.

Close to the car park in the town centre, the convivial **Huxleys** (☎ 01386-840537, 🖥 cafehuxleys.co.uk; Mon-Thur 10am-8pm, Fri-Sat 10am-9pm, Sun 10am-4pm, winter Mon & Tue to 5pm; 🐾) serves Italian treats from antipasti to seafood pasta from £15. Arno's Bouillabaisse with prawns, mussels, clams and white fish, potatoes and aioli is £19 or, alternatively, a Huxleys burger is £16. A terrace under willow trees makes a popular summer alternative to the restaurant. Bread and cakes come from their bakery next door.

Da Luigi Bistro (☎ 01386-840934, 🖥 daluigi.co.uk; Mon 5-10pm, Tue-Sun noon-10pm – Tue-Fri breakfasts from 10am; 🐾) is on the High St with some seating right on the pavement so you can watch the world go by. It's a popular Italian with pizzas (£11.50-15.50) and all the usual favourites plus good-value two or three course set lunches or dinners.

At Woolmarket House, **Michael's Mediterranean** (☎ 01386-840826, 🖥 michaelsmediterranean.co.uk; daily from 10am for brunch, noon-2.30pm & 5-8.30pm) is excellent. It's mainly Spanish and Greek cuisine. Try a halloumi & chorizo pitta pocket (£11.95), mezedakia (£19.95 for nine hot/cold hors d'oeuvres for sharing), moussaka with salad (£17.50) or huevos rancheros (£12.95).

ROUTE GUIDE AND MAPS

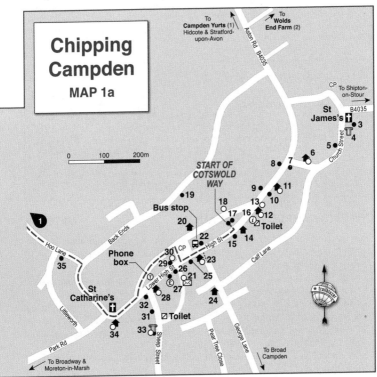

Chipping Campden

MAP 1a

To Campden Yurts (1) Hidcote & Stratford-upon-Avon

To Wolds End Farm (2)

Aston Rd B4035

CP To Shipton-on-Stour

St James's ⛪ 3

B4035

4

5 ● 6

8 ● 7 ●

START OF COTSWOLD WAY

● 19

Bus stop

18

20

22

Phone box

30 CP

29

35

St Catharine's ⛪

32

31 ☐ Toilet

34

33

0   100   200m

Hoo Lane

Back Ends

Lower High St

High St

9 ● ● 11

13 ● 10

17 16 ● 12

ℹ Toilet

14

15

21 25

27 £

26 23

28

24

Call Lane

George Lane

Pear Tree Close

Sheep Street

Littleworth

Park Rd

To Broadway & Moreton-in-Marsh

To Broad Campden

🧭 trailblazer

The town also has some excellent **pubs**. *Eight Bells Inn* (see Where to stay; food Mon-Sat noon-2.30pm & 6-9pm, Sun noon-8.30pm), which retains the atmosphere of a traditional pub, offers plenty of options. Wherever you eat – in the bar, the restaurant or the courtyard garden – you should eat well, particularly on a Sunday with their magnificent roasts (£21.45).

At *Lygon Arms* (see Where to stay; food Mon-Sat noon-9pm, Sun 12.30-8pm) the menu features lamb and beef from the family farm, as well as sandwiches home-made soup and jacket potatoes.

The atmosphere at the *Red Lion Tavern* (☎ 01386-840760, 🖥 redliontavern.co.uk; **fb**; 🐾; food Mon-Thur noon-2pm & 6-8.45pm, Fri noon-2.30pm & 6-9.30pm, Sat noon-3pm & 6-9.30pm, Sun noon-3pm & 6-8.45pm) is relaxed and friendly, and there's a courtyard bar if you'd rather be outside with a pint of IPA. The menu is primarily traditional English, with daily specials that reflect seasonal produce:

expect to pay from £16.95 for a main course, with lighter bites at lunch such as pork belly or halloumi ciabatta costing £9.95. Over summer weekends in the afternoons there may be a DJ or live jazz band in the beer garden.

If you fancy a curry, head for the Indian *Maharaja* (☎ 01386-849281, 🖥 www.maharajacatering.net, daily 5.30-10.30pm) at the *Volunteer Inn* (see Where to stay). They also do takeaways (10% discount). The pub itself sticks to the beer, which can be savoured in summer in the garden.

The *Noel Arms* (☎ 01386-840317, **fb**; see Where to stay; food Mon-Fri noon-3pm & 6-9pm, Sat & Sun noon-9pm) is also a good place to go for a curry – their regular curry feast is every last Thursday of the month (6-9pm). Every second Thursday of the month is Street Food Night. Usual pub classics such as fish & chips (£17) are always available.

❏ OLIMPICK GAMES

Chipping Campden displays its frivolous side in the form of Robert Dover's Olimpick Games (🖥 olimpickgames.co.uk), held on Dover's Hill (Map 1) every May on the Friday after the Whitsun Bank Holiday. Dating back to 1612, it's a noisy affair, with bands, cannon fire and fireworks, culminating in a torchlit procession into the town for dancing in the square. If events such as sack races, a tug of war and even shin-kicking would raise an eyebrow at the Olympics, there's also the more conventional shot put, part of the Championship of the Hill, as well as wrestling and cross-country races. The following day is the **Scuttlebrook Wake**, more of a village fête in style, with a Scuttlebrook Queen, maypole dancing and colourful floats.

CHIPPING CAMPDEN TO BROADWAY   MAPS 1-3

This first **6-mile (9.6km, 2¾-3¼hrs)** stretch of the Cotswold Way, characterised by agricultural land and open hills, is a great introduction to the trail as a whole.

The start – or finish – of the trail is marked by a circular limestone plaque set into the flagstones at the foot of the Market Hall (see p75). Designed, like its partner outside Bath Abbey (see p166), by artist Iain Cotton, it is engraved with the names of places along the trail, encircled by a line from TS Eliot's *Four Quartets*: 'Now the light falls across the open fields leaving the deep lane shuttered with branches dark in the afternoon.'

A gradual ascent leads across farmland to **Dover's Hill**, at 738ft (225m) the first of many high points along the walk, affording the first of several superb

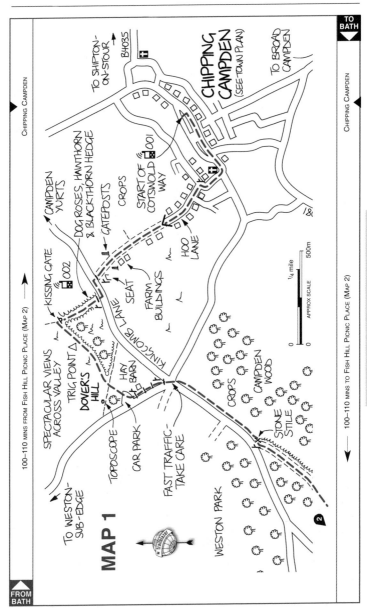

MAP 1

TO BATH

FROM BATH

100–110 MINS FROM FISH HILL PICNIC PLACE (MAP 2)

100–110 MINS TO FISH HILL PICNIC PLACE (MAP 2)

TO SHIPTON-ON-STOUR

B4035

CHIPPING CAMPDEN (SEE TOWN PLAN)

TO BROAD CAMPDEN

CAMPDEN YURTS

DOG ROSES, HAWTHORN & BLACKTHORN HEDGE

GATEPOSTS

CROPS

START OF COTSWOLD WAY

001

KISSING GATE

002

SPECTACULAR VIEWS ACROSS VALLEY

TRIG POINT △

DOVER'S HILL

HAY BARN

HOO LANE

SEAT

FARM BUILDINGS

KINGCOMBE LANE

TOPOSCOPE

CAR PARK

FAST TRAFFIC- TAKE CARE

TO WESTON-SUB-EDGE

WESTON PARK

CAMPDEN WOOD

CROPS

CROPS

STONE STILE

2

180

APPROX SCALE

0   ¼ mile

0   500m

ROUTE GUIDE AND MAPS

views. Get your bearings (and your breath) at **Broadway Tower** (see box on p84), the second-highest point along the trail, before the steep descent to Broadway.

BROADWAY [MAP 3a, p87]

Named for its wide central street, once the main road between Worcester and London, Broadway is to many tourists (and there are a lot of them) synonymous with the Cotswolds.

A broad green at the western end of the High St sets a somewhat bucolic tone, enhanced by trees lining the road and rows of stone cottages, giving rise to an excess of clichés and tourist shops. And yet, despite

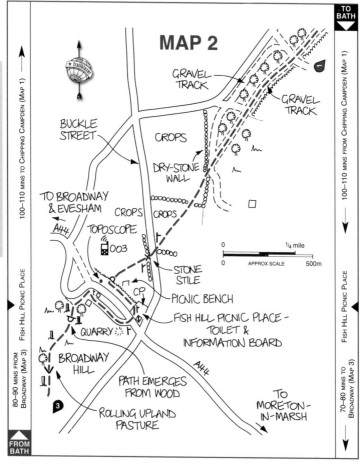

MAP 2

TO BATH

ROUTE GUIDE AND MAPS

100–110 MINS TO CHIPPING CAMPDEN (MAP 1)

100–110 MINS FROM CHIPPING CAMPDEN (MAP 1)

GRAVEL TRACK

GRAVEL TRACK

BUCKLE STREET

CROPS

DRY-STONE WALL

TO BROADWAY & EVESHAM

A44

CROPS CROPS

TOPOSCOPE

003

0   ¼ mile

0   APPROX SCALE   500m

STONE STILE

PICNIC BENCH

CP

FISH HILL PICNIC PLACE – TOILET & INFORMATION BOARD

FISH HILL PICNIC PLACE

FISH HILL PICNIC PLACE

QUARRY   F

BROADWAY HILL

A44

80–90 MINS FROM BROADWAY (MAP 3)

70–80 MINS TO BROADWAY (MAP 3)

PATH EMERGES FROM WOOD

TO MORETON-IN-MARSH

3

ROLLING UPLAND PASTURE

FROM BATH

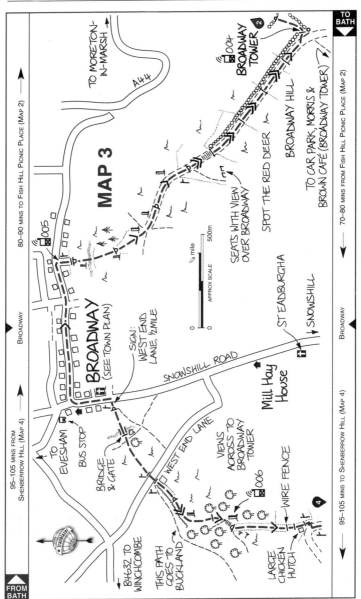

MAP 3

TO MORETON-IN-MARSH

A44

BROADWAY TOWER 2

004 BROADWAY TOWER

TO BATH

BROADWAY HILL

TO CAR PARK, MORRIS & BROWN CAFÉ (BROADWAY TOWER)

SPOT THE RED DEER

SEATS WITH VIEW OVER BROADWAY

005

BROADWAY (SEE TOWN PLAN)

SIGN: WEST END LANE, ½ MILE

SNOWSHILL ROAD

STEADBURGHA

SNOWSHILL

Mill Hay House

TO EVESHAM

BUS STOP

BRIDGE & GATE

WEST END LANE

VIEWS ACROSS TO BROADWAY TOWER

006

WIRE FENCE

4

LARGE CHICKEN HUTCH

THIS PATH GOES TO BUCKLAND

B4632 TO WINCHCOMBE

½ mile

500m

APPROX SCALE

¼ mile

0

BROADWAY

70–80 MINS FROM FISH HILL PICNIC PLACE (MAP 2)

← 95–105 MINS TO SHENBERROW HILL (MAP 4)

FROM BATH

ROUTE GUIDE AND MAPS

the high number of visitors, the town retains a considerable charm, particularly outside the summer months.

Celebrating Broadway's links with the Arts and Crafts Movement (see box on p76), **Gordon Russell Design Museum** (☎ 01386-854695, 🖥 gordonrusselldesign museum.org; Tue-Sun 10am-4pm, closed for two weeks in Jan; £7) pays tribute to a man who from 1918 committed his working life on this site to designing and making furniture.

Broadway Museum & Art Gallery (☎ 01386-859047, 🖥 broadwaymuseum .org.uk; daily 10am-4pm; £5), in partnership with the Ashmolean in Oxford, harks back to an earlier period. It is housed in a beautifully preserved 17th-century house, which is no small part of its attraction. As at the main Ashmolean in Oxford, it includes a 'cabinet of curiosities', as well as a fine collection of 18th-century paintings, with an emphasis on the local area. The top floor

showcases temporary exhibitions featuring artists such as Whistler.

Somewhat unusually, Broadway's original parish church of **St Eadburgha** (Map 3) is marooned in a serene location well over half a mile (1.1km) to the south, towards Snowshill. Severely damaged in the 2007 floods, it has been restored and makes an interesting detour. Today, its former role is filled by **St Michael & All Saints**, close to the town and an attractive backdrop to the trail as it leaves Broadway.

Those with a nostalgic bent might make time for a trip on the **Gloucestershire Warwickshire Steam Railway** (GWSR; ☎ 01242-621405, 🖥 gwsr.com). Axed by Beeching in the 1960s, the line – which skirts the town to the west – was bought in 1981 and restored by volunteers. In 2018 a further section of track between Toddington and Broadway was reopened, bringing the total length from Broadway to its southern

---

❑ BROADWAY TOWER [Map 3, p83]

With its turreted top and walls of oolitic limestone, the tall tower that looms into view as you cross the fields on the outskirts of Broadway is an unlikely sight, apparently protecting only the sheep that graze nearby. Built in 1799 as a folly for Lady Coventry by the 6th Earl of Coventry, it sits atop Broadway Hill, a beacon hill which, at 1024ft (312m), is the second highest point in the Cotswolds. In its heyday, it was a lively retreat, attracting several Pre-Raphaelite artists, among them the Socialist and artist William Morris (1834-96), who was a regular visitor from his home at Kelmscott. Rejected by the National Trust in 1949, the tower is now in private hands, but it is open to the public (☎ 01386-852390, 🖥 broadwaytower.co.uk; daily 10am-5pm; from £14 or £4 for entry just to the grounds and for car parking).

According to Morris's daughter, May, men used to bathe on the roof of the tower, which was described as 'the most inconvenient and the most delightful place ever seen'. Today's visitors can climb up to the roof, too, but only for the scenery: in good weather there are superb 360° views of up to 16 counties! Some 200m north of the tower, and somewhat incongruous in this setting, is a **Cold War nuclear bunker** (Apr-Oct weekends & bank hol Mon; 45-minute tour £12, or £20 to include entrance to the tower; no under 12s), which used to be manned by the Royal Observer Corps.

Morris & Brown Café (☎ 01386-852945; daily 9am-5pm, 9.30am-4.30pm in winter; 🐾) in the grounds is next to a small but swanky gift shop where you can also buy tickets for the tower. The décor is contemporary, the food likewise: panini and ciabatta from £7.95 are set alongside 'soup of the moment', and dishes that include quiche and salad (£12.50). And lots of tea and cakes.

Completed in 2018 with a grant from the European Agricultural Fund for Rural Development, there's also the **Tower Barn Visitor Centre** with another café, *Espresso Bar* (☎ 01386-572284; daily 9.30am-5pm, shorter hours in winter).

terminal at Cheltenham Racecourse to 14 miles; for timetables and special events, see the website.

Transport

Several **bus** services (see pp48-50) stop here providing connections with Chipping Campden, Cheltenham and Evesham. The most useful for walkers is Pulhams No 606. Other services include NN Cresswell's R4 and Stagecoach's Nos 1/1A.

The GWSR (see opposite) provides rail access to places on/near the path but services are limited.

Broadway's **taxi** firms include Cotswold Horizons (☎ 01386-858599) and Broadway Taxis (mob ☎ 07407 707044, 🖥 www.broadwaytaxis.co.uk).

Services

Almost everything in Broadway happens on the High St, though the smart **tourist information centre** (☎ 01386-852937, 🖥 broadway-cotswolds.co.uk; Mon-Sat 10am-1.30pm, but the staff are all volunteers so the hours can be variable) is set back behind the Mid-Counties Co-op **supermarket** (Mon-Sat 7am-9pm, Sun 10am-4pm). The supermarket also plays host to the **post office** (Mon-Fri 9am-5.30pm, Sat 9am-12.30pm) and nearby is an **ATM**. Across the road on the High St itself is the more personal and very well-stocked Broadway Deli (🖥 broadwaydeli.co.uk, Mon-Sat 8am-5pm, Sun 9am-5pm), with fresh fruit and veg, freshly baked bread and all sorts of goodies. They also have a *café* here.

Close at hand, Blandford Books (☎ 01386-858588; hours vary but generally Mon-Sat 9.30am-5.30pm, Sun 10.30am-5.30pm; winter daily 10am-4pm) stocks a good range of **books** and is particularly strong on local titles. Those browsing for **antiques** will find plenty to delay them along the street, too.

For **medical** matters, the New Barn Close Surgery (☎ 01386-853651, 🖥 newbarnclose.co.uk; Mon-Fri 8am-6.30pm), is now on Station Rd, 500m from the centre of the village. Back on the High St, there's a **pharmacy** (Mon-Fri 9am-6pm, Sat to 5.30pm).

A footpath from the High St leads through to the public **toilets** in the car park on Church Close.

Where to stay

There's no shortage of places to stay in this picture-postcard village that draws foreign visitors in their droves. Finding something within a tight budget is much harder – and unless you're planning to walk in the depths of winter, you'd be well advised to book ahead.

A couple of **pubs** offer accommodation. At the pleasant *Horse & Hound* (☎ 01386-852287, 🖥 horseandhoundbroadway.com; **fb**; 5D/1Qd, all en suite; 🐾; 🐕 bar area only and on a lead), at the top of the High St, a room above the pub costs £62.50-100pp. Note that in the winter the pub is closed all day on Monday and Tuesday.

Room-only rates at the 17th-century *Crown & Trumpet* (☎ 01386-853202, 🖥 crownandtrumpet.co.uk; **fb**; 1T/4D, all en suite; 🐾; 🐕 bar area only), on Snowshill Rd, are from £49pp (sgl occ room rate); cooked breakfast (£12.50pp) available if booked in advance. At weekends there is a two-night minimum stay for advance bookings.

Tucked away behind the High St, at 2 Kiel Close, *The Lodge at Broadway* (☎ 01386-852007, 🖥 thelodgebroadway.co.uk; 8D/1Q, all en suite; 🐾), is a modern place that charges from £68pp (sgl occ room rate). It's room only but as it's right in the centre of the village there are lots of places very close for breakfast or brunch and you'll get a 10% discount.

At the other end of the High St away from any traffic but also on the Cotswold Way, is the award-winning *Olive Branch* (☎ 01386-853440, 🖥 theolivebranch-broadway.com; 1S private bathroom, 3D/2T or D/1Tr/1Qd, all en suite; 🐾; (🄻), built in 1592 and offering B&B for over 50 years. Today, rooms are fitted out in an elegant but cottagey style (three with a bath) with a range of extras. Rates are from £75-87.50pp depending on the room (sgl £130). Advance bookings at weekends must be for two nights but if there is availability near the time they will accept a single-night stay.

Windrush House (off Map 3a; ☎ 01386-853577, 🖳 windrushhouse.com; 2D or T/2D, all en suite; Mar-Dec) has very comfortable rooms, some with king-size beds. Run by friendly and helpful owners, they charge from £60pp a night (sgl occ from £100). Advance bookings at weekends must be for two nights; single nights are sometimes available.

About half a mile from the trail, is **The Old Stationhouse** (off Map 3a; ☎ 01386-852659, 🖳 oldstationhousebroadway.co.uk; 3D, all en suite; ➘), occupying the old stationmaster's lodgings down a private drive between the railway bridge and the petrol station. B&B in the comfortable rooms costs from £85pp (sgl occ from £140) and gets rave reviews but the minimum stay is two nights.

Russell's of Broadway (☎ 01386-853555, 🖳 russellsofbroadway.co.uk; 6D/1D or T, all en suite; ➘) has rooms above the excellent restaurant. They charge from £85pp for the smaller rooms and £130pp for the larger. There's also a luxurious suite with jacuzzi bath from £315 for two people. Rates include breakfast.

The renowned **Lygon Arms** (pronounced 'Ligon' not 'Liegon'; ☎ 01386-852255, 🖳 lygonarmshotel.co.uk; 7S/70D or T/9Tr, all en suite; ➘; 🐾) where prices start at £105-175pp (sgl from £195) was where Oliver Cromwell wisely chose to spend the night before the Battle of Worcester in 1651. As well as a restaurant and bar there's a pool and spa.

On the green in the centre of the village and dating back to 16th century, **The Broadway Hotel** (☎ 01386-852 401, 🖳 broadway-hotel.co.uk; 19D or T all en suite; ➘, 🐾), is a luxurious place to stay with very comfortable beds and a good restaurant. They charge from £66.50pp to £172.50pp.

And if you fancy being truly decadent, you could swap your boots for Queen Anne-style splendour at **Mill Hay House** (see Map 3, p83; ☎ 01386-852498, 🖳 mill hay.co.uk; 3D, all en suite; ➘). B&B costs from £137.50-197.50pp (sgl occ full room rate); you could choose the 'gourmet break-

fast' which includes boiled eggs with lumpfish caviar). Note there is a minimum two-night stay policy throughout the year. It lies on Snowshill Rd less than half a mile south of the trail.

Where to eat and drink

The popular **Market Pantry** (☎ 01386-858318, 🖳 marketpantry.co.uk; **fb**; Wed-Sat 9am-5pm, Sun 10am-4pm) serves breakfast, lunch and tea, wraps, toasted sandwiches, excellent sausage rolls and delicious cakes. The **café** at Broadway Deli (🖳 broadwaydeli.co.uk, Mon-Fri 8am-3pm, Sat 8am-4pm, Sun 9am-3pm) serves a brunch menu all day. It's good with generous servings but quite pricey.

On the High St, **Number 32** (☎ 01386-306670, 🖳 number32broadway.co.uk; **fb**; daily 8.30am-4pm), is a good choice: think eggs Benedict, pancakes with maple syrup, sandwiches, superfood salads, and tapas. They even do takeaways.

Not surprisingly, with so many tourists around, tea is high on the agenda here. **Tisanes Tea Rooms** (☎ 01386-853296, 🖳 tisanes-tearooms.com; **fb**; daily 10am-5pm), on The Green, is perfectly traditional complete with waitresses in white pinnies and traditional bow window, though the option of gluten-free dishes is rather more contemporary.

The nearby **Hunters** (☎ 01386-858522, 🖳 huntersofbroadway.co.uk; **fb**; Mon-Fri 10am-4pm, Sat & Sun 10am-4.30pm) falls into a similar category, its menu including substantial takeaway sandwiches, baguettes and salad boxes.

More modern but still cosy is **Leaf & Bean** (☎ 01386-859151, 🖳 leafbeanbroad way.com; daily 10am-5pm), whose range of fancy sandwiches/paninis includes chicken, chorizo and red onion, and masala potato toastie.

A busy addition to the restaurant scene in Broadway is **Flipside** (☎ 01386-852277, 🖳 flipsideburgers.co.uk; Wed-Mon noon-9pm, to 8.30pm Sun) at 6 The Green. Their 7oz freshly ground beef gastro burgers with fries or salad cost £15-18. The meaty range does include one vegan option. You can even order online – click and collect.

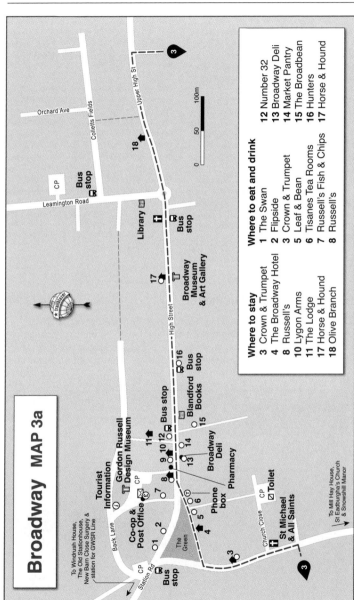

Broadway MAP 3a

To Windrush House,
The Old Stationhouse,
New Barn Close Surgery &
station for GWSR Line

Back Lane

Station Rd

CP

Bus stop

Tourist
Information

Co-op &
Post Office

Gordon Russell
Design Museum

CP

11

Bus stop

The Green

Phone
box

Pharmacy

Blandford
Books

Broadway
Deli

High Street

Church Close

CP

Toilet

St Michael
& All Saints

To Mill Hay House,
St Eadburgha's Church &
Snowshill Manor

Broadway
Museum
& Art Gallery

17

Library

Leamington Road

CP

**Bus
stop**

Orchard Ave

Colletts Fields

Upper High St

18

Bus stop

0   50   100m

Where to stay
3 Crown & Trumpet
4 The Broadway Hotel
8 Russell's
10 Lygon Arms
11 The Lodge
17 Horse & Hound
18 Olive Branch

Where to eat and drink
1 The Swan
2 Flipside
3 Crown & Trumpet
5 Leaf & Bean
6 Tisanes Tea Rooms
7 Russell's Fish & Chips
8 Russell's

12 Number 32
13 Broadway Deli
14 Market Pantry
15 The Broadbean
16 Hunters
17 Horse & Hound

The Broadbean (☎ 01386-306670, 🖳 thebroadbeanbroadway.co.uk; **fb**; Mon-Fri 6-9pm, Sat noon-4pm & 6-9pm) offers tapas-style dishes from around the Mediterranean. It's an unassuming place but good value and filled with lots of happy diners.

Along a passageway leading from the High St, *Russell's Fish & Chips* (☎ 01386-858435, 🖳 russellsfishandchips.co.uk; **fb**; Mon noon-2.30 & 5-7pm, Tue-Sat noon-2.30pm & 5-8.30pm) does exactly what it says, either to eat in or take away and from £14. The relaxed sibling of Russell's (see below), it has tables both inside and out.

Continuing upmarket, *Russell's* itself (☎ 01386-853555, 🖳 russellsofbroadway .co.uk/restaurant; Mon-Tue 8.30-10am & noon-2pm, Wed-Sat 8.30-10am & noon-2.15pm & 5.30-9pm, Sun noon-6.15pm) offers a fixed-price menu at £30-40 (not available on either Sat evening or Sun).

There's an à la carte menu, too, albeit best kept for very special occasions.

A popular option for a meal is *The Swan* (☎ 01386-852278, 🖳 theswanbroad way.co.uk; food Mon-Fri noon-10pm, Sat 9.30am-10pm, Sun 9.30am-9pm; 🐾 bar area only), where comfy chairs and heavy wooden tables feel right at home in the old building. Relaxed and informal, it offers a varied menu, including pub favourites well done. Similarly traditional, the *Horse & Hound* (see Where to stay; food Tue-Fri noon-2.30pm & 6-8.30pm, Sat noon-3pm & 6-8.30pm, Sun noon-3pm, 🐾 bar area only), does good pub food and keeps at least three guest ales on tap (see box p23). Another good CAMRA-recognised pub is the *Crown & Trumpet* (see Where to stay; food Mon-Thur noon-2.30pm & 6-8pm, Fri-Sun noon-8pm) where there's also occasional live music.

BROADWAY TO WINCHCOMBE   MAPS 3-8

This **12-mile (19.6km, 5½-6½hrs)** stretch should fulfil the expectations of anyone who has leafed through glossy coffee-table books on the Cotswolds. Here are the rolling hills, the fine views and the cottages of time-weathered stone. This is rural England at its best, with **Stanton** (Map 5) the quintessential Cotswold village.

❑ SNOWSHILL MANOR   [off Map 4]

Even those least interested in museums will find something appealing about a man who amassed a collection that ranged from Samurai armour to stringed instruments to boneshaker bicycles. Charles Paget Wade was just such a collector, cramming his house, 2½ miles (4km) south of Broadway, with a seemingly random range of over 22,000 items. Even the gardens, with their terraces, ponds and outdoor rooms, were the subject of his apparently boundless enthusiasm.

Today, Snowshill Manor (☎ 01386-852410, 🖳 nationaltrust.org.uk; mid Mar-Oct daily 11am-5.30pm, Manor House 11.30-4.30pm; Nov weekends only, manor and gardens £13, NT members free) is in the hands of the National Trust, which struggles to keep pace with the number of visitors to what is a relatively small house.

For walkers on the Cotswold Way, the house is best approached along the tracks leading east/south-east from Shenberrow Hill; it's a distance of around three-quarters of a mile (1.2km). The *tea room* in the grounds makes a detour particularly appealing but, with timed tickets to visit the house and last entry an hour before closing, you may need to be flexible to avoid disappointment.

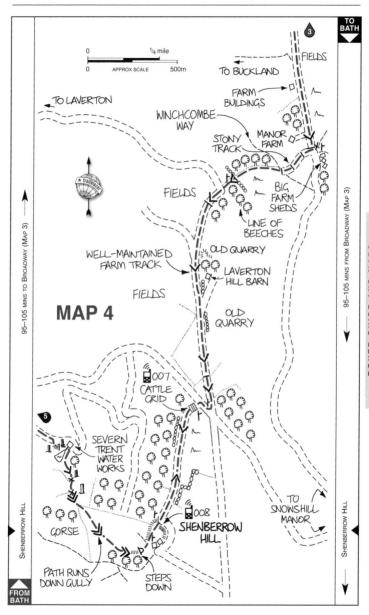

TO BATH

TO BUCKLAND

FIELDS

3

TO LAVERTON

FARM BUILDINGS

WINCHCOMBE WAY

STONY TRACK

MANOR FARM

FIELDS

BIG FARM SHEDS

LINE OF BEECHES

WELL-MAINTAINED FARM TRACK

OLD QUARRY

LAVERTON HILL BARN

FIELDS

MAP 4

OLD QUARRY

007 CATTLE GRID

5

SEVERN TRENT WATER WORKS

TO SNOWSHILL MANOR

008 SHENBERROW HILL

GORSE

PATH RUNS DOWN GULLY

STEPS DOWN

0   ¼ mile

0   APPROX SCALE   500m

95–105 MINS TO BROADWAY (MAP 3)

95–105 MINS FROM BROADWAY (MAP 3)

ROUTE GUIDE AND MAPS

SHENBERROW HILL

SHENBERROW HILL

FROM BATH

Some steep ups and downs bring in several cultural highlights, too: **Stanway House** (see below); the site of the Iron-Age **Beckbury Camp** (Map 6), where a stone monument known locally as 'Cromwell's seat' is reputed to mark where Thomas Cromwell watched Hailes Abbey burn; and the ruins of **Hailes Abbey** itself (Map 7; see box on p93) – which are well worth exploring. From Hailes it's an easy and pleasant walk to the fine old wool town of **Winchcombe**.

STANTON [MAP 5]

Broadway may attract the tourists, but for true Cotswold beauty Stanton is hard to beat. At the heart of the village is the **church of St Michael & All Angels**, its tall spire clearly visible in the valley from the surrounding hills.

Pulhams No 606 **bus** (see pp48-50) stops at Stanton North Turn – the most northerly of the junctions on the B4632, about half a mile from the village.

There are two **B&Bs** in the village and an excellent **pub**, *The Mount Inn* (☎ 01386-584316, ⌨ themountinn.co.uk; **fb**; **food** Easter to end Aug daily noon-2pm & 6-9pm, Sep to Easter Tue-Sat noon-2pm & 6-9pm, Sun noon-3pm; 🐾), but note that it closes in the afternoon. Up a steep hill, yet only a stone's throw from the trail, it boasts an inglenook fireplace, Donnington Brewery beers (their fish is battered with Donnington ale) and superb views. Evening reservations are strongly recommended. You can order online but note that this is only for when you're in the pub. And there's even a dogs' menu!

Within just 200m of the pub is *Shenberrow Hill* (☎ 01386-584468, ⌨ broadway-cotswolds.co.uk/shenberrowhill bb; 1D/1D or T, all en suite; 🐾), not to be confused with the complex of buildings at the top of Shenberrow Hill (Map 4). B&B costs from £80pp in the double and from £87.50pp in the twin (sgl occ rates on request).

Right in the heart of the village, *The Vine* (☎ 01386-584250, ⌨ broadway-cotswolds.co.uk/thevine; 1D en suite, 1T/1Tr private facilities but shared toilet; 🐾; Ⓛ; 🐴) offers B&B from £55pp (sgl occ £90-110). The owner specialises in horseriding and there's a riding centre here, too, so you could swap your walking boots for a few hours in the saddle!

Unfortunately The Old Post House B&B closed at the end of 2023 but **Airbnb** (⌨ airbnb.co.uk) lists several places in and around the village.

STANWAY [MAP 5]

If you're passing through in June, July or August on a Tuesday or Thursday between 2pm and 5pm, do drop into the Jacobean **Stanway House** (⌨ www.stanwayfountain.co.uk; fountain £7, house & fountain £11 – cash only). Set in a restored 18th-century water garden, with its own tea room, it claims to have the tallest gravity fountain in the world which, at 300ft (91m), normally 'plays' at 2.45pm and 4pm. At other times you'll have to be content with the sight of the imposing gatehouse and the neighbouring church.

Spare a glance, too, for the thatched cricket pavilion set on staddle stones near by. It was a gift from *Peter Pan* author JM Barrie, who used to rent the house during the summer months.

A further attraction on the Stanway estate is the restored **Stanway Watermill** (⌨ www.stanwayfountain.co.uk/the-water mill.html; £3), which now produces wholemeal Cotswold flour. It opens to visitors at the same times as the house, plus 10am-noon on Thursday all year.

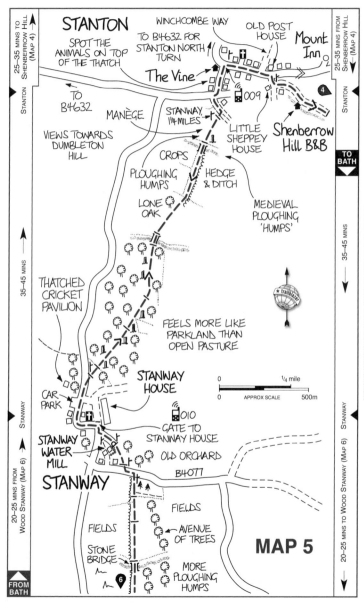

WOOD STANWAY [MAP 6]

Blink and you could miss the sleepy hamlet of Wood Stanway but it does have a **B&B**. The 17th-century **Wood Stanway Farmhouse** (☎ 01386-584318, 🖥 wood stanwayfarmhouse.co.uk; email: greensbedandbreakfast@gmail.com; 1D/1T/1Qd, all en suite; �; (L); 🐾), is 30 yards down the road to the right as you come through the gate. It has open views across farmland and the hills and B&B costs from £55pp (sgl occ £75). The nearest pub is 1¼ miles (2km) away in Toddington, but a three-course evening meal for around £25pp can be prebooked.

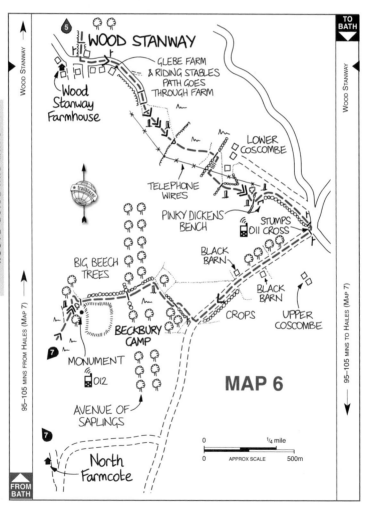

WOOD STANWAY

WOOD STANWAY

TO BATH

WOOD STANWAY

WOOD STANWAY

ROUTE GUIDE AND MAPS

5

GLEBE FARM
& RIDING STABLES
PATH GOES
THROUGH FARM

Wood
Stanway
Farmhouse

★ trailblazer

LOWER
COSCOMBE

TELEPHONE
WIRES

PINKY DICKENS
BENCH

STUMPS
011 CROSS

BLACK
BARN

BIG BEECH
TREES

BLACK
BARN

UPPER
COSCOMBE

CROPS

BECKBURY
CAMP

7

MONUMENT
012

MAP 6

AVENUE OF
SAPLINGS

7

North
Farmcote

95–105 MINS FROM HAILES (MAP 7)

95–105 MINS TO HAILES (MAP 7)

0   ¼ mile
0   APPROX SCALE   500m

FROM
BATH

NORTH FARMCOTE   [MAP 6]

One of a handful of working farms offering B&B within reasonable reach of the Cotswold Way is *North Farmcote* (☎ 01242-602304, ☐ northfarmcote.co.uk; 1D/1T, both en suite, 1T private bathroom; ☛; Mar-end Oct); it is in a glorious location just over quarter of a mile (0.2km) from the trail (see Map 7 for access, and follow the sign for **Farmcote Herbs**). B&B costs from £55-70pp (sgl occ from £90). If the owners aren't busy they will drive guests to the nearest pub, a couple of miles away at Ford, for an evening meal. They require a minimum two-night stay for advance booking at weekends between May and the end of October.

HAILES   [MAP 7, p94]

Hailes or Hayles, or Hales – which really does have three spellings – takes its name from the **abbey** (see box below).

Hailes Abbey Halt is a request stop for some of the GWSR **train** services (see p84). If you wish to alight here you must tell the guard before you leave Toddington or Winchcombe and you must travel in the front two coaches of the train. To join the train at Hailes Abbey you just need to hail the train as it approaches.

The trail descends parallel to the orchards of *Hayles Fruit Farm* (☎ 01242-602123, ☐ haylesfruitfarm.co.uk; fb; ☛). This has one of the few **campsites** along the entire Cotswold Way that is actually on the trail, so make the most of it.

(cont'd on p96)

❏ HAILES ABBEY   [Map 7, p94]

Hailes Abbey (☎ 01242-602398, ☐ english-heritage.org.uk; daily Jul-Aug 10am-6pm, Wed-Sun late Mar-Jun & Sep-early Nov 10am-5pm; £6.80-7.70, English Heritage and National Trust members free) dates back to the 13th century. It owes its construction to a vow made by Richard, Earl of Cornwall (1209-72), should he survive a storm at sea during his return from a military campaign. The ship returned safely to harbour, and the then earl, son of King John and brother of Henry III (who was responsible for the construction of Westminster Abbey), founded the abbey in 1246.

The site, that of an existing settlement, was chosen carefully. Limestone was readily available for building, there was good grazing for sheep, and a reliable water supply, with which the monks created a series of fishponds. The building itself was an elaborate affair, in contrast with the traditional simplicity of the Cistercian brotherhood – and indeed with the austerity of the earlier parish church, which lies across the road, and is still in use. The importance and grandeur of the abbey lay largely in its possession of the Holy Blood relic, which was housed in its own specially designed shrine and which brought considerable income into the abbey's coffers.

Initially, the population at the new abbey comprised a prior, 20 monks and 10 lay brothers, who moved here from Beaulieu Abbey in Hampshire, but many of the community died in 1361 during a recurrence of the Black Death. The monastery was dissolved in 1539, one of the last to be closed on Henry VIII's orders, and the abbey destroyed. The remainder of the estate was given by the king to Katherine Parr. Later, the buildings were adapted as a country house, but by 1794 that, too, lay in ruins. Today, it is the ruined cloisters that most vividly conjure up some sense of the ordered life once led by the monks. All that remains of the abbey are the footings, yet these – together with artefacts found on the site, on display in the excellent visitor centre – give a powerful indication of the scale and drama of the original building. In the words of St Bernard, *Bonum est nos hic esse*: 'It is good for us to be here.'

ROUTE GUIDE AND MAPS

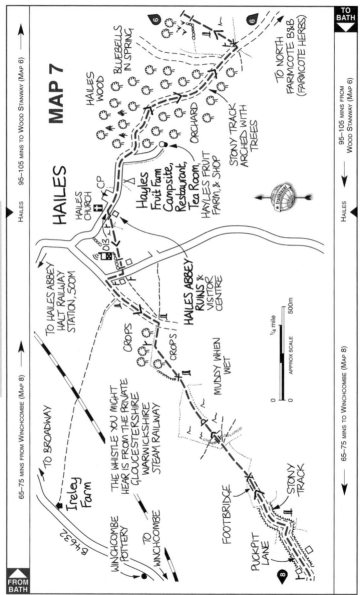

MAP 7

HAILES

95–105 MINS TO WOOD STANWAY (MAP 6)

BLUEBELLS IN SPRING

HALES WOOD

ORCHARD

TO NORTH FARMCOTE B&B (FARMCOTE HERBS)

STONY TRACK ARCHED WITH TREES

HALES CHURCH

CP

Hayles Fruit Farm Campsite, Restaurant, Tea Room, HAYLES FRUIT FARM, & SHOP

013

HAILES ABBEY RUINS & VISITOR CENTRE

TO HAILES ABBEY HALT RAILWAY STATION, 500M

CROPS

CROPS

MUDDY WHEN WET

1/4 mile

500m

APPROX SCALE

0

TO BROADWAY

Ireley Farm

THE WHISTLE YOU MIGHT HEAR IS FROM THE PRIVATE GLOUCESTERSHIRE WARWICKSHIRE STEAM RAILWAY

WINCHCOMBE POTTERY

TO WINCHCOMBE

B4632

FOOTBRIDGE

STONY TRACK

PUCKPIT LANE

65–75 MINS FROM WINCHCOMBE (MAP 8)

TO HALES ABBEY HALT RAILWAY STATION, 500M — TO BROADWAY

65–75 MINS TO WINCHCOMBE (MAP 8)

HAILES

95–105 MINS FROM WOOD STANWAY (MAP 6)

TO BATH

FROM BATH

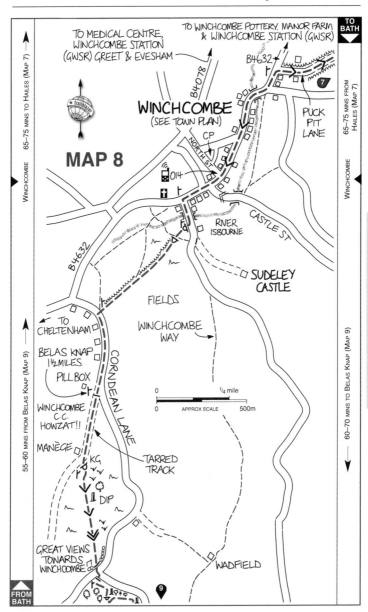

TO BATH

TO MEDICAL CENTRE,
WINCHCOMBE STATION
(GWSR) GREET & EVESHAM

TO WINCHCOMBE POTTERY, MANOR FARM
& WINCHCOMBE STATION (GWSR)

B4078

B4632

WINCHCOMBE
(SEE TOWN PLAN)

MAP 8

NORTH ST

CP

☎ 014

PUCK
PIT
LANE

7

65–75 MINS TO HALES (MAP 7)

65–75 MINS FROM HALES (MAP 7)

WINCHCOMBE

WINCHCOMBE

CASTLE ST

RIVER
ISBOURNE

B4632

SUDELEY
CASTLE

FIELDS

WINCHCOMBE
WAY

TO
CHELTENHAM

BELAS KNAP
1½ MILES

PILLBOX

WINCHCOMBE
C.C.
HOWZAT!!

MANÈGE

KG

DIP

GREAT VIEWS
TOWARDS
WINCHCOMBE

CORNDEAN LANE

TARRED
TRACK

WADFIELD

9

0   ¼ mile
APPROX SCALE
0   500m

55–60 MINS FROM BELAS KNAP (MAP 9)

60–70 MINS TO BELAS KNAP (MAP 9)

ROUTE GUIDE AND MAPS

FROM
BATH

(cont'd from p93) ***Hayles Fruit Farm Campsite*** is a large, fairly level, grassy site, with shower and toilet facilities, where you can pitch a tent for £9.50pp per night. They also have several unfurnished **bell tents** sleeping 3-5 people (£55); these should be booked in advance. Just up the hill is their excellent **farm shop** (Apr-Dec daily 9am-5pm, Jan-Mar closed Mon), where you can buy good cakes and delicious apple juice, as well as ice-cream, fresh bread and the makings for a substantial breakfast. There's also a welcoming **tea room and restaurant** (closed Mondays otherwise same hours as shop; hot food served 9am-3pm).

If you'd prefer a **B&B**, ***Ireley Farm*** (☎ 01242-602445, 💻 ireleyfarm.com; 1T private bathroom/2D, both en suite; ☛; Ⓛ) could fit the bill although accommodation for just one night may not always be possible. You'll pay from £60pp (sgl occ £60). Access is via a footpath from Hailes of just over half a mile (0.8km); the farm is also within walking distance of Winchcombe Pottery (see p97).

WINCHCOMBE [MAP 8a, p99]

The ancient Saxon borough of Winchcombe, one-time capital of the kingdom of Mercia, later enjoyed status as a focal point for pilgrims. Its abbey has long since gone, but the town – emphatically not a village – of Winchcombe remains a significant presence in the Cotswolds.

More recently, the town hit the world presses when, on the night of 28 Feb 2021, a fireball was seen over the Cotswolds. In the morning a family in Winchcombe discovered a 300g 4.6 billion-year-old meteorite embedded in their driveway. A piece is now on display in the town museum.

For walkers along the Way, Winchcombe is an ideal place to stay or to stop for a bite to eat at one of a number of pubs, restaurants and tea rooms. Even if you're short of time, it's worth taking a look inside the wool church of **St Peter's**.

If you've longer to spare, you might want to check out **Sudeley Castle** (Map 8; see box below), or one of two small museums. At **Winchcombe Museum** (💻 winchcombemuseum.org.uk; Apr-Oct Tues-Sun 10am-4pm), next to the **old stocks** and the tourist information office (see opposite), exhibits about the town's history rub shoulders with a collection of police paraphernalia. They were joined recently by a section of the **Winchcombe Meteorite** (see 💻 winchcombemeteorite.org).

❑ SUDELEY CASTLE [Map 8, p95]

The history of Sudeley Castle (☎ 01242-604244, 💻 sudeleycastle.co.uk; Mar-end Oct daily 10am-5pm, Nov-mid Dec to 4pm, last admission 3pm; £19.50, discount to English Heritage members) can be traced back as far as King Ethelred, in the 10th century. Although nothing of his manor house remains, the estate's royal connections run like a thread through its chequered past, from Edward IV to Queen Elizabeth I. The buildings visible today, including the Dungeon Tower and St Mary's Church, were constructed by Baron Sudeley from the mid 15th century. It is in the church that Katherine Parr, the sixth of Henry VIII's wives, is buried, having lived at Sudeley following the king's death. A century later, the castle fell into disuse, becoming increasingly dilapidated until it was bought and restored during Victoria's reign by members of the Dent family. The castle today is the private home of their descendants.

Visitors may look round the church and tour the estate, with its beautiful rose gardens, a pheasantry, and a wonderful wooden fort that will make you wish you were 10 years old again. A number of rooms in the castle are also accessible to the public, including the library, the morning room, and Chandos bedroom. The **visitor centre** (daily 10am-5pm) includes a shop and ***restaurant*** (to 4.30pm).

Just over half a mile (1km) north of Puck Pit Lane on the B4632, to the left just after the railway bridge, you'll find **Winchcombe Pottery** (Map 7, p94; ☎ 01242-602462, 🖳 winchcombepottery.co .uk; Mon-Fri 9am-5pm, Sat & bank hols 10am-4pm, May-Sep Sun noon-4pm), where traditionally crafted pots are still turned, fired and sold on the premises. Anyone interested in a ride on the **Gloucestershire Warwickshire Steam Railway** (see p84) should note that the actual station for this is not in Winchcombe but in Greet, about a mile away.

Cotswold Voluntary Wardens lead a heavily oversubscribed annual series of **11 consecutive walks** for those who would like to complete the trail in stages, one of them based from Winchcombe; for details, see p29.

See box p16 for details of the festivals held here in May.

Transport

Winchcombe is well placed on Pulhams No 606 north–south **bus** route running through the Cotswolds. The 606 stops at Winchcombe School (Greet Rd) and Old Police station (North St). Pulhams also operate the limited No 656 service and Stagecoach the W service; both stop at the war memorial (Gloucester St) and on Gretton Rd (stop called Delavale Rd). For details, see pp48-50.

Services

There's a small but helpful **tourist information centre** (☎ 01242-602925; Easter-Oct Tue-Sun 10am-4pm, Nov-Easter Sat 10am-4pm, Sun 10am-3pm) on the corner of North St. Useful websites are 🖳 winch-combewelcomeswalkers.com and 🖳 winch combe.co.uk. The museum is also here.

Coventry Building Society has a branch with an **ATM** on the High St; where High St morphs into Hailes St there's a **newsagent** (Mon-Sat 6am-5pm, Sun 6am-1pm) that sells drinks and snacks, but most other tourist amenities are found along North St. This lies at right angles to the trail from the tourist information centre and is where you'll find several independent

shops of interest including North's **bakery** (Mon-Fri 7am-4.30pm, Sat to 4pm) for fresh rolls and sandwiches, or the excellent **delicatessen** Williams of Winchcombe (see Where to eat), where sandwiches are made to order or to eat in.

There's a **supermarket**, Morrisons Daily (open daily 7am-10pm), which also plays host to the **post office** and an **ATM**; and there's a second supermarket, Co-op Food Market (Mon-Sat 7am-9pm, Sun 10am-4pm), with its own ATM, just off North St on Greet Rd.

There's a **shoe repairer** (☎ 01242-604602; Mon-Fri 8am-12.30pm) at Winchcombe Pottery (see above), so if your boots need some attention, it's worth going out of your way.

Winchcombe **medical centre** (☎ 01242-602307, 🖳 winchcombemedical.nhs .uk; Mon-Fri 8am-6.30pm) is about a quarter of a mile north of the town, along Greet Rd, and there's a **pharmacy** (Mon-Fri 9am-6pm, Sat to 5.30pm) on the High St.

Where to stay

Winchcombe has a good assortment of small pubs and inns and a few B&Bs, most of them fairly central. **Campers**, though, will need to walk some three-quarters of a mile (1.2km) from the trail to *Manor Farm* (off Map 8a; ☎ 01242-602423, 🖳 janetday423@gmail.com; 🐾) where it's around £10pp (toilet/shower facilities are available). To get there from the Cotswold Way, turn right at the end of Puck Pit Lane, go under the railway bridge and turn immediately left (past the pottery) on Becketts Lane to **Greet**. Just before you arrive at the B4078/Evesham Rd, turn right up Market Lane; the farm is about a quarter of a mile (0.4km) up that road on the left-hand side.

There's B&B at attractive Georgian *Blair House* (☎ 01242-603626, 🖳 blair-housewinchcombe.co.uk; 1S/1T shared bathroom, 1D en suite; 🍷; WI-FI). It's at 41 Gretton Rd and charges are from £55pp (sgl from £75) for B&B.

Of the **pubs** and inns, *White Hart Inn* (☎ 01242-602359, 🖳 whitehartwinchcombe .co.uk; 3T/3T or D/5D, most en suite; 🍷;

Ⓛ; 🐾), on High St, is right on the trail and ideal for walkers, with three designated 'ramblers' rooms' (2T/1D) which share a bathroom and cost from around £30pp. The other (en suite) rooms are divided into standard (from around £50pp) and superior (from £60pp). Single occupancy of any room costs upwards of £50 and expect to pay the room rate in peak periods. There may be good deals on some booking websites. They sometimes also use some of the rooms at *Wesley House* (3D/1D or T/1T, all en suite; 🐾) right next door.

Set back from the main road on Abbey Terrace, near Coventry Building Society, *The Plaisterers Arms* (☎ 01242-602358, **fb**; 2T/3D, all en suite; ●; Ⓛ; 🐾) has B&B for around £45pp (sgl occ from £45 though room-rate at weekends). If you have a dog you will need to bring bedding for it.

Close to the shops on North St is *The Lion Inn* (☎ 01242-603300, ▭ thelion winchcombe.co.uk; **fb**; 2D or T/6D, all en suite; ●; 🐾), where B&B in comfortably refurbished rooms with a blissful lack of TV costs from around £60pp (sgl occ room rate). For a convivial evening, just head downstairs to the excellent bar.

Where to eat and drink

'Winchcombe welcomes walkers' proclaims the sign, and nowhere more so than in its wide range of places to eat. On North St, the licensed deli *Williams of Winchcombe* (see Services; ☎ 01242-604466, **fb**; Mon-Thu 8am-5.30pm, Fri & Sat 8am-6pm, Sun 10am-4pm) serves sandwiches and cakes as well as breakfasts; the pork pies topped with apple or cranberry sauce are wonderful. Nearby, there's *The Greasiest Spoon* (☎ 01242-652222) Mon-Sat 10am-3pm, Sun 10am-1pm) for breakfasts, sandwiches and jacket potatoes.

The *Old Bakery Coffee & Wine Bar* (☎ 01242-437632, ▭ theoldbakerywinch

combe.com; Wed noon-4, Thu-Sat noon-9.45) is an excellent little café and wine bar run by a friendly husband and wife team. There's a nice terrace, home-baked cakes and a great selection of wines with bowls of soup or chilli, pork pies or a charcuterie/ cheese board to accompany them.

Those with an acquisitive nature might be drawn to *Tea Rooms* at **Winchcombe Antiques Centre** (☎ 01242-300556, ▭ winchcombeantiquescentre.co.uk; summer Mon-Sat 10am-4.15pm, Sun 11am-3.15pm, winter Sat & Sun only), off the High St, where you'll pass rooms enticingly jammed with antiques to reach the simple basement café for tea and cakes, or a light lunch.

For more hearty fare, try one of the pubs. On the main street is *The Plaisterers Arms* (see Where to stay; food Mon-Fri noon-2.30pm & 6-9pm, Sat noon-3pm & 6-9pm, Sun 12.30-3pm; shorter hours in winter), which does a good range of ciabattas at lunchtime and substantial mains in the evening. They've a lovely garden, too, and as a diversion, more than 40 different gins!

Further along is *Corner Cupboard* (☎ 01242-602303, ▭ cornercupboardwinch combe.co.uk; food Tue-Fri noon-3pm & 6-8.30pm, Sat noon-2.30pm & 6-9pm, Sun noon-4pm), a pub where the Sunday lunch is particularly good and real ales are prominent. The food gets great reviews, too.

In a class of its own is *The Lion Inn* (see Where to stay; food daily noon-3pm & 6-9pm); the atmosphere is relaxed but the food – from a lunchtime pub snack of beer-battered anchovies with curried mayonnaise and burnt lime (£6.50) to a venison steak with soused pear and red wine sauce at dinner (£24.95) – is taken very seriously.

The restaurant at the *White Hart Inn* (see Where to stay; food daily 8am-9pm, Fri & Sat to 9.30pm), is unfussy, generous and tasty – which is music to most walkers' ears. They serve breakfast, coffee and after-

Symbols used in text (see also p74)
🐾 Dogs allowed subject to prior arrangement (see pp184-6)
● Bathtub in, or for, at least one room   **fb** indicates a Facebook page
Ⓛ packed lunch available if requested in advance

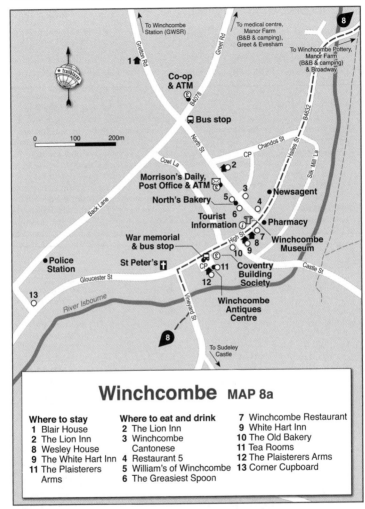

Winchcombe MAP 8a

Where to stay
1 Blair House
2 The Lion Inn
8 Wesley House
9 The White Hart Inn
11 The Plaisterers
   Arms

Where to eat and drink
2 The Lion Inn
3 Winchcombe
   Cantonese
4 Restaurant 5
5 William's of Winchcombe
6 The Greasiest Spoon

7 Winchcombe Restaurant
9 White Hart Inn
10 The Old Bakery
11 Tea Rooms
12 The Plaisterers Arms
13 Corner Cupboard

ROUTE GUIDE AND MAPS

noon teas, too. It's also the home of the Winchcombe Pizza Co.

Nearby, ***Winchcombe Restaurant*** (☎ 01242-604856, 🖳 winchcomberestaurant. co.uk; daily 6-11pm) does excellent Indian cuisine with reasonable prices and a 10% discount on takeaways. For takeaways, there's also ***Winchcombe Cantonese***

Chinese Takeaway (Wed-Mon 5-10.30pm).

For a special occasion, there's ***Restaurant 5*** (☎ 01242-604566, 🖳 5north-streetrestaurant.co.uk; Wed-Sun 12.30-1.30pm, Tue-Sat 7-9pm) on North St. Try dishes such as quail with bacon jam, pumpkin, cherries and sherry (£24) or celebrate with the set 7-course menu which is £78.

WINCHCOMBE TO CLEEVE HILL   MAPS 8-10

The next **6 miles (9.5km, 3-3½hrs)** take in one of the highlights of the Cotswold Way: **Cleeve Common** (Map 10), passing the ancient and impressive long barrow of **Belas Knap** (Map 9; see box below). Considered to be the largest single area of unimproved limestone grassland in Gloucestershire, the

---

❏ BELAS KNAP   [Map 9]

Sheltering in the corner of a field, at the edge of the woods, the ancient long barrow (see box on p134), or burial ground, of Belas Knap rises up from the ground rather like a beached whale, some 180ft (55m) long and 18ft (5.5m) high. Dating back to around 2500BC, it was used for successive burials, possibly over several centuries, until it was deliberately blocked. Archaeologists have uncovered the remains of 38 human skeletons, as well as animal bones, flints and pottery. At the northern end, an apparent entrance in fact leads nowhere, but the reason for this is unclear.

The grass-covered mound – for such is its appearance today – is dotted with cowslips and daisies, but you can clearly see the thin layers of stone, neatly stacked like sheaves of paper, that were used in its construction.

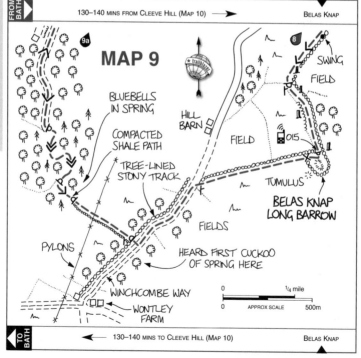

ROUTE GUIDE AND MAPS

FROM BATH ►

130–140 MINS FROM CLEEVE HILL (MAP 10) ⟶   ▼ BELAS KNAP

MAP 9

9a

8

SWING FIELD

BLUEBELLS IN SPRING

HILL BARN

FIELD

015

COMPACTED SHALE PATH

TREE-LINED STONY TRACK

TUMULUS

BELAS KNAP LONG BARROW

FIELDS

PYLONS

HEARD FIRST CUCKOO OF SPRING HERE

WINCHCOMBE WAY

WONTLEY FARM

0   ¼ mile
0   APPROX SCALE   500m

◄ TO BATH

⟵ 130–140 MINS TO CLEEVE HILL (MAP 10)   ▲ BELAS KNAP

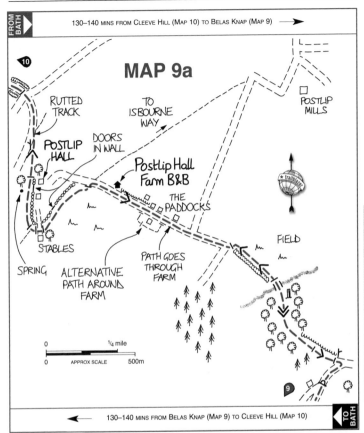

130–140 MINS FROM CLEEVE HILL (MAP 10) TO BELAS KNAP (MAP 9) ⟶

MAP 9a

RUTTED TRACK

TO ISBOURNE WAY

POSTLIP MILLS

DOORS IN WALL

POSTLIP HALL

Postlip Hall Farm B&B

THE PADDOCKS

FIELD

STABLES

PATH GOES THROUGH FARM

SPRING

ALTERNATIVE PATH AROUND FARM

0   ¼ mile

0   APPROX SCALE   500m

9

130–140 MINS FROM BELAS KNAP (MAP 9) TO CLEEVE HILL (MAP 10) ⟵

TO BATH

ROUTE GUIDE AND MAPS

common, an SSSI (see p61), rises to the highest point on the trail, **Cleeve Hill**, at 1066ft (325m). Wild and windswept, its closely cropped turf is shared by sheep, cattle, golfers and walkers, but it's a successful partnership; there is plenty of space for all.

Much of the trail from this point runs along the edge of the Cotswold escarpment, with a grandstand view of **Cheltenham Racecourse** (Map 11a) on the plains below. If visibility is poor, take especial care along this stretch; it would be all too easy to stray too close to the edge.

❑ **Important note – walking times**
All times in this book refer only to the time spent walking. You will need to add 20-30% to allow for rests, photography, checking the map, drinking water etc.

POSTLIP [MAP 9a, p101]

The Cotswold Way neatly sidesteps the hamlet of Postlip, but the section between Belas Knap and Cleeve Common does skirt around the edge of the privately owned Postlip Hall; see box on p16 for details of the Cotswold Beer Festival which is usually held here.

There's a perfectly positioned **B&B** right on the trail here at *Postlip Hall Farm* (☎ 01242-603351, 🖳 cotswoldsfarmstay.co .uk/postlip-hall-farm-winchcombe; 1T or

D/1D, both en suite; ⓛ; Feb-Nov), but with no evening meal available you may have to walk or consider a taxi to The Rising Sun (see below) on Cleeve Hill. The house itself is built of stone and sheltered behind high hedges on a working farm. Rooms cost from £50pp (single occupancy full room rate), for B&B. Nearby, look out for the *popup café*, Postlip Pitstop at The Paddocks in case it's open.

CLEEVE HILL [MAP 10]

Right by the trail, and up on Cleeve Hill itself, the bar at *Cleeve Hill Golf Club* (☎ 01242-672025, 🖳 cleevehillgolfclub.co.uk; drinks and snacks daily 8am-6pm (to 9pm Wed-Sat), hot food Tue-Sun 9am-3pm; 🐾) is open to non-members for tea, coffee and light lunch. You can eat in the clubhouse, on the veranda or on the grass looking up to Cleeve Hill and the golf course, choosing from a menu that includes breakfasts (full English), sandwiches and toasted paninis to pizzas. Their chunky chips (£3.50) are excellent. The *Cotswold Way Café* (☎ 01242-672025, 🖳 flynnsonthehill.co.uk), just outside, is part of the same enterprise.

All three hotels on Cleeve Common are clustered fairly close together about a quarter of a mile (0.4km) down the hill from the trail, along the busy B4632 but with views across to the Malvern Hills. **To avoid walking along the road, you can take one of the footpaths that lead down from the trail**, bringing you out at the back of the hotels. First up is the elegant *Cleeve Hill Hotel* (☎ 01242-672052, 🖳 cleevehill hotel.co.uk; 7D/5D or T/1Qd, all en suite; ▬; ⓛ; 🐾), which dates back to the early 1900s when it was first opened by a Mr Petty. Now run by a friendly helpful owner,

some rooms are suites or have half-tester beds; B&B costs from around £67.50pp (sgl occ full room rate).

Slightly further down the hill, *Malvern View* (☎ 01242-672017, 🖳 malvernview .com; 6D all en suite, 1D or T private bathroom; ▬; ⓛ; 🐾) has very comfortable rooms of varying sizes; rates from around £70pp for B&B; note there's a two-night minimum stay policy in the main season (Mar-end Sep). Book direct for best rates.

Just a couple of hundred yards further down, there's the rather larger *Rising Sun* (☎ 01242-676281, 🖳 greenekinginns.co .uk; 1S/4T/17D/2Tr, all en suite; ▬; ⓛ; 🐾). **B&B** rates are complex but range from £40pp (sgl from £75, sgl occ room rate). Dining (**food** daily 11am-9pm, 8pm on Sunday) is pretty relaxed, whether in the restaurant or bar or outside on the terrace. As well as lunchtime favourites there's an inexpensive menu with mains from £11-20, and a daily specials board. Sometimes they also have live music.

Stagecoach's W **bus** and Pulhams (Mon & Fri only) No 656 stop on the B4632 at the top of Stockwell Lane, opposite the first two hotels, and also by the Rising Sun; see pp48-50.

CLEEVE HILL TO LECKHAMPTON HILL MAPS 10-15

The 9½-mile **(15km)** section of the trail that skirts around Cheltenham takes about 4¾ to 5½ hours to complete. If it seems from on high as though the town goes on forever, much of the walking is across open common land with exceptionally rewarding views. Those interested in natural history are in for a treat, with ancient beeches and large-leaved limes in **Lineover Wood** (Map 13; the word means 'lime bank'), and the protected areas of **Prestbury Hill Reserve**

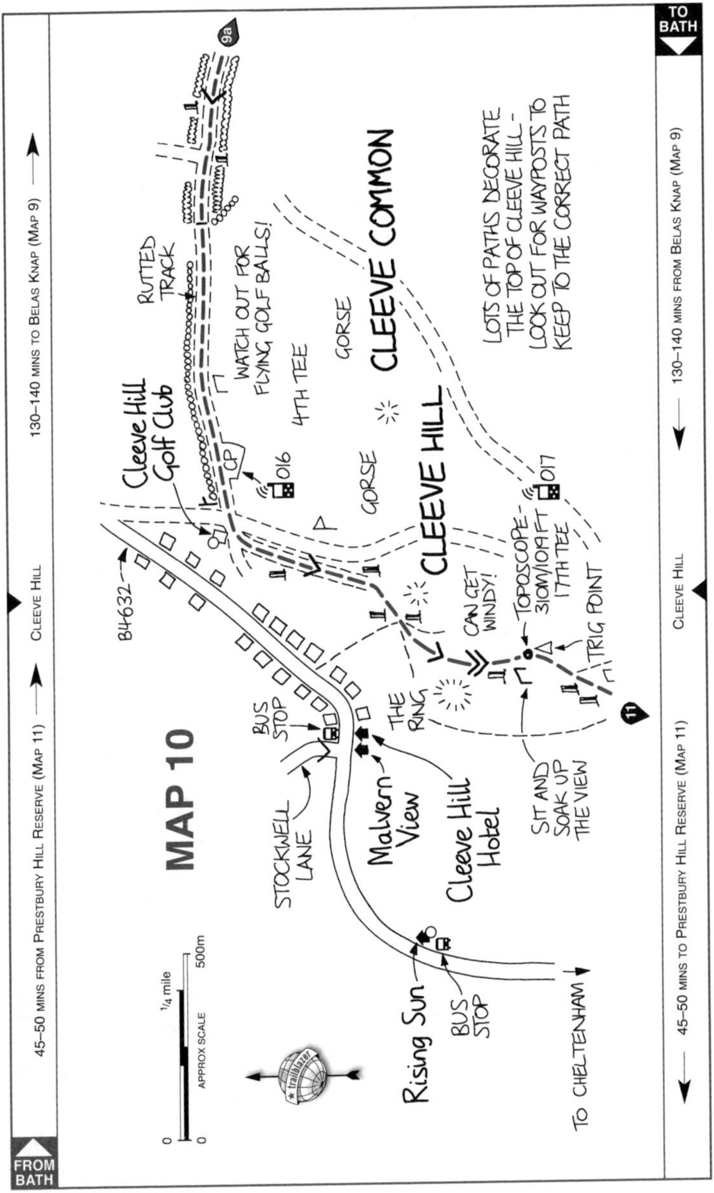

MAP 10

TO CHELTENHAM

Rising Sun

BUS STOP

STOCKWELL LANE

BUS STOP

Malvern View

Cleeve Hill Hotel

THE RING

SIT AND SOAK UP THE VIEW

CAN GET WINDY!

TOPOSCOPE-330M/1084FT 17TH TEE

TRIG POINT

017

CLEEVE HILL

GORSE

GORSE

4TH TEE

CP

016

WATCH OUT FOR FLYING GOLF BALLS!

Cleeve Hill Golf Club

RUTTED TRACK

B4632

CLEEVE COMMON

LOTS OF PATHS DECORATE THE TOP OF CLEEVE HILL – LOOK OUT FOR WAYPOSTS TO KEEP TO THE CORRECT PATH

9a

TO BATH

FROM BATH

¼ mile

500m

APPROX SCALE

Trailblazer

45–50 MINS FROM PRESTBURY HILL RESERVE (MAP 11) → CLEEVE HILL → 130–140 MINS TO BELAS KNAP (MAP 9) →

130–140 MINS FROM BELAS KNAP (MAP 9) ← CLEEVE HILL ← 45–50 MINS TO PRESTBURY HILL RESERVE (MAP 11)

ROUTE GUIDE AND MAPS

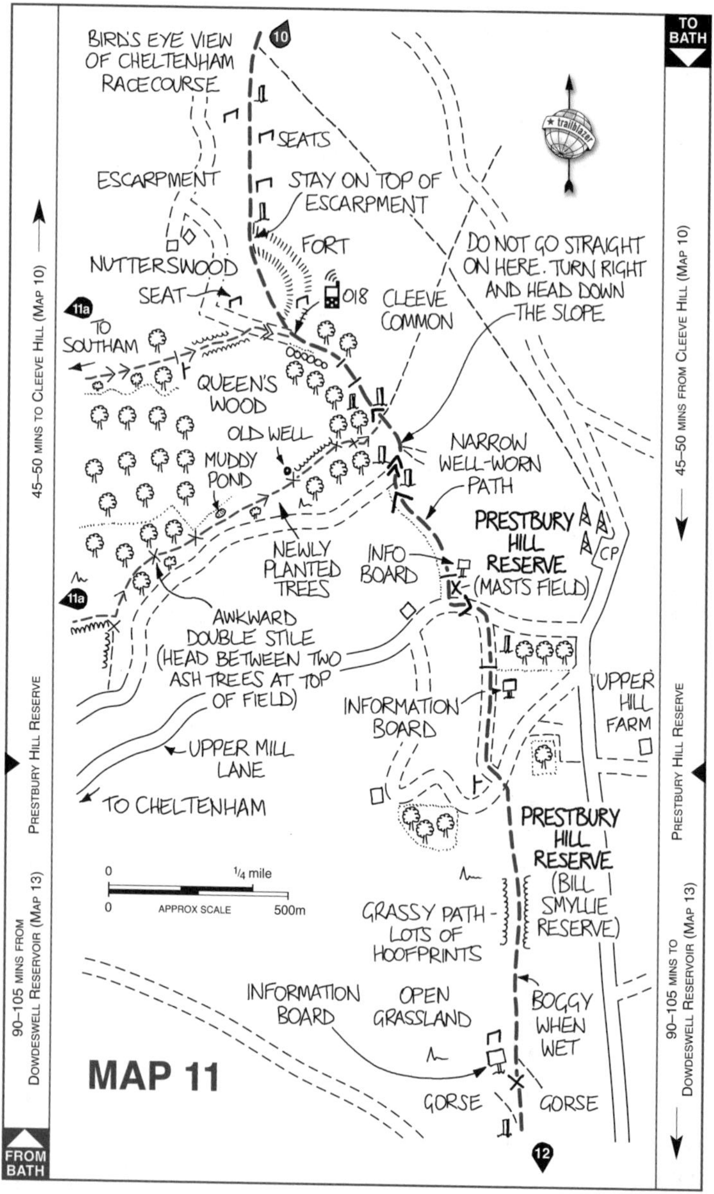

BIRD'S EYE VIEW
OF CHELTENHAM
RACECOURSE

10

TO
BATH

SEATS

ESCARPMENT

STAY ON TOP OF
ESCARPMENT

NUTTERSWOOD
SEAT

FORT

DO NOT GO STRAIGHT
ON HERE. TURN RIGHT
AND HEAD DOWN
THE SLOPE

11a

TO
SOUTHAM

018

CLEEVE
COMMON

QUEEN'S
WOOD

OLD WELL

MUDDY
POND

NARROW
WELL-WORN
PATH

11a

NEWLY
PLANTED
TREES

INFO
BOARD

PRESTBURY
HILL
RESERVE
(MASTS FIELD)

CP

AWKWARD
DOUBLE STILE
(HEAD BETWEEN TWO
ASH TREES AT TOP
OF FIELD)

INFORMATION
BOARD

UPPER
HILL
FARM

UPPER MILL
LANE

TO CHELTENHAM

PRESTBURY
HILL
RESERVE
(BILL
SMYLLIE
RESERVE)

0   1/4 mile
APPROX SCALE
0   500m

GRASSY PATH -
LOTS OF
HOOFPRINTS

MAP 11

INFORMATION
BOARD

OPEN
GRASSLAND

BOGGY
WHEN
WET

GORSE   GORSE

12

45–50 MINS TO CLEEVE HILL (MAP 10)

45–50 MINS FROM CLEEVE HILL (MAP 10)

ROUTE GUIDE AND MAPS

PRESTBURY HILL RESERVE

PRESTBURY HILL RESERVE

90–105 MINS FROM
DOWDESWELL RESERVOIR (MAP 13)

90–105 MINS TO
DOWDESWELL RESERVOIR (MAP 13)

FROM
BATH

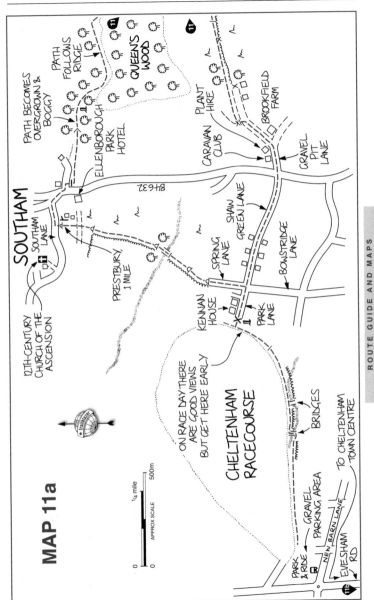

MAP 11a

ROUTE GUIDE AND MAPS

(Map 11; incorporating both Masts Field and Bill Smyllie Reserve), **Charlton Kings Common** (Map 14) and **Leckhampton Hill** (Map 15), each sheltering several rare flowers and butterflies.

Leckhampton Hill itself is the site of one of the many hill forts (see box on p122) that line the escarpment, and of the much-photographed **Devil's Chimney**. This tall outcrop of rock towers over a disused quarry, giving rise to a legend involving the Devil hurling stones from this spot at worshippers as they made their way to church on a Sunday. More prosaic suggestions as to its provenance include erosion (somewhat unlikely), and the possibility that it was created as a bawdy joke by 18th-century quarry workers. Whatever its history, the chimney has been regularly climbed by local youngsters over the years and even survived an earthquake in the 1920s. Today, it is securely fenced to help protect it from (very real) erosion. To reach it look for the path (signed) off the main trail, by the southern edge of the hill fort.

Walking between Cheltenham and the Cotswold Way
[Map 11a, p105]

While the most direct route from Cheltenham to the Cotswold Way is probably along the busy London Rd, this is hardly attractive walking territory. Far more interesting is to head north out of town through the park towards the racecourse, from where a network of footpaths along the edge of Queen's Wood leads up to Cleeve Common – some of it coinciding with the Gustav Holst Way (see opposite). If you fancy returning a different way, you can descend along the woodland path to Southam and thence back to the racecourse, a circular trip of just over 5 miles (8.25km).

CHELTENHAM   [MAP 11b, p108]

Cheltenham was swept into the popular consciousness by George III, who first came to take the waters in 1788. Its Regency architecture, with whitewashed houses rather than the natural dressed stone typical of Georgian Bath, continues to attract visitors, but today the town's primary attractions are considerably broader than its architecture or spa waters. Although Cheltenham is some distance from the trail, many visitors to the town will want to sample at least a section of the Cotswold Way, while some walkers along the trail may wish to work the town into their trip in some way, so the information given here is intended as a starting point.

Tourist information can be found online at ⌨ visitcheltenham.com or by visiting The Cheltenham Pod (High St, outside M&S) which is staffed at weekends (Sat, Sun & public holidays 11am-3pm). On weekdays head to reception area of the

Municipal Offices (Mon, Tue, Thur & Fri 9am-5pm, Wed 10am-5pm) where maps, town guides and leaflets are available.

Cheltenham is also home to several festivals (see box pp15-16), and regularly hosts live concerts. For more information see ⌨ cheltenhamtownhall.org.uk.

What to see and do

Cheltenham was built with pleasure in mind, laid out with wide promenades, formal gardens and elegant houses fronted by intricate metal balconies.

The town's Regency architecture can best be viewed by walking in the **Montpellier district** then on through the central area and north alongside **Pittville Park**. Significant among the buildings is **Pittville Pump Room** which, with its distinctive columns and decorated dome, stands at the head of the park. Completed in 1830, it was restored in 1960, and remains in regular use for private-hire functions and events including concerts and an artisan market. Although the main building is no longer open to the general public, in the orangery their *Heritage Café* (☎ 01242-528764, 🖳 pittvillepumproom.org.uk/heri tage-cafe; **fb**; daily 9.30am-5pm) serves a range of hot and cold food with views over the park.

The Wilson, Cheltenham's **Art Gallery and Museum** (☎ 01242-237431, 🖳 www.cheltenhammuseum.org.uk/explore thewilson; Tue-Sat 10am-6pm, Sun 10am-4pm; free except for special exhibitions: £4 donation suggested), on Clarence St, is certainly a dramatic space – from the uber-modern entrance hall to a new permanent art gallery. There's also their archive department (known as the Paper Store), and space for temporary exhibitions. Of major importance is an exhibition of furniture, together with silver, textiles, ceramics and paintings, from the Arts and Crafts Movement; don't miss the remarkably intricate piano created by CR Ashbee for his wife. Other artefacts span the period from ancient Egypt to the 20th century, with a small exhibition dedicated to Edward Wilson of Antarctic fame, who was born in the town, and for whom the gallery is named. For a coffee or light lunch there's *The Wilson Kitchen* (🖳 www.cheltenham museum.org.uk/thewilsonkitchen, **fb**; Tue-Sat 10am-6pm, Sun 10am-4pm).

The Gloucestershire Guild (☎ 07562-516545, 🖳 guildcrafts.org.uk; **fb**; Mon-Sat 10am-5pm) at 18 Rotunda Terrace, Montpellier St, continues the Arts and Crafts theme through displays and sales of work by members of the Gloucestershire Guild of Craftsmen.

Further north, **Holst Victorian House** (☎ 01242-524846, 🖳 holstvictorian house.org.uk; Tue-Sat 10am-4pm; £10), 4 Clarence Rd, is set in a small Regency townhouse, displaying a drawing room of that period and a Victorian kitchen. It celebrates the life of the composer Gustav Holst, internationally renowned for his *Planets* suite, which was first performed in London in 1918. Holst was born in this house in 1874, was educated in the town,

and returned in the late 1920s, remaining until his death in 1934. The composer's love of his native countryside is celebrated in the waymarked 35-mile (56km) Gustav Holst Way, from Cranham to Wyck Rissington, which in parts runs parallel to the Cotswold Way.

Prestbury Park, just north of the town, has been home to **Cheltenham Racecourse** (☎ 01242-513014, 🖳 thejockeyclub.co.uk/cheltenham) since 1831. Before that, race meetings were held on Cleeve Common, where horses are still regularly exercised. The course hosts around 16 meetings a year between October and May, with the highlight being the Cheltenham Festival, the famous race meeting in the National Hunt racing calendar held over four days in mid March (see box p15). A footpath alongside the course affords a close-up view of the races, though be warned: it's a popular spot!

Transport
Cheltenham is well served by trains, coaches and buses.

Both GWR and Cross Country **train services** (see box p46) call at Cheltenham Spa, which is about a mile (1.6km) west of the town centre. Stagecoach's D bus service operates frequently between the railway station, Clarence St (but not the bus station) and the Racecourse Park & Ride, making it ideal for walkers heading up onto the Cotswold Way.

National Express **coaches** (see box p47), and some other **buses**, go to Royal Well bus station behind the Promenade. Probably of greatest use to walkers are Pulhams' No 606 service (departs from Pittville St), but their No 801 (Royal Well bus station) and P & Q (Pittville St) and Marchants L also call here. Stagecoach's No 51, 66 & 166 stop on the Promenade; their B service operates (from Pittville St & Clarence St) to Charlton Kings and Marchants' L service (from North St) to Leckhampton. For details, see pp48-50.

There are licensed **taxi** ranks at the station, Montpellier and The Promenade but also private hire companies such as Starline Taxis (☎ 01242-250250).

ROUTE GUIDE AND MAPS

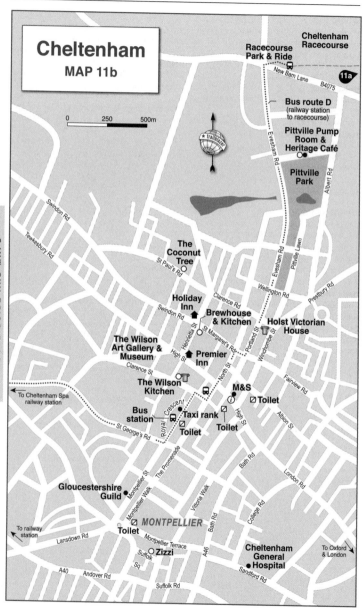

Cheltenham
MAP 11b

0   250   500m

Racecourse Park & Ride

Cheltenham Racecourse

New Barn Lane

B4075

11a

Bus route D
(railway station to racecourse)

Pittville Pump Room & Heritage Café

Pittville Park

Evesham Rd

Pittville Lawn

Albert Rd

Swindon Rd

Tewkesbury Rd

St Paul's Rd

The Coconut Tree

Clarence Rd

Wellington Rd

Prestbury Rd

Holiday Inn

Swindon Rd

Brewhouse & Kitchen

St Margaret's Rd

Portland St

Windhcombe St

Holst Victorian House

The Wilson Art Gallery & Museum

Henrietta St

High St

Premier Inn

North St

Clarence St

Fairview Rd

The Wilson Kitchen

← To Cheltenham Spa railway station

M&S

Toilet

Albion St

Bus station

Royal Crescent

Taxi rank

Toilet

Toilet

St George's Rd

High St

Bath Rd

London Rd

The Promenade

Gloucestershire Guild

Montpellier St

Montpellier Walk

Victoria Walk

College Rd

MONTPELLIER

Toilet

Lansdown Rd

Montpellier Terrace

Bath Rd

A46

To railway station

Suffolk Sq

Zizzi

Cheltenham General Hospital

A40

Andover Rd

Suffolk Rd

Sandford Rd

To Oxford & London

Where to stay

While it is beyond the scope of this guide to cover Cheltenham's hotels in detail, here are two reliable chains that are conveniently located. Both have over 100 rooms with a mix of doubles and twins, all with en-suite bathrooms. Rates vary hugely from day to day.

Premier Inn Cheltenham Town Centre (☎ 0333 321 9326, 🖳 premierinn .com), Henrietta St ; average prices around £50-110 per room.

Holiday Inn Express Cheltenham Town Centre (☎ 0800 8080 0800, 🖳 ihg .com/holidayinnexpress), 33 Dunalley St; average prices around £70-140 per room.

Where to eat and drink

Cheltenham has numerous restaurants, from Michelin starred establishments to most of the usual chains. Here are a few convenient places; there are many others close to them.

The Coconut Tree (☎ 01242-465758, 🖳 thecoconut-tree.com; **fb**; Mon-Thur noon-11pm, Fri-Sat noon-1am, Sun noon-10pm), 59 St Pauls Rd, is a popular, good-value Sri Lanka restaurant.

Brewhouse & Kitchen (☎ 01242-509946, 🖳 brewhouseandkitchen.com; **fb**; Mon-Fri 11am-10pm, Sat 10am-10pm, Sun 11am-9pm), Henrietta St, is usefully-located in the northern part of the town. It's part of a chain of pubs that also sell their own craft beers and serve inexpensive pub grub. They offer brunches until 1pm.

In the attractive Montpellier district *Zizzi* (☎ 01242-252493, 🖳 zizzi.co.uk; **fb**; daily 11.30am-10pm), St James Church, 3 Suffolk Sq, is part of the relatively predictable pizza/pasta chain, but the star is the setting: a large converted church with stained-glass windows looking down on an outsize pizza oven in place of the altar.

HAM HILL   [MAP 12, p110]

Continuing along the Cotswold Way, you'll come to *Colgate Farm* (mob ☎ 07980-607867, 🖳 colgatefarm.co.uk), a working livery farm with a history of rearing polo ponies and that offers **camping**.

You can pitch a tent here for £10 per person per night. You pay on arrival and they don't take advance bookings as there's acres of space. There are toilets, hot show-

ers, a kitchen with a microwave and some food available to buy at cost, a dry room, free wi-fi, and firepits with free wood. Dogs 'that wag their tails' may stay for free.

As they say on their website, 'it's a working farm not a caravan park' – precisely what most walkers looking to pitch a tent for a night are looking for.

CHARLTON KINGS   [off MAP 13]

On the A40 main road into Cheltenham, there are a couple of places to stay. The first is just under a mile from the trail junction at Koloshi Restaurant where there's a bus stop for buses into Cheltenham via Charlton Kings. You could also walk along the road as there's a pavement by it but it's a busy road. Under new ownership, the *Charlton Boutique Hotel* (☎ 01242-651051, 🖳 thecharlton.co.uk; 2T/ 9D/1Tr, all en suite; ▼), offers accommodation from £45pp (sgl occ full room rate) in comfortable modern rooms, including a triple room with three single beds. There's also a restaurant –

Oncore Dining – here, open daily 9-11am, noon-2pm and 5-9.30pm (to 8pm on Sunday).

Near the hotel and still on the main road is East End Service Station, where there's an **ATM** and Londis **shop** (daily 7am-9.30pm) with a *Costa Express*, though you'll find more variety at East End Stores across the road (Mon-Sat 7am-8pm, Sun 8am-7pm).

About a mile further along the A40 towards Cheltenham is *The London Inn* (☎ 01242-525606, 1S/2T/3D/2Tr, all en suite; ▼; **fb**), a pub with rooms. B&B here costs

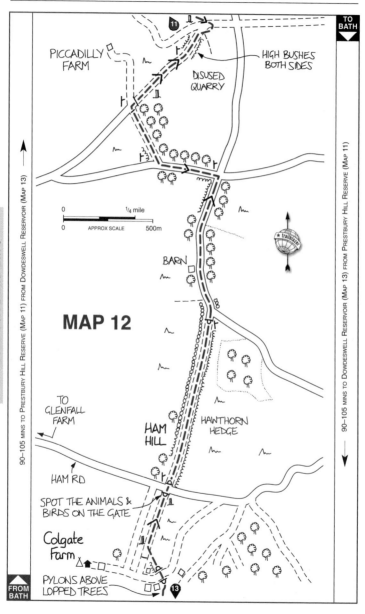

TO BATH
11
PICCADILLY FARM
HIGH BUSHES BOTH SIDES
DISUSED QUARRY
0 1/4 mile
0 APPROX SCALE 500m
trailblazer
BARN
MAP 12
TO GLENFALL FARM
HAM HILL
HAWTHORN HEDGE
HAM RD
SPOT THE ANIMALS & BIRDS ON THE GATE
Colgate Farm
PYLONS ABOVE LOPPED TREES
13
FROM BATH
90–105 MINS TO PRESTBURY HILL RESERVE (MAP 11) FROM DOWDESWELL RESERVOIR (MAP 13)
90–105 MINS TO DOWDESWELL RESERVOIR (MAP 13) FROM PRESTBURY HILL RESERVE (MAP 11)

from £45pp (sgl from £60). There's good pub grub and specials during the week – eg a pint and pizza for £10 – and there's live music some evenings.

Another good pub is *The Royal* (☎ 01242-228937, 🖥 royalpub.co.uk; food Mon-Sat noon-2.30pm & 6-8.30pm, Sun to 7pm; 🐕 in bar area) at 54 Horsefair St, about three-quarters of a mile towards Charlton Park from East End Service Station. Royal pie of the day £14.50, burgers from £13, steaks from £19, salads from £6/11 for small/large. You may need to book for supper at the weekend.

Several **bus** services call here (Pulham's No 801 as well as their P & Q and Stagecoach's B service); for details see pp48-50.

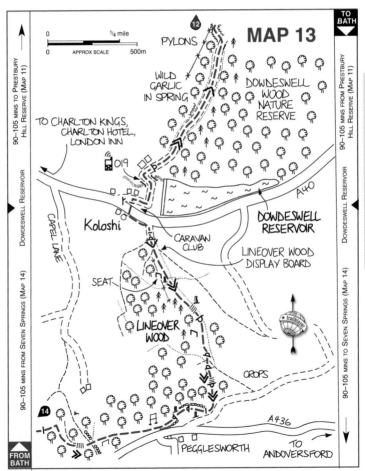

NEAR DOWDESWELL RESERVOIR
[MAP 13, p111]

At the bottom of the hill on the busy A40 road is *Koloshi* (☎ 01242-516400, 🖳 koloshi.co.uk), a popular Indian restaurant and takeaway. If you were passing around lunchtime you could order some nans (from £2.50) and a few side dishes (from £4.50) such as palak paneer (spinach with Indian cottage cheese) and char-dal tarka (lentils) for a quick meal. However, do note that the restaurant (**food** Tue-Sun noon-2.30pm & 5.30-10pm) is closed on a Monday.

Pulham's No 801 **bus** (see pp48-50) stops outside Koloshi on request. Since there is no official bus stop here, if you want to be picked up be sure to stand somewhere conspicuous and where it can safely pull over – just outside the restaurant car park is best.

SEVEN SPRINGS   [MAP 14]

There is really little more than a pub and a small roadside diner, though there is a café at the shooting range just up the road.

Parked in a layby by one of the sources of the Thames (see box p114) *Suzie's* (Mon-Fri 7am-1.30pm) is a little red burger van where Suzie dishes up great breakfasts and hot and cold drinks. There are good burgers made with meat from a local butcher. Note that it's cash only.

More permanent is the *Seven Springs* (☎ 01242-870219, 🖳 hungryhorse.co.uk; food daily 11am-9pm; small 🐾 on lead).

Part of the Hungry Horse chain, it has a huge menu at bargain prices, with glossy pictures to match; finesse is not the order of the day. Alongside pub favourites from £8.99, there are baguettes, wraps and hot dogs.

Alternatively, just off the A436 (see Map 14) there's the *café* (☎ 01242-870391, 🖳 iancoley.co.uk; food Tue-Sat 9am-5pm; 🐾 on lead) at Ian Coley Sporting. They serve breakfasts and light lunches. A panini with chicken and pesto, crisps and salad is £5.50 and there's a good range of coffee.

LECKHAMPTON HILL TO BIRDLIP   MAPS 15-17

From Leckhampton Hill it's a fairly straightforward **5¾-mile (9.25km)** walk to Birdlip, taking about **2¾ to 3¼ hours**. The route primarily follows the line of the escarpment, with attendant views in good weather. The Star Bistro at Ullenwood (see below) makes an excellent lunch stop and there's also a café at **Crickley Hill** (see p117), where it's worth lingering both to explore the hill fort and surrounding area.

By now you'll be becoming aware of the roar of heavy machinery as work progresses on the rerouting of the A417 by the Air Balloon roundabout where the former pub has now closed. Works are planned to last until 2027 and a new Cotswold Way crossing is planned but for the moment you'll need to follow the diversion signs.

ULLENWOOD   [MAP 15, p115]

The good people at National Star College in the grounds of Ullenwood Manor have set up a couple of ventures that are perfect for walkers along the Cotswold Way. **Campers** will find relative comfort in the four wooden **camping pods** at *Ullenwood StarGlamping* (☎ 01242-527631, 🖳 nationalstar.org; 🐾) and food, in the form of a hamper, is available by prior arrangement. As well as two pods sleeping up to

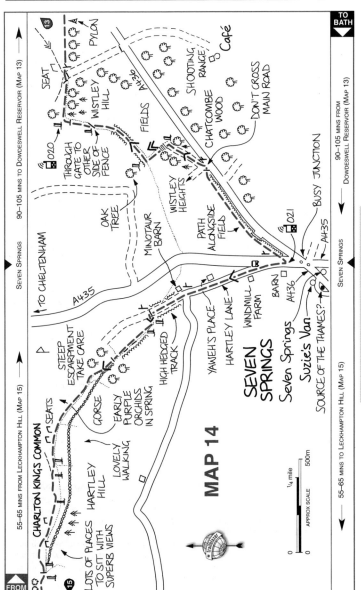

MAP 14

¼ mile

500m

APPROX SCALE

0

0

TO BATH

FROM BATH

15

90–105 MINS TO DOWDESWELL RESERVOIR (MAP 13)

SEVEN SPRINGS

55–65 MINS FROM LECKHAMPTON HILL (MAP 15)

90–105 MINS FROM DOWDESWELL RESERVOIR (MAP 13)

SEVEN SPRINGS

55–65 MINS TO LECKHAMPTON HILL (MAP 15)

CHARLTON KINGS COMMON

SEATS

LOTS OF PLACES TO SIT WITH SUPERB VIEWS

HARTLEY HILL

LOVELY WALKING

GORSE

EARLY PURPLE ORCHIDS IN SPRING

STEEP ESCARPMENT TAKE CARE

HIGH HEDGED TRACK

YAWEH'S PLACE

HARTLEY LANE

WINDMILL FARM

SEVEN SPRINGS

Seven Springs

Suzie's Van

SOURCE OF THE THAMES?

BARN

A436

BUSY JUNCTION

A435

021

PATH ALONGSIDE FIELDS

WISTLEY HEIGHTS

MINOTAUR BARN

OAK TREE

TO CHELTENHAM

A435

THROUGH GATE TO OTHER SIDE OF FENCE

020

SEAT

WISTLEY HILL

FIELDS

PYLON

Café

A436

CHATCOMBE WOOD

SHOOTING RANGE

DON'T CROSS MAIN ROAD

two (£60 for one or two people), and a third up to four (£80), there's the oak-timbered Shire House (1D; £60 for one or two). Expect toilets and showers, of course, but you'll need to bring your own towels though bedding can be hired if you don't have a sleeping bag.

On the same site is *StarBistro* (☎ 01242-339988; Mon-Fri 9am-4pm; 🐾 only on their covered patio), which serves coffee, lunch and afternoon tea during the

week (hot food till 2pm), except on bank holidays. Pre-booking may be required for afternoon tea. The bistro is staffed by youngsters with disabilities from the college, working with a resident chef. The food is excellent – the bao buns highly recommended. Everyone was friendly and helpful and it makes a good lunch stop.

There's a tempting range of cakes and also a small **shop** selling sandwiches, filled rolls, fruit and snacks.

❏ SEVEN SPRINGS – THE TRUE SOURCE OF THE THAMES?

Mention Seven Springs to those who've done the Cotswolds Way and the chances are, if they remember the place at all, it will be as a rather busy, noisy roundabout; indeed, many will consider it to be a contender for the least attractive part of the entire trail. But the place does – possibly – boast one rather important distinction. For some people consider this place to be the true source of the River Thames.

Most people consider the source of the Thames to be at Trewsbury Mead, south-west of Cirencester. It is here that the Thames Path starts, and Ordnance Survey maps have always had it labelled as the Thames's true source. Even the local pub, about half a mile away, is called Thames Head Inn.

This site, near Kemble, was first identified as the source of England's most important river way back in 1546 by John Leland, and if you visit the site today you'll find an impressive stone monument stating:

'THE CONSERVATORS OF THE RIVER THAMES
1857-1974
THIS STONE WAS PLACED HERE TO MARK THE
SOURCE OF THE RIVER THAMES'

All of which sounds pretty conclusive. But to those in the know, the claims of Seven Springs are even stronger. On the opposite side of the A436 to the Seven Springs pub, seven small trickles of water drip down a mossy wall into a pool. These, of course, are the Seven Springs after which the area was named. Study the stonework more closely and you'll discover a carving in the stone that reads '*Hic tuus o Tamesine Pater septemceminus fons*', which translates, rather poetically, as 'Here, O Father Thames, is your sevenfold spring'.

But it that true? Well, the water from these springs combines to form a small river called the Churn. This in turn feeds the Thames. And when a river has more than one source, it is usual to declare the one that is the highest as the true source. Seven Springs sits, according to my GPS, at around 207m, whereas the Trewsbury Mead site is over 100m lower at 106m. So there is a strong case to be made for declaring Seven Springs as the true source of the Thames – and relegating the site at Trewsbury Mead to that of a mere tributary.

It's doubtful, of course, that Seven Springs will ever be officially considered the start of the Thames. Which is actually a bit of a pity. For if it *were* ever viewed as the official source it would add about another 15 miles to the river, which would make it longer than the Severn – and thus the longest river in the UK!

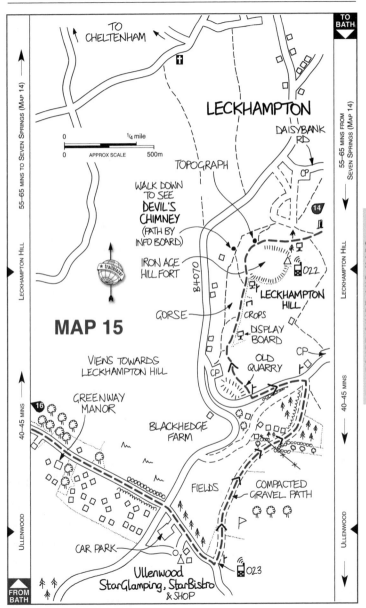

TO BATH

TO CHELTENHAM

LECKHAMPTON

DAISYBANK RD

CP

55–65 MINS TO SEVEN SPRINGS (MAP 14)

55–65 MINS FROM SEVEN SPRINGS (MAP 14)

TOPOGRAPH

0   ¼ mile
0   500m
APPROX SCALE

WALK DOWN TO SEE DEVIL'S CHIMNEY (PATH BY INFO BOARD)

14

IRON AGE HILL FORT

B4070

022

LECKHAMPTON HILL

LECKHAMPTON HILL

MAP 15

GORSE

CROPS

DISPLAY BOARD

CP

VIEWS TOWARDS LECKHAMPTON HILL

OLD QUARRY

CP

40–45 MINS

GREENWAY MANOR

16

BLACKHEDGE FARM

COMPACTED GRAVEL PATH

FIELDS

ULLENWOOD

ULLENWOOD

CAR PARK

023

Ullenwood StarGlamping, StarBistro & SHOP

FROM BATH

ROUTE GUIDE AND MAPS

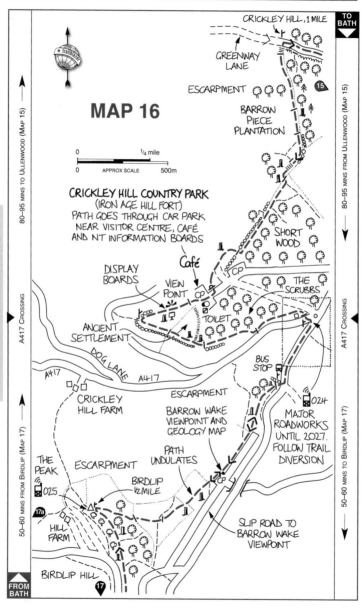

MAP 16

0   ¼ mile

0   APPROX SCALE   500m

TO BATH

FROM BATH

CRICKLEY HILL, 1 MILE

GREENWAY LANE

ESCARPMENT

BARROW PIECE PLANTATION

15

80–95 MINS TO ULLENWOOD (MAP 15)

80–95 MINS FROM ULLENWOOD (MAP 15)

CRICKLEY HILL COUNTRY PARK
(IRON AGE HILL FORT)
PATH GOES THROUGH CAR PARK
NEAR VISITOR CENTRE, CAFÉ
AND NT INFORMATION BOARDS

Café

SHORT WOOD

CP

DISPLAY BOARDS

VIEW POINT

CP

THE SCRUBBS

CP

TOILET

ANCIENT SETTLEMENT

A417 CROSSING

A417 CROSSING

DOG LANE

A417

A417

BUS STOP

ESCARPMENT

CRICKLEY HILL FARM

BARROW WAKE VIEWPOINT AND GEOLOGY MAP

024

MAJOR ROADWORKS UNTIL 2027. FOLLOW TRAIL DIVERSION

PATH UNDULATES

THE PEAK

025

17a

ESCARPMENT

BIRDLIP ½ MILE

CP

HILL FARM

BIRDLIP HILL

17

SLIP ROAD TO BARROW WAKE VIEWPOINT

50–60 MINS FROM BIRDLIP (MAP 17)

50–60 MINS TO BIRDLIP (MAP 17)

AROUND CRICKLEY HILL [MAP 16]

Popular locally with families and dog walkers, **Crickley Hill Country Park** (🖳 natio naltrust.org.uk) covers 143 acres (58 ha) protecting both the site of an ancient hill fort (see box on p122) and a natural environment which attracts a broad diversity of birds, butterflies and wild flowers, including the rare bee orchid (see pp63-4). There's a *café* (daily Apr-Sep 9am-4.30pm, Oct-Mar 9am-4pm) here run by Gloucestershire Wildlife Trust. There's soup, sandwiches, pasties, ice cream, milkshakes and a range of hot drinks but note that they accept card payments only. A wildlife trust noticeboard lists recent bird sightings.

Community Connexions' No 21 **bus** (Wed & Fri 1/day, see pp48-50) heads northbound through here towards Gloucester. Owing to the current roadworks you'll need to check for the location of the temporary bus stop. If you're planning to stay in this area, note that Little Witcombe (see p119) is almost as close to Birdlip Hill as it is to Cooper's Hill.

BIRDLIP [MAP 17, p118]

Although the Cotswold Way passes within 200m of Birdlip, it is easy to miss the tiny village entirely. But negotiate the steep and busy road and you'll come to the stone-built *Royal George Hotel* (☎ 01452-862506, 🖳 greenekinginns.co.uk; 24D/8T/2Tr, all en suite; ☛; ⓛ; 🐾). Rates vary daily and are usually best for online bookings, but expect to pay from around £40pp (sgl occ full room rate); special deals are regularly available. If you book online on their website you get a 20% discount on meals. **Meals** (daily noon-9pm, main dishes from £11) can be taken in the restaurant, or more informally in the bar or garden, or on the terrace.

Community Connexions' No 21 **bus** (Wed & Fri 1/day, see pp48-50) stops here about 100m up the road from the hotel.

BIRDLIP TO PAINSWICK MAPS 17-20

For much of the next **6¾ miles (11km, 3¼-3¾hrs)** you'll continue along the Cotswold escarpment through a woodland fringe, which opens out occasionally to reveal hillside areas such as **Cooper's Hill** (Map 18), site of the annual cheese-rolling competition (see box below), and tantalising glimpses north-west to the Malvern Hills. Be particularly careful to follow the waymarked path up here,

---

❏ CHEESE ROLLING [Map 18, p120]

Picture the scene at Cooper's Hill near Brockworth on the Whitsun Bank Holiday Monday at the end of May. At the top, a group of contestants is set on chasing a giant Double Gloucester cheese down the almost sheer hillface for no other reason than to win the cheese – and the glory. Add in the unpredictable English weather and it's a spectacle that will gladden the heart of anyone who thought British eccentricity was dying out. It's a risky affair, with paramedics kept busy throughout the five races, but that hasn't stopped the proceedings – yet.

In 2010, as international popularity threatened to swamp this once strictly village event, the official line was that it was cancelled for safety reasons. While it looked like the end, participants were less easily convinced. Cheese rolling has a long history in this neck of the woods, and local rivalries are not that easily put down. The event went ahead anyway, as it has done every year since, so if you're timing your walk at the end of May, be prepared to share the hill with some 4000 spectators. Winners in 2023 came from the UK, USA, Canada and Japan.

ROUTE GUIDE AND MAPS

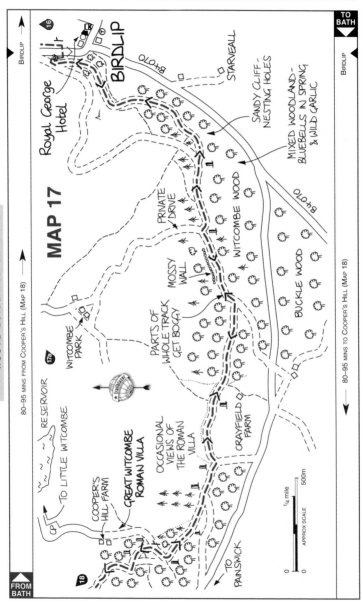

TO BATH
BIRDLIP →

BIRDLIP

FROM BATH

BIRDLIP

MAP 17

80—95 MINS FROM COOPER'S HILL (MAP 18) →

80–95 MINS TO COOPER'S HILL (MAP 18)

Royal George Hotel

BIRDLIP

16

STARVEALL

B4070

SANDY CLIFF – NESTING HOLES

MIXED WOODLAND – BLUEBELLS IN SPRING & WILD GARLIC

WITCOMBE WOOD

PRIVATE DRIVE

B4070

BUCKLE WOOD

MOSSY WALL

WITCOMBE PARK

17a

PARTS OF WHOLE TRACK GET BOGGY

CRAYFIELD FARM

RESERVOIR

TO LITTLE WITCOMBE

OCCASIONAL VIEWS OF THE ROMAN VILLA

GREAT WITCOMBE ROMAN VILLA

COOPER'S HILL FARM

CP

18

TO PAINSWICK

¼ mile

500m

0

0

APPROX SCALE

and not to wander off the edge of the escarpment in misty weather; the rough picket fence would do little to break a fall.

Painswick Beacon (Map 19), site of an Iron-Age hill fort (see box on p122) follows, before you reach one of the trail's architectural highlights: **Painswick**. It was east of the town, in the Slad Valley, that the three-year-old Laurie Lee was famously 'set down from the carrier's cart', thus beginning his evocative autobiographical work, *Cider with Rosie*. While the world has moved on, many of the views along this part of the route are probably little changed – at least superficially – since Lee's childhood.

LITTLE WITCOMBE   [MAP 17a]

There are two main ways down to Little Witcombe, one each side of Birdlip – see Map 17. West of Birdlip, a steep walk down from the trail brings you to **Great Witcombe Villa** which was constructed during Roman times, but abandoned around the 5th century AD. The foundations are still clearly visible, but almost as interesting is an unmown section of grass which in summer yields numerous wild flowers, including the pyramidal orchid (see p63).

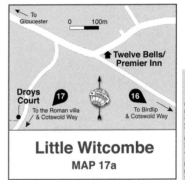

Little Witcombe
MAP 17a

Just a short walk across the main road is *Twelve Bells* (☎ 01452-862521, 🖳 beefeater.co.uk; breakfasts Mon-Fri 6.30-10.30am, Sat & Sun 7-11am; Mon-Sat 11.30am-10pm, Sun noon-10.30pm), part of the Beefeater chain. The adjacent *Premier Inn* (☎ 0333 321 9326, 🖳 premierinn.com; 59D, all en suite; ☞) is a dependable choice, with some of the rooms having space for additional children (though not adults). Pricing varies widely and depends in part on whether you have a Saver rate (where you pay when you book) or a Flex rate (where you can cancel up to 1pm on the day you are booked), but can be as little as £59 for the room (albeit generally only

for a Sunday night and for a Saver rate). Breakfast – taken at the pub – is all you can eat and costs £7.99 for a continental breakfast, or £9.99 for a full English cooked to order. They also have a 'meal deal' at £25.99, which includes a two-course evening meal and drink and an all-you-can-eat breakfast.

Community Connexions' No 21 **bus** (Wed & Fri 1/day, see pp48-50) stops here.

CRANHAM CORNER [MAP 18, p120]

Not so much a village as a point on the map where the road to Cranham (and the Way) meets the A46, Cranham Corner is nevertheless served by a **bus**, Stagecoach's No 166; see pp48-50. The village itself, almost a mile (1.3km) east of the trail, was where Gustav Holst (see p107) lived for a period and in 1906, while here, he composed the first setting to music of *In the Bleak Midwinter*, a poem by Christina Rosetti.

Between Cooper's Hill and Cranham Corner you could take one of the paths down to **Prinknash Abbey**, a Roman Catholic community of Benedictine monks and visit the chapel and the excellent non-profit *café* (☎ 01452-812066, 🖳 prinknash abbey.org; daily 10am-4pm) run by Cranham locals.

A few steps from the trail on the A46 is the Royal William pub sadly currently

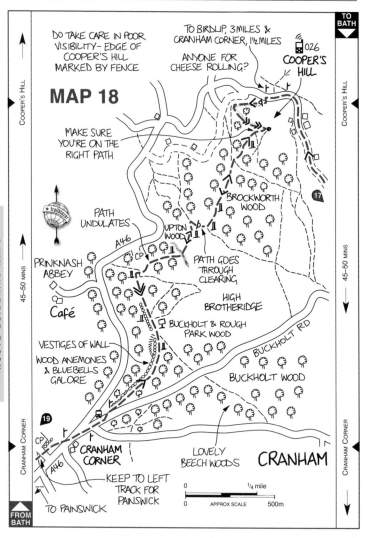

MAP 18

TO BATH

CRANHAM CORNER

COOPER'S HILL

45–50 MINS

COOPER'S HILL

ROUTE GUIDE AND MAPS

45–50 MINS

CRANHAM CORNER

FROM BATH

TO BIRDLIP, 3 MILES & CRANHAM CORNER, 1½ MILES

ANYONE FOR CHEESE ROLLING?

📱026 COOPER'S HILL

DO TAKE CARE IN POOR VISIBILITY – EDGE OF COOPER'S HILL MARKED BY FENCE

MAKE SURE YOU'RE ON THE RIGHT PATH

trailblazer

PATH UNDULATES

A46

PRINKNASH ABBEY

Café

VESTIGES OF WALL

WOOD ANEMONES & BLUEBELLS GALORE

17

BROCKWORTH WOOD

UPTON WOOD

CP

PATH GOES THROUGH CLEARING

HIGH BROTHERIDGE

BUCKHOLT & ROUGH PARK WOOD

BUCKHOLT RD

BUCKHOLT WOOD

19

CP

CRANHAM CORNER

A46

KEEP TO LEFT TRACK FOR PAINSWICK

TO PAINSWICK

LOVELY BEECH WOODS

CRANHAM

0   ¼ mile
0   APPROX SCALE   500m

☐ **Important note – walking times**
All times in this book refer only to the time spent walking. You will need to add 20-30% to allow for rests, photography, checking the map, drinking water etc.

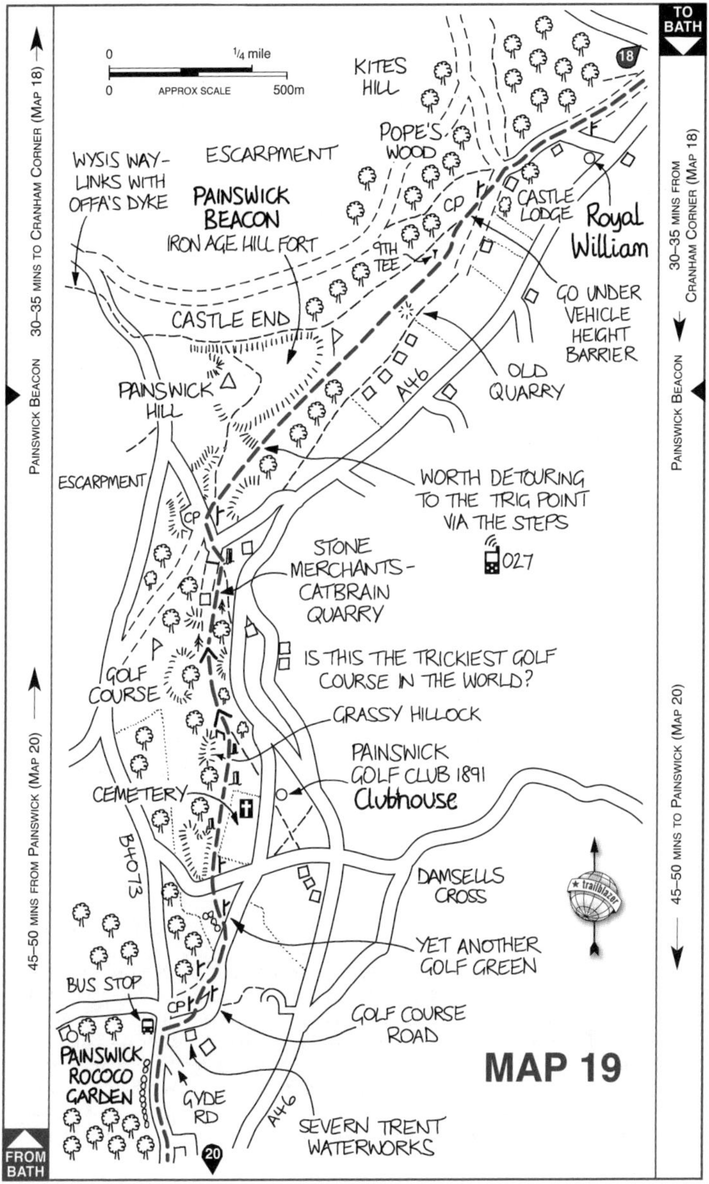

MAP 19

KITES HILL

POPE'S WOOD

ESCARPMENT

WYSIS WAY - LINKS WITH OFFA'S DYKE

PAINSWICK BEACON
IRON AGE HILL FORT

9TH TEE

CP

CASTLE LODGE

Royal William

CASTLE END

GO UNDER VEHICLE HEIGHT BARRIER

PAINSWICK HILL

OLD QUARRY

A46

ESCARPMENT

CP

WORTH DETOURING TO THE TRIG POINT VIA THE STEPS

027

STONE MERCHANTS - CATBRAIN QUARRY

IS THIS THE TRICKIEST GOLF COURSE IN THE WORLD?

GOLF COURSE

GRASSY HILLOCK

PAINSWICK GOLF CLUB 1891
Clubhouse

CEMETERY

B4073

DAMSELLS CROSS

YET ANOTHER GOLF GREEN

BUS STOP

CP

GOLF COURSE ROAD

PAINSWICK ROCOCO GARDEN

GYDE RD

A46

SEVERN TRENT WATERWORKS

MAP 19

0   1/4 mile
0   500m
APPROX SCALE

TO BATH
18

FROM BATH
20

30-35 MINS TO CRANHAM CORNER (MAP 18)

PAINSWICK BEACON

45-50 MINS FROM PAINSWICK (MAP 20)

30-35 MINS FROM CRANHAM CORNER (MAP 18)

PAINSWICK BEACON

45-50 MINS TO PAINSWICK (MAP 20)

ROUTE GUIDE AND MAPS

closed. Until late 2023 it was a popular independently-run pub and it may reopen. Just over a mile south and some three-quarters of a mile (1.3km) north of Painswick, is Painswick Golf Club with its friendly *Clubhouse* (Map 19; ☎ 01452-812180, ▢ painswickgolf.com; Tue & Thur-Sun 10am-3pm; 🐾). Open for sandwiches, drinks and cakes, it has a sunny balcony with glorious views over the Slad valley. Note that larger groups of walkers should phone ahead.

PAINSWICK   [MAP 20a, p125]

The small town of Painswick, which harks back to the Domesday Book, may come as something of a surprise for those more familiar with the Cotswold villages further north. The off-white stone of the buildings, many built by wool merchants during the 18th century, comes without the golden hue found to the north and the whole style is more elegant.

If you've the energy, count the 99 yew trees in the grounds of **St Mary's Church** (legend has it that the Devil won't let the 100th one grow), seek out the tea-caddy gravestones, or look for the **spectacle stocks** by the churchyard wall. And while you're there, note the clock on the tower, erected to celebrate the millennium.

The Arts and Crafts Movement (see box on p76) was influential here in the early 20th century and the tradition continues.

Today's artists exhibit at **The Painswick Centre** (☎ 01452-814567, ▢ painswick-centre.com; daily 10am-4pm; free), on Bisley St, which has regular artists in residence, there's a good *café* (see p126) and also here is the community cinema, **Wick-Flix**. On Thursdays 7.45-9am there's a **farmers' market** here.

Though it's not often open – occasionally at weekends or you can email ahead to ask to look round – the **Ashton Beer Collection** (mob ☎ 07828-930050, ▢ ashtonbeercollection.wixsite.com/beer; May-Oct Sat & Sun 11am-4pm or by appointment), housed in the old Christ Church on Gloucester St, whose central window was designed by Sir Edward Burne-Jones and made by William Morris's company. Here, John Ashton Beer has displayed around 600 items from his Arts and Crafts collection,

---

❏ HILL FORTS

Painswick Beacon (Map 19), also known as Kimsbury Camp, is just one of 35 **Iron-Age hill forts** that have been identified in Gloucestershire, this one dating back to around 400BC. From the layman's perspective, it is arguably the fort that gives greatest vent to the imagination along the Cotswold Way, with steep sides leading up to the fort area from where there are extensive views. Although golf has been played here since 1891, and quarrying has left its mark, the outline of the fort on the ground can still clearly be seen. Today, steps have been cut into the hill to prevent further damage to the ramparts.

Other notable hill forts along the Cotswold Way include those at **Leckhampton Hill** (Map 15, p115), **Crickley Hill** (Map 16, p116), **Haresfield Beacon** (Map 21, p127) and – just off the trail – **Uley Bury** (Map 26, p136). Some of the earlier settlements, including the one at Crickley Hill, are at least 5000 years old, although the hill fort there is far more modern, occupied around 500BC. Although little of these sites is visible on the ground today, there are some excellent interpretive panels along the trail, including an artist's impression at Crickley Hill of how a hill fort might have looked.

The thin soil on these sites, and the fact that they have never been ploughed, means not only that it is relatively easy to make out the lines of the forts on the ground, but also that they are particularly rich environmentally, and several – including Painswick Beacon – have been designated as SSSIs (see p61).

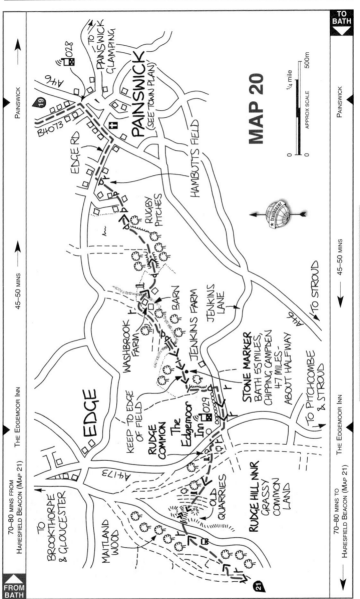

TO
BATH

PAINSWICK

TO
PAINSWICK
GLAMPING

028

A46

19

B4073

EDGE RD

PAINSWICK
(SEE TOWN PLAN)

MAP 20

¼ mile

500m

0

0

APPROX SCALE

PAINSWICK

HAMBUTTS FIELD

RUGBY
PITCHES

TO STROUD

45–50 MINS

45–50 MINS ──→

WASHBROOK
FARM

BARN

JENKINS FARM

JENKINS
LANE

A46

TO
PITCHCOMBE
& STROUD

STONE MARKER
BATH 55 MILES,
CHIPPING CAMPDEN
47 MILES–
ABOUT HALFWAY

KEEP TO EDGE
OF FIELD

RUDGE
COMMON

029

The
Edgemoor
Inn

A4173

EDGE

TO
BROOKTHORPE
& GLOUCESTER

70–80 MINS FROM
HARESFIELD BEACON (MAP 21)

The Edgemoor Inn

MAITLAND
WOOD

OLD
QUARRIES

RUDGE HILL NNR
GRASSY
COMMON
LAND

21

FROM
BATH

70–80 MINS TO
HARESFIELD BEACON (MAP 21)

The Edgemoor Inn ──→

ROUTE GUIDE AND MAPS

lovingly assembled over four decades.

As well as the Artburst art festival in August there's also the Painswick Church Clypping and Puppydog Pie (aka Painswick Feast – and no actual puppies involved) on a Sunday in late September (see p16).

Transport
Stagecoach's Nos 66 & 166 **buses** (see pp48-50) stop outside St Mary's church. For a **taxi**, try RM Goddard (☎ 01452-812240), or Painswick Taxis (☎ 07833-444607).

Services
Painswick's **tourist information centre** (☎ 01452-812278, Apr-Oct Mon-Fri 10am-4pm, Sat 10am-1pm) is in the Gravedigger's Hut on the southern side of St Mary's churchyard and is run by volunteers.

There is no bank in the town, but there's an **ATM** at the small Premier **village shop** (Mon-Sat 7am-8pm, Sun 8am-5pm) on St Mary's St. Sadly, the **post office** (Wed & Fri 9.30-11.30am) has been moved into the Town Hall from its beautiful half-timbered building on New St, dating back to the 15th century.

There's a doctor's **surgery** (☎ 01452-812545, 🖳 painswicksurgery.nhs.uk; Mon-Fri 8.30am-6pm) to the north of the town at Hoyland House on Gyde Rd, off Gloucester St, and the handy Painswick **Pharmacy** (Mon-Fri 9am-1pm & 2-6pm, Sat 9am-noon) on New St.

Where to stay
There's **camping** half a mile east of the village at *Painswick Glamping* (☎ 07866-520636, 🖳 painswickglamping.co.uk; **fb**; Mar-Oct; 🐾), for £12/15pp in low/high season. It's at Beech Farm and there are showers, toilets and a cooking area. They also have a pod (1D, £84 for 2) and shepherd hut (1D, £87 for 2) but, unlike for camping, there's a two-night minimum stay policy.

Most of Painswick's places to stay are near the town centre. Two **B&Bs** are close to each other on Gloucester St, along the trail. At friendly *Troy House* (☎ 01452-812339, 🖳 troyguesthouse.co.uk; 2D/2Tr, all en suite; 🍸; Ⓛ; Feb-Dec), where each triple room can be set up as a double or single or three singles. You'll pay from £55pp in the doubles and from £42 in the triples. Opposite is *St Anne's* (☎ 01452-812879, 🖳 st-annes-painswick.co.uk; **fb**; 1T/2D, all en suite; Ⓛ; 🐾), a well-run cottagey place with flowers in the rooms. They also have drying facilities and a utility room with a large sink for washing off kit and filling water bottles. Rates are from £55pp (sgl occ £90). They offer a pick up and drop off at Leckhampton if you stay two nights.

Also on the trail is *Falcon* (☎ 01452-222820, 🖳 falconpainswick.co.uk; 2T/2D/7D or T, all en suite; 🍸; Ⓛ; 🐾), New St, a 16th-century coaching inn with a 21st-century twist. Rooms can be booked online and prices fluctuate, but expect to pay £45-70pp (sgl occ room rate).

❏ PAINSWICK ROCOCO GARDEN [Map 19, p121]
Not far from the trail, this garden (☎ 01452-813204, 🖳 www.rococogarden.org.uk; **fb**; daily late Jan to end Feb, Wed-Sun Mar to mid-July, daily mid-July to Aug, Wed-Sun Sep & Oct, Nov & Dec weekends only 10am-4pm (5pm in summer); £10.50) is claimed to be the only complete English Rococo garden still in existence. It was planted in the 1740s, but so quickly did the fashion change that the original was soon replanted and the garden was later abandoned. Over 240 years later, in 1984, restoration was put in hand thanks to a painting made in 1748 showing the original design. Flights of fancy characterise a fairly structured and geometric layout, with fruit and vegetables forming a part of the whole rather than hidden away. A maze created to commemorate the garden's 250th anniversary is an added attraction; the gardens are renowned for their display of snowdrops in early spring and for the bluebell walk.

Coffee, tea, cakes and light lunches are served in the *café* (food to 4pm, lunch noon-2pm; 🐾).

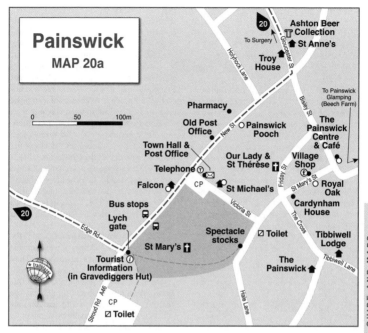

At *Tibbiwell Lodge* (☎ 01452-812748 or mob ☎ 07872-310393, 🖥 tibbiwell lodge.com – phone if website not yet working; 1T private facilities, 1D/ 1Tr, both en suite; ✿; Ⓛ; 🐾; Mar-late Nov), a short way down Tibbiwell Lane, there's an interesting choice of rooms with rates from around £50pp. The room that can sleep up to three people has a balcony and the double has a terrace; both of these rooms look over the valley. Useful facilities include a drying room and boot wash area.

Top of the range in accommodation terms, *The Painswick* (☎ 01452-813688, 🖥 thepainswick.co.uk; 7D/9D or T, all en suite; ✿; 🐾) is an imposing three-storey stone building on a quiet lane – and pretty much as good as it gets when it comes to B&Bs on the trail. Luxurious and stylish, the rooms are so popular that it can be difficult to book despite the high room-only rates that start at about £85pp but can easily rise to £130pp or more, for B&B. If

you're treating yourself go for one of their packages which includes dinner as they have an excellent restaurant.

St Michael's (☎ 01452-812712, 🖥 stmichaelsbistro.co.uk; 5D, all en suite; ✿; Ⓛ; 🐾 restaurant only) is an upmarket B&B and restaurant that gets top reviews. The décor in the rooms is striking to say the least – the suite, for example, features retro '70s furnishings including a hanging perspex bubble chair, portable record player and 'vintage' board games – but there's no denying the quality and comfort of this place. B&B rates start at £65pp (sgl occ full room rate) for the smaller rooms or £125pp for the suites. It's worth checking on 🖥 booking .com as significant discounts may be available particularly for single occupancy. Some come without breakfast – and you wouldn't want to miss that here!

Cardynham House (🖥 kateandtoms .com/houses/cardynham-house) is now only available for groups of up to 24 people.

ROUTE GUIDE AND MAPS

Where to eat and drink

The *Arts Café* (☎ 01452-814567; **fb**; food Mon-Sat 10am-4pm, Sun 10-2pm; 🐾), at the Painswick Centre is perfect for a coffee and cakes or a light lunch (paninis or filled bagels), with friendly staff and a good range of hot drinks. There's also a shop here selling some of the art produced at the centre.

Also popular is the dog-friendly *Painswick Pooch* (☎ 01452-812560, 🖳 thepainswickpooch.wixsite.com/thepainswickpooch; Sat-Thurs 10am-4pm; 🐾) with daily wraps and bagels, cakes, 'walker packs' (packed lunches) and their orange & lavender signature cake. For your pet they have beds, chaise longues, water bowls and Scoops ice cream. At the end of 2023, sadly, they were up for sale though still operating.

Thankfully, Painswick's two venerable inns are still going strong and remain highlights. You'll get a warm welcome at the *Royal Oak* (☎ 01452-813129; food Wed-Sat noon-2.30pm & 6-9pm, Sun noon-3pm; 🐾), on St Mary's St, which remains a proper real-ale pub (with beers from Stroud or Butcombe breweries, see box p23). Cosy, stone built and often with a roaring fire. There's standard pub fare but it's well-prepared and good value. More stylish is *Falcon* (see Where to stay; Mon-Fri noon-2.45pm & 6-9pm, Sat-Sun noon-9pm, -8pm Sun), where you'll dine in relaxed but contemporary surroundings with excellent service. Locals and visitors flock here for the diverse menu (so you may need to book), but many walkers will appreciate their delicious bar snacks (pork & leek Scotch egg, £7). Try the pigeon breast for starters (£9) or the 14-hour slow-roasted venison for mains (£22).

St Michael's Bistro & Restaurant (see Where to stay; food Tue 6.30-10pm, Wed-Sun noon-3pm & 6.30-10pm), is now headed by Marin, the chef who used to run the restaurant at Cardynham House, with Catalina front of house. The style is 'traditional English and simple European', with locally sourced ingredients and a great range of dishes that are good value. Light lunches include baguettes served with chips and salad (around £7.50) or more substantial dishes such as pan-fried lamb's liver with bacon and onions. In the evening you could try the chef's speciality: Beef Stroganoff (£16.95).

The Painswick Restaurant (see Where to stay; open for afternoon tea Mon-Sat noon-3.30pm, Sun lunch noon-3pm, dinner daily 5.45pm-9pm or 5.45pm-7.30pm for tasting menu) is the place to go for a celebratory dinner. How about loin of Cotswold venison with beetroot, BBQ maitake, fig and port (£33)? At lunchtime they serve what they call 'afternoon tea' but since it includes a Scotch egg, pork pie, sandwiches, a scone and cake (£25) it would make a rather good lunch. Add a glass of champagne or two and it would be an even better lunch but might put an end to the day's walking.

PAINSWICK TO STONEHOUSE (CANAL CROSSING)   MAPS 20-23

This **9-mile (14.6km, 4¼-5hr)** section marks the halfway point along the Cotswold Way; indeed, you'll pass a stonemarker (Map 20) stating 'Bath 55' on one side – and 'Chipping Campden 47' on the other – which clearly *isn't* halfway, but it's close. After the open countryside of the first few miles the trail enters a narrow strip of woodland, following the edge of the escarpment as it twists and turns around **Haresfield Beacon** (Map 21). With unimpeded (not to mention spectacular) views in almost every direction, and sheer slopes on two sides, it's no surprise that it was chosen as the site of an Iron-Age hill fort (see box on p122).

The descent through woods and fields to **Stroudwater (Ebley) Canal** (Map 23) gives little indication of the urban sprawl to the east that is the town of Stroud. No wonder, then, that the appearance of first the railway, then two busy

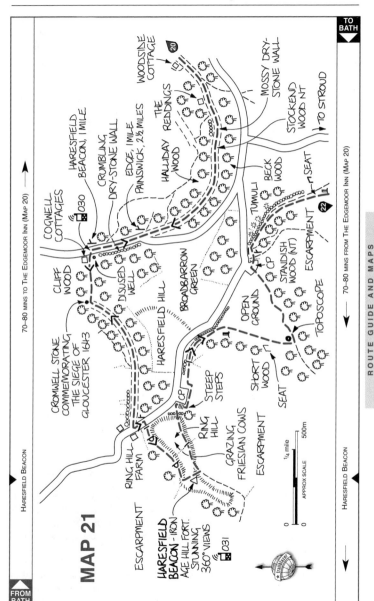

TO BATH

MAP 21

HARESFIELD BEACON

HARESFIELD BEACON

FROM BATH

70-80 MINS TO THE EDGEMOOR INN (MAP 20)

70-80 MINS FROM THE EDGEMOOR INN (MAP 20)

HARESFIELD BEACON - IRON AGE HILL FORT. STUNNING 360° VIEWS.
031

ESCARPMENT

CROMWELL STONE COMMEMORATING THE SIEGE OF GLOUCESTER 1643

RING HILL FARM

RING HILL

GRAZING FRIESIAN COWS

ESCARPMENT

STEEP STEPS

CP

SHORT WOOD

SEAT

OPEN GROUND

CLIFF WOOD

HARESFIELD HILL

DISUSED WELL

BROADBARROW GREEN

STANDISH WOOD (NT)

TOPOSCOPE

COGWELL COTTAGES
030

HARESFIELD BEACON, 1 MILE

CRUMBLING DRY-STONE WALL

EDGE, 1MILE
PAINSWICK, 2½ MILES

HALLIDAY WOOD

THE REDDINGS

WOODSIDE COTTAGE

20

MOSSY DRY-STONE WALL

STOCKEND WOOD NT

TO STROUD

BECK WOODS

TUMULI

ESCARPMENT

SEAT

CP

22

¼ mile

500m

APPROX SCALE

0

0

parallel roads, jars the senses. Yet the canal between these, just a few metres above sea level and the lowest point along the route, is one of the few areas of water along the Cotswold Way and introduces a very different environment.

EDGE [MAP 20, p123]

Right on the Cotswold Way on the busy A4173, opposite the entrance to Edge Common (part of Rudge Hill National Nature Reserve), *The Edgemoor Inn* (☎ 01452-813576, 🖥 edgemoorinn.uk; food Mon-Sat noon-2pm & 6.30-8.30pm, Sun 12-2pm) could be a good staging post. Expect daily specials on the menu, main courses from £13.50, a good choice of vegetarian food and a range of real ales. You may need to book ahead for their Sunday lunch. Dogs are only allowed on the patio.

RANDWICK [MAP 22]

On the western outskirts of Stroud are the villages of Randwick and Westrip (see below), a short but steep walk down from the trail.

The local **pub** up the hill in **Randwick** does a good job of satisfying walkers' hunger pangs. *Vine Tree Inn* (☎ 01453-763748, 🖥 thevinetreerandwick.co.uk; **fb**; food served Tue 5.30-9pm, Wed-Fri noon-2pm & 5.30-9pm, Sat noon-9pm, Sun noon-6pm; 🐾), where lunchtime ciabattas at £8.50 vie with glazed ham, egg & chunky chips (£14). Note that the pub is closed all day on Monday and till Tuesday evening.

Cotswold Green's No 230 **bus** (only on Tue: 2/day, see pp48-50) from Stroud stops here.

WESTRIP [MAP 22]

Further south, Westrip boasts *The Carpenters Arms* (☎ 01453-766028, 🖥 thecarpentersarmswestrip.co.uk; **fb**; food Tue-Thu noon-2.30 & 5-8.30pm, Fri-Sun noon-8.30pm; 🐾), a real-ale and cider pub where the food (pub classics) is excellent value – mains from £9. There's live music some nights and they won the 2023 Gloucestershire Cider Pub of the Year Award.

STONEHOUSE [MAP 23, p131]

As the Cotswold Way emerges into the valley that links Stonehouse to the west and Ebley to the east, there's little to delay the walker. Stonehouse **railway** station, a little over half a mile (1km) from the trail, off the B4008, is served by GWR (see p84) and offers straightforward access to the Cotswold Way at this point. Stagecoach's **bus** Nos 62 & 65 (see pp48-50) stop on the B4008 (Bath Rd) near the station.

See box p16 for details of Frocester Festival which is held near here in August.

STONEHOUSE (CANAL CROSSING) TO PENN WOOD MAPS 23-24

At this point, the Cotswold Way offers two options. The **shorter route**, which runs close to King's Stanley, is only 1½ miles (2.4km) long, taking about **40-50 minutes** to walk. Predominantly urban with an agricultural fringe, its attractions are of a practical nature, with a couple of B&Bs, a pub and a useful shop in King's Stanley itself.

The more **scenic route**, which follows in part the restored **Stroudwater (Ebley) Canal** then goes on to cross Selsley Common, is almost **4 miles (6.5km, 1½-2hrs)**, so about twice the distance. Unless time is of the essence, opt for the longer walk; the rewards are infinitely greater, with the common

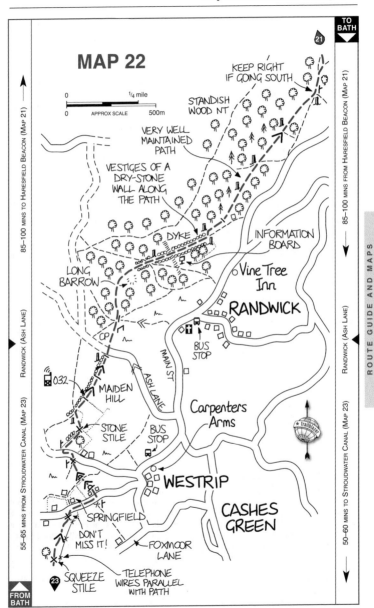

MAP 22

0 — 1/4 mile
0 — 500m
APPROX SCALE

TO BATH

21

KEEP RIGHT IF GOING SOUTH

STANDISH WOOD NT

VERY WELL MAINTAINED PATH

VESTIGES OF A DRY-STONE WALL ALONG THE PATH

DYKE

INFORMATION BOARD

Vine Tree Inn

RANDWICK

LONG BARROW

CP

BUS STOP

032

MAIDEN HILL

STONE STILE

BUS STOP

MAIN ST

ASH LANE

Carpenters Arms

WESTRIP

SPRINGFIELD

DON'T MISS IT!

FOXMOOR LANE

SQUEEZE STILE

TELEPHONE WIRES PARALLEL WITH PATH

CASHES GREEN

23

FROM BATH

85–100 MINS TO HARESFIELD BEACON (MAP 21)

RANDWICK (ASH LANE)

55–65 MINS FROM STROUDWATER CANAL (MAP 23)

85–100 MINS FROM HARESFIELD BEACON (MAP 21)

RANDWICK (ASH LANE)

50–60 MINS TO STROUDWATER CANAL (MAP 23)

ROUTE GUIDE AND MAPS

trailblazer

itself one of the trail's highlights. Open and windswept, it offers glorious walking at any time of the year, but is at its best in summer when the grass is thick with orchids and other wild flowers.

Both routes converge in **Penn Wood**, just a quarter of a mile (0.45km) or so above (almost literally) Middleyard.

EBLEY [on SCENIC ROUTE, MAP 23]

Less than quarter of a mile (0.4km) east of the oak tree where the re-routed Cotswold Way turns away from Ebley Canal is **Ebley Wharf**, a development across the bridge from Ebley Mill. *Kitsch Coffee and Wine Bar* (☎ 01453-350930; Mon-Fri 9am-6pm, Sun 10am-3pm) is here and can provide

sanctuary if it's raining. For a supermarket head a further half-mile along the main road to the **Cainscross** branch of the Co-op (Mon-Sat 7am-10pm, Sun 10am-4pm).

Cotswold Green's No 230 **bus** service calls at Ebley here (only Tue, 2/day; see pp48-50).

SELSLEY [off MAP 23; MAP 24, p133]
[on SCENIC ROUTE]

The village of Selsley is notable for the Victorian **All Saints' Church** (Map 24), clearly visible on the hill from the canal and a little way from the heart of the community. The church was influential in the development of the Arts and Crafts Movement (see box on p76), its stained-glass windows being one of the first commissions for William Morris's design company. Work was contributed by Dante Gabriel Rossetti and Edward Burne-Jones, as well as by Morris himself. The church lies alongside **Selsley Common**, itself a haven for any number of wild flowers, including the pyramidal orchid (see p63).

Both lodging and sustenance are on hand in the centre of the village at *The Bell Inn* (off Map 23; ☎ 01453-753801, 🖳 the bellinnselsley.com; 1D/1Tr, both en suite; (L); 🐾), a couple of hundred yards (200m)

from the trail. There are two classy bedrooms with king-size beds, contemporary bathrooms and plenty of mod cons. Rates are from £50pp in the smaller room, or £55pp in the larger, which has a separate living room with sofa bed. There's also a **self-contained apartment** with double bed and kitchen area for stays of two nights or more. There's an excellent **restaurant** (Mon 6-8.30pm, Tue-Sat noon-2.30pm & 6-9pm, Sun noon-3pm), mains in the evening are £16-23, or – perhaps more manageable at lunchtime – sandwiches (eg crayfish with lemon mayonnaise) made with their own sourdough bread with fries & salad are £10.

Stagecoach's No 65 **bus** service (see pp48-50) stops by The Bell Inn and their No 62 by All Saints' Church. Cotswold Green's No 65A Sat service also calls here.

KING'S STANLEY   [MAP 24, p133]
[on SHORTER ROUTE]

Only a short walk west of the trail across playing fields, King's Stanley offers most of the services essential to walkers.

The **Co-op** (Mon-Sat 7am-10pm, Sun 8am-10pm) has all the necessities, including a **post office** counter (open the same hours) and a useful **ATM**. Opposite is a small **newsagent**, Yew Tree Stores.

For B&B, try *Orchardene* (☎ 01453-822684, 🖳 orchardene.co.uk, for email use:

orchardene77@gmail.com; 1T en suite/ 1D with private bathroom; 🐾; (L); 🐾), reached by heading away from the shops along Castle St. A 19th-century stone house down a narrow drive, it's a friendly place offering local organic food, including their own honey. B&B comes in at £55pp (sgl occ room rate).

For **food** in the evening, now that the King's Head has closed, there's just the Chinese takeaway, *Ben's* (☎ 01453-

ROUTE GUIDE AND MAPS

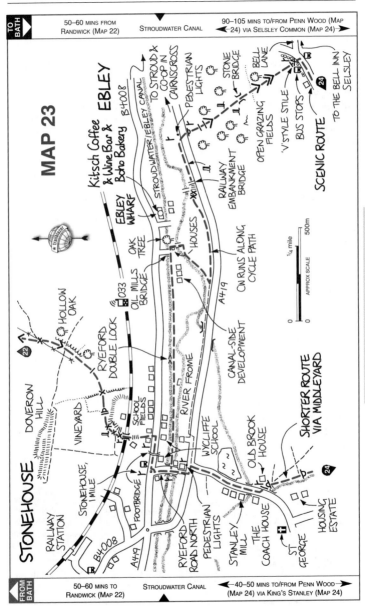

MAP 23

EBLEY

STONEHOUSE

Kitsch Coffee & Wine Bar & Boho Bakery

B4008

STROUDWATER/EBLEY CANAL

TO STROUD & CO-OP IN CAINSCROSS

EBLEY WHARF

PEDESTRIAN LIGHTS

STONE BRIDGE

BELL LANE

TO THE BELL INN SELSLEY

24

'V' STYLE STILE

BUS STOPS

OPEN GRAZING FIELDS

SCENIC ROUTE

RAILWAY EMBANKMENT BRIDGE

OAK TREE

HOUSES

CW RUNS ALONG CYCLE PATH

OIL MILLS BRIDGE

033

A419

RYEFORD DOUBLE LOCK

HOLLOW OAK

22

DOVERON HILL

VINEYARDS

SCHOOL FIELDS

RIVER FROME

CANAL-SIDE DEVELOPMENT

WYCLIFFE SCHOOL

OLD BROOK HOUSE

SHORTER ROUTE VIA MIDDLEYARD

24

STONEHOUSE, 1 MILE

FOOTBRIDGE

RYEFORD ROAD NORTH

PEDESTRIAN LIGHTS

STANLEY MILL

THE COACH HOUSE

ST GEORGE

HOUSING ESTATE

RAILWAY STATION

B4008

A419

¼ mile

500m

0

0

APPROX SCALE

828855, 🖳 benstakeaway.co.uk; Tue-Sun 4.30-11pm), almost hidden down a narrow street that runs between Shute St and the playing fields. It's good value with set meals from £12.80 but closed on a Monday

evening, so you may have to take a taxi somewhere for supper.

Stagecoach **bus** No 62 (see pp48-50) stops by the war memorial and on Bath Rd.

MIDDLEYARD [MAP 24]
[on SHORTER ROUTE]

The Cotswold Way runs through Middleyard, a small ribbon of old and new stone houses up the hill from King's Stanley, yet within easy walking distance of the larger village's facilities.

Backing on to farmland, with direct access clearly signposted from the trail, the aptly named *Valley Views* (☎ 01453-827458, 🖳 valley-views.com; 1D private bath; ✒; Ⓛ; Mar-end Oct), 12 Orchard Cl, is a modern, very comfortable house. Owner Pam

gets rave reviews for this long-running establishment but is now only letting this one room. B&B costs £45pp (sgl occ from £80).

Just off the road to Selsley is *Greencourt Loft* (**fb**; 1D + sofabed & futon; en suite; Ⓛ; 🐾), above the garage at Greencourt House. Featuring on several booking websites including AirBnb, rates are from around £45pp including breakfast.

Stagecoach **bus** No 62 stops on Broad St near Coombe Lane (see pp48-50).

PENN WOOD TO DURSLEY   MAPS 24-27

Further ribbons of steeply banked beech woods characterise this **6½-mile (10.4km, 3¼-4hrs)** stretch, broken up by two significant highlights as well as a couple of interesting long barrows.

The views from **Coaley Peak** (Map 25) look not just west to the Severn, but onward to Cam Long Down and the Tyndale Monument – a taste of things to come. **Cam Long Down** (Map 27) itself is all too short, the steep climb up being richly rewarded with 360° views: a place to be savoured before the descent into **Dursley**. Be careful up here if the weather is poor, though; there are some sheer drops.

❏ WHAT IS A LONG BARROW?

Essentially another name for a communal burial ground, the long barrow is known locally as a '*tump*'. These were the graveyards of the Neolithic people, early settlers who were the first to farm the land over 5000 years ago. In addition to human remains, archaeologists have identified the remains of fires that indicate some form of ritual or religious activity.

Of almost 100 long barrows in the Cotswolds, several are along the Cotswold Way including **Nympsfield Long Barrow** (Map 25) near Coaley Peak, dating from 2500BC, and others at Leckhampton Hill and in Standish Wood. Notable among them are **Belas Knap** (Map 9; see box on p100) and – just off this stretch of the route – **Uley Long Barrow** (Map 26), more evocatively known as **Hetty Pegler's Tump**. Best approached along the road rather than by scrambling up the steep hill through the woods, Hetty Pegler is worth the detour, since here you can crawl inside the chamber itself. You'll need a torch – but don't spend too long, for folklore has it that, if you do, the fairies will start to work their magic on the passing of time.

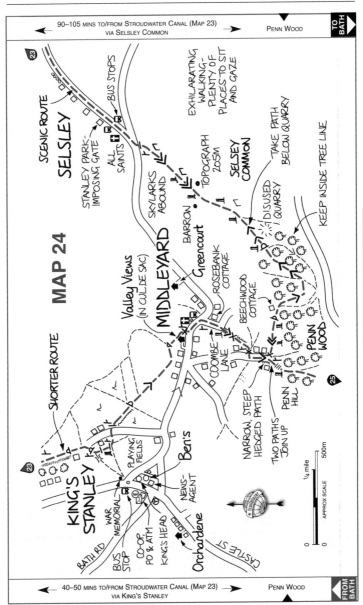

90–105 MINS TO/FROM STROUDWATER CANAL (MAP 23) via SELSLEY COMMON

PENN WOOD

TO BATH

MAP 24

SCENIC ROUTE SELSLEY

STANLEY PARK– IMPOSING GATE

BUS STOPS

ALL SAINTS

EXHILARATING WALKING– PLENTY OF PLACES TO SIT AND GAZE

SKYLARKS ABOUND

TOPOGRAPH 205M

SELSEY COMMON

TAKE PATH BELOW QUARRY

DISUSED QUARRY

KEEP INSIDE TREE LINE

Valley Views (IN CUL DE SAC)

BARTON

MIDDLEYARD

Greencourt

ROSEBANK COTTAGE

BEECHWOOD COTTAGE

PENN WOOD

SHORTER ROUTE

COOMBE LANE

PENN HILL

25

NARROW, STEEP HEDGED PATH

TWO PATHS JOIN UP

KING'S STANLEY

PLAYING FIELDS

Ben's

NEWS-AGENT

WAR MEMORIAL

BATH RD

CO-OP, PO & ATM

KING'S HEAD

BUS STOP

Orchardene

CASTLE ST

STROUDWATER

1/4 mile

APPROX SCALE

0   500m
0

ROUTE GUIDE AND MAPS

40–50 MINS TO/FROM STROUDWATER CANAL (MAP 23) via KING'S STANLEY

PENN WOOD

FROM BATH

The area is also home to two of the trail's most interesting long barrows (see box p132), at **Nympsfield** (Map 25) and **Uley** (Map 26), and two very different mansions: **Woodchester Mansion** (see box below) and **Owlpen Manor** (off Map 26; see box p138), although the latter is no longer open to the public.

ULEY [MAP 26, p136]

Although it's over half a mile (1km) from the Cotswold Way, Uley does at least justify the diversion. Probably many people's idea of a proper village, it boasts a pub, a decidedly imposing church, St Giles, and a **post office cum shop** (☎ 01453-861592, 🖳 uleycommunitystores.co.uk; Mon-Fri 8am-5.30pm, Sat 8am-1pm, Sun 9am-noon; post office Mon, Tue, Thur & Fri 9am-1pm & 2-.5.30pm, Wed 9am-1pm & 2-4.30pm, Sat 9am-12.30pm); it even has its own brewery (see box p23) and a posh manor house – Owlpen Manor – a short distance away. The village is also notable for the hill fort of Uley Bury which is much closer to the trail.

The highlight of the village for many, however, is the Prema Arts Centre where *The Vestry Café* (☎ 01453-861177, 🖳 prema.org.uk/cafe; **fb**; Wed-Sat 9am-4pm;

🐾); it has an inventive menu including the delicious Vestry hash (hash brown potato topped with a poached egg). Note, however, that the café closes for 2-3 weeks during the summer school holidays.

The whitewashed *Old Crown* (☎ 01453-860502, 🖳 theoldcrownuley.co.uk; **fb**; 1T/2D, all en suite; ⓛ; 🐾), with a terrace garden at the rear, does **B&B** from £40-50pp. They now also have a three-bedroom apartment (1T/2D). There's a good **pub menu** (food Tue-Fri noon-2pm & 6-9pm, Sat & Sun noon-9pm but also Mon in summer) and plenty of real-ale choices to accompany your meal. Live music some weekends.

Stagecoach's No 65 and Cotswold Green's No 65A **bus** services (see pp48-50) stop near the post office.

❏ WOODCHESTER MANSION AND PARK [Map 25]

Despite its imposing architecture, the three-storey Victorian **Woodchester Mansion** (☎ 01453-861541, 🖳 woodchestermansion.org.uk; £11, NT & English Heritage members £1 discount), near Nympsfield, was never finished, its rooms being inhabited by five species of bat, but never by humans. It is usually open to the public from Easter to October (Fri-Sun & bank hols 11am-5pm), but do check their website first. Visitors may explore the house, including the drawing room, which was the only room to be completed, and upstairs along boarded corridors. Lunches, tea and coffee in their *tea room* should help to restore a sense of normality.

The mansion is set in the grounds of **Woodchester Park**, a peaceful wooded valley with a chain of lakes that is owned by the National Trust (☎ 01453-860037, 🖳 nationaltrust.org.uk; daily dawn-dusk; parking £3, NT members free). Designated as an SSSI (see p61), the estate is notable not just for the bats, but for a broad diversity of birds and wild flowers. Waymarked trails through the grounds are accessible to the public all year.

Visitors arriving on foot can access the mansion along the main drive; otherwise entry is via the National Trust car park to the south, from where it's a 10- to 15-minute walk to the house.

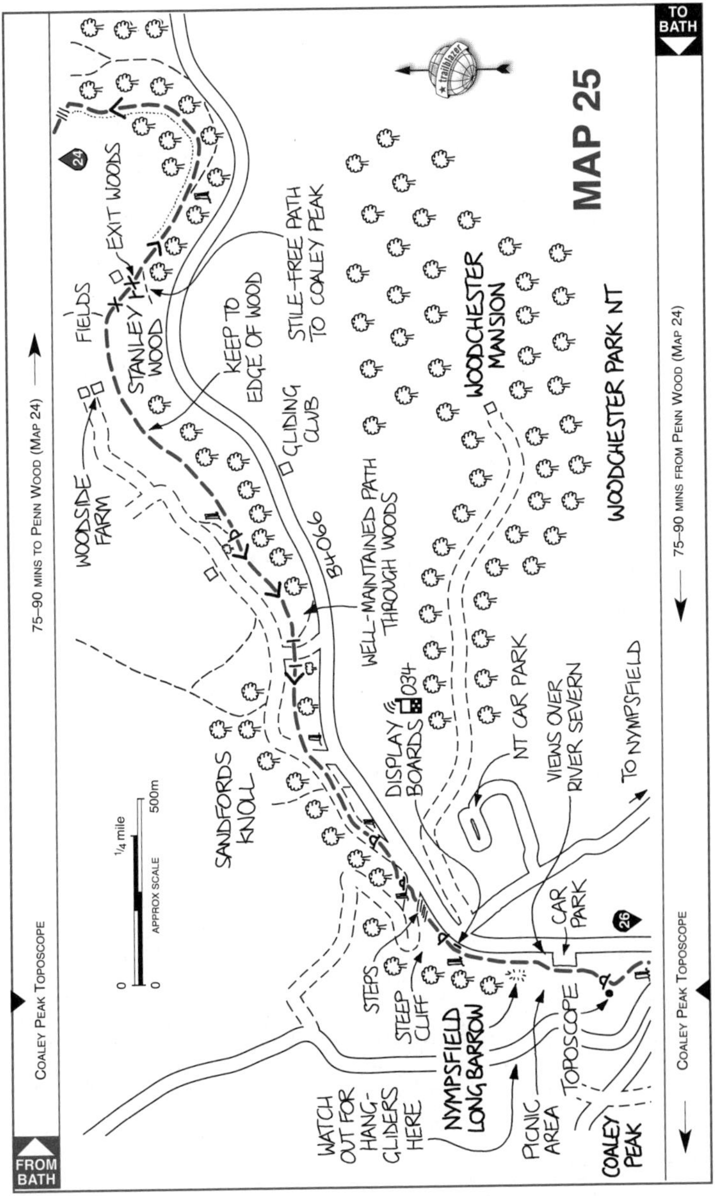

MAP 25

COALEY PEAK TOPOSCOPE

24

FIELDS

EXIT WOODS

STANLEY WOOD

KEEP TO EDGE OF WOOD

GLIDING CLUB

STILE-FREE PATH TO COALEY PEAK

WOODSIDE FARM

B4066

WOODCHESTER MANSION

WOODCHESTER PARK NT

WELL-MAINTAINED PATH THROUGH WOODS

DISPLAY BOARDS

NT CAR PARK

VIEWS OVER RIVER SEVERN

TO NYMPSFIELD

SANDFORDS KNOLL

STEPS

STEEP CLIFF

NYMPSFIELD LONG BARROW

PICNIC AREA

TOPOSCOPE

CAR PARK

26

WATCH OUT FOR HANG-GLIDERS HERE

COALEY PEAK

¼ mile

APPROX SCALE

500m

0

0

ROUTE GUIDE AND MAPS

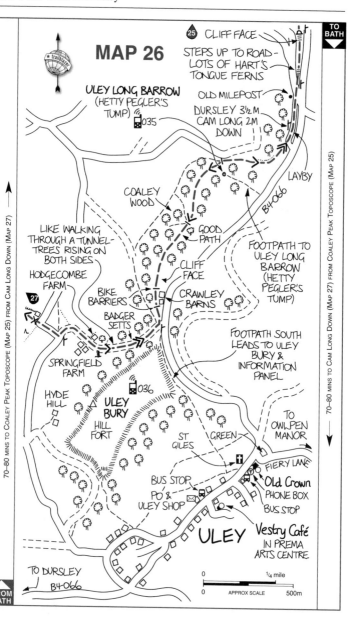

ROUTE GUIDE AND MAPS

70–80 MINS TO COALEY PEAK TOPOSCOPE (MAP 25) FROM CAM LONG DOWN (MAP 27)

70–80 MINS TO CAM LONG DOWN (MAP 27) FROM COALEY PEAK TOPOSCOPE (MAP 25)

TO BATH

FROM BATH

MAP 26

25   CLIFF FACE

STEPS UP TO ROAD - LOTS OF HART'S TONGUE FERNS

ULEY LONG BARROW (HETTY PEGLER'S TUMP) 035

OLD MILEPOST

DURSLEY 3½ M CAM LONG 2M DOWN

LAYBY

B4066

COALEY WOOD

GOOD PATH

FOOTPATH TO ULEY LONG BARROW (HETTY PEGLER'S TUMP)

LIKE WALKING THROUGH A TUNNEL - TREES RISING ON BOTH SIDES

CLIFF FACE

CRAWLEY BARNS

HODGECOMBE FARM

27

BIKE BARRIERS

BADGER SETTS

FOOTPATH SOUTH LEADS TO ULEY BURY & INFORMATION PANEL

SPRINGFIELD FARM

036

HYDE HILL

ULEY BURY

HILL FORT

TO OWLPEN MANOR

ST GILES

GREEN

FIERY LANE

Old Crown

PHONE BOX

BUS STOP

PO & ULEY SHOP

BUS STOP

ULEY   Vestry Café IN PREMA ARTS CENTRE

TO DURSLEY B4066

0   ¼ mile
0   APPROX SCALE   500m

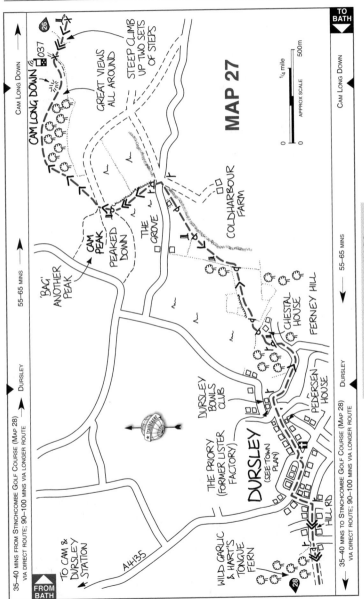

❏ OWLPEN MANOR   [off Map 26, p136]

Almost hidden from view in a valley along a short avenue of trees, Owlpen Manor
(☎ 01453-860261, 🖳 owlpen.com) is an enchanting Tudor manor house, complete
with great hall, dating in part back to 1450. It was abandoned early in the 19th century, but was rescued in 1926 in line with the principles of the Society for the
Protection of Ancient Buildings (🖳 spab.org.uk), a body formed by William Morris.
While most of the furniture and decoration date to an earlier era, the Arts and Crafts
Movement founded by Morris is also represented. Outside, the formal gardens with
their neatly clipped yews lead to beech woods with a series of walks, while above
looms an elaborate Victorian church.

Sadly, the manor, which remains in private hands, is not open to the public except
for private functions and group tours (May-Oct; £26.50 including a cream tea).

DURSLEY   [MAP 27a]

Like many other Cotswold towns, Dursley
was founded on the wool trade; today its
weaving skills have turned towards billiard-
table baizes and the covers for tennis balls.

It was also home to the **Lister** family,
of agricultural engineering fame. **Mikael
Pedersen**, the Danish inventor whose
patented cream separator that was produced
by Lister, was invited over from Denmark
to help set up production in the 1890s. He
liked Dursley so much he stayed and went
on to design a revolutionary bicycle – with
hub gears, a lightweight tubular frame and
a comfortable suspended saddle – produced
here from the 1890s until the 1920s.

As manufacturing industries closed
down over the last 20 years, the town has
been subject to considerable redevelop-
ment. Now, as houses and shops have mate-
rialised on the building sites that marred the
centre, so the town has settled into a new
phase, marked by a strong sense of community. As you walk down pedestrianised Parsonage St note the nods to the town's industrial past in the bench ends and the giant
engine con rods embedded in the pavement.

At one end of the pedestrianised
Parsonage St, which boasts a decent range
of traditional shops and facilities, stand the
pillared Georgian **Market House** and the
parish church of **St James the Great**. Cars
follow the newer road that runs almost parallel, lined with a supermarket and a leisure
complex. For the walker, Dursley has one
further card up its sleeve: the CAMRA

award-winning Old Spot pub (see p140),
which is one of the best along the trail.

To get an idea of the town's history
and its industrial past with examples of several Lister machines and an early Dursley
Pedersen bicycle, pop into the **Heritage
Centre** (☎ 01453-543550, 🖳 dursleyhc
.org.uk, Tue-Sat 10am-noon).

See box on p16 for details of the walking festival held here in October.

Transport

GWR **trains** (see p84) run to Cam &
Dursley station, nearly three miles (4.8km)
north of the town.

The town's **bus station** is on May
Lane, squeezed between the modern, tint-
ed-glass library and the Old Spot – the old
and the new. Stagecoach's No 65 bus calls
at various places in Dursley but only stops
at the railway station in the early morning
and late afternoon/early evening, while
their No 60 & Cotswold Green's 65A services call at the bus station but *not* the railway station. See pp48-50.

For **taxi** services, try A 2 B Taxis (☎
01453-548483), or Cam & Dursley Taxis
(mob ☎ 07577-753530, 🖳 www.camand
dursleytaxis.co.uk).

Services

While the town has no **tourist information**
centre as such, staff at the **library** (Mon &
Thur 9.30am-5pm, Tue & Fri to 6.30pm,
Wed to 2pm, Sat to 4pm) are extremely

helpful and they have a good selection of leaflets for visitors. There's an **ATM** at Sainsbury's (see below) The **post office** (Mon-Fri 8.30am-5.30pm, Sat 8.30am-3pm) is by Market House, at the end of Parsonage St.

A large Sainsbury's **supermarket** (Mon-Sat 8am-10pm, Sun 10am-4pm) &

ATM may have brought a new dimension to Dursley, but its traditional shops along the pedestrianised Parsonage St are more than hanging on. This is where you'll find an independent **bakery**, and a **butcher** with good cheese and pies. Crisps, sandwiches and drinks can also be bought at Hewitt's, the **newsagent**. A **farmers' market** is held

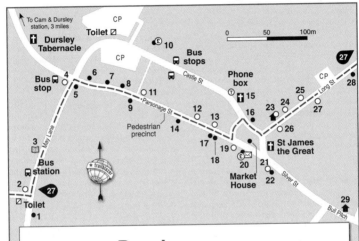

Dursley MAP 27a

Where to stay and eat
2 The Old Spot Inn
4 Della Casa
11 Gravity Fish & Chips
12 The King's Head
13 Dursley & Cam's Kebab & Pizza House
19 Bank Café
21 Indie's Deli
23 Ye Olde Dursley Hotel
24 Bengal Lounge
25 Dil Raj
26 The Everest
27 Golden Wall
29 Ormond House (The Garden Flat)

Other
1 May Lane Surgery & Pharmacy
3 Library
5 Dursley Family Pharmacy
6 Bike shop
7 Dursley Cobblers
8 Bakery
9 Butcher
10 Sainsbury's & ATM
14 Simply Foot Care
15 Methodist Centre
16 Heritage Centre
17 Boots Pharmacy
18 Hewitt's (newsagent)
20 Post Office
22 Newsagent
28 Raglan House (former home of Mikael Pedesen)

at Market House on the second Saturday of each month (9am to 1pm).

If you've any problems with your **boots**, Dursley Cobblers (☎ 01453-542918; Mon, Tue, Thur & Fri 9am-5pm, Wed & Sat to 4pm), on Parsonage St, may be able to repair them. If the situation has got really bad, salvation may come in the form of **Simply Foot Care** (☎ 07920-018416, ▣ simplyfootcare.uk; Mon-Tue, Thur & Fri 9am-4pm, Sat to 1pm), which can deal with corns, calluses, toenail trimming – or simply sell you a pair of orthopaedic slippers.

Although there's a **pharmacy** attached to May Lane surgery almost right on the trail, more central are two other chemists – Boots (Mon-Sat 9am-5.30pm) and the Dursley Family Pharmacy (Mon-Fri 9am-5.30pm, Sat to 5pm) – along Parsonage St.

Where to stay

There's a shortage of **B&B** accommodation in Dursley.

Well recommended is *The Garden Flat* (☎ 01453-545312; 1T; ▼; Mar-end Oct), a self-contained annexe of **Ormond House**, at 13 Bull Pitch (a continuation of Silver St) but note that there's a 2-night minimum stay policy. Large, light and airy, with its own entrance, kitchen and bathroom, it looks over a pretty garden and costs from £45pp (sgl occ £47.50) for B&B; the fridge is stocked with basic ingredients so that guests can cook their own breakfast.

Back in town, *Ye Olde Dursley Hotel* (☎ 01453-542821, ▣ yeoldedursley@outlook.com; **fb**; 1D/3T, en suite; ▼; 🐾 bar only or plus £20 for deep clean after dog in bedroom), on Long St, is a friendly place. The rooms are fine though the public areas are rather shabby but it's good value for single occupancy: £48. Based on two people it's £42pp, plus £10 for breakfast. The downside is that this is a busy pub, particularly at weekends. To book a room phone or use the email above.

Where to eat and drink

Arguably one of the best reasons for stopping in Dursley is to pay a visit to *The Old Spot Inn* (☎ 01453-542870, ▣ oldspot inn.co.uk; **fb**; food Mon-Sat noon-3pm, Sun noon-4pm). Regularly featured among the top CAMRA awards, it is a stronghold among ale drinkers (see box on p23). Doorstop sandwiches are £9 and there's usually a 'Plenty Pie of the Day' (£14) served with mash. Their Sunday roast is so popular that it runs to two sittings (noon and 2.15pm).

For breakfast, lunch or a cup of tea during the day, the choice has burgeoned in recent years. Near Market House, try *Bank Café* (☎ 01453-543920, ▣ bankcafe.uk; **fb**; 🐾; Mon-Sat 9am-4.30pm, Sun 9.30am-4pm), where squashy sofas meet functional chairs and tables in a big old banking hall. Despite being the smartest place in town, it's also one of the few that allows dogs.

Pick up a bap, wrap, salad box or burger at *Indie's Deli* (☎ 01453-542036; Mon-Sat 9am-3pm) or eat in at this friendly little café at 26 Silver St.

Heading to the Mediterranean, *Della Casa* (☎ 01453-549679, ▣ www.della casarestaurant.com; Mon-Fri noon-3pm & 5-10pm, Sat noon-10.30pm, Sun noon-9pm), on Parsonage St, is cool and classy. It focuses on classic Italian cuisine including pizzas (from £10.75) and risotto – try their seafood signature dish Risotto Branzino (£16.55).

For a pub, other than The Old Spot (above), there's Ye Olde Dursley Hotel (see Where to stay; food Mon-Sat 10am-9pm, Sun 11am-5pm but hours do vary depending on demand) where you're looking at standard pub fare; there's also a beer garden and a games room here. There's also *The King's Head* (☎ 01453-619182) in the middle of pedestrianised Parsonage St.

Indian and Asian cuisine is represented by three restaurants on Long St. The best is *The Everest* (☎ 01453-519600, ▣ everestofnepal.com; Tue-Sun 5.30-10pm, to 9pm on Sun) which gets great reviews, particularly for its Nepalese cuisine; momos from £5.50. Also popular is *Dil Raj* (☎ 01453-543472, ▣ dilrajdursley.co.uk; **fb**; daily noon-2pm, Sun-Thur 5.30-11.30pm, Fri & Sat to midnight) and there's also *Bengal Lounge* (☎ 01453-519711/2,

🖥 bengal loungedursley.co.uk; daily 5.15-10.30 pm).

At *Gravity Fish & Chips* (☎ 01453-933989; 🖥 gravityfishandchips.com; **fb**; Mon-Sat 11.30am-9.30pm) on Parsonage St you can dine in or take away and they also run a Greek Street Food van you may see parked near Sainsburys.

Other takeaways include the Chinese *Golden Wall* (🖥 goldenwalldursley.co.uk, Sun, Tue-Thur & bank hol Mon 5-9pm, Fri & Sat to 9.30pm) on Long St and *Dursley & Cam's Kebab and Pizza House* (☎ 01453-544188; daily 3pm-midnight) at 57 Parsonage St.

DURSLEY TO WOTTON-UNDER-EDGE   MAPS 27-30

The Cotswold Way offers another choice at this stage. The **longer (scenic) route**, a **6¾-mile (11km, 3¼-3¾hrs)** stretch, climbs steeply from Dursley and circumnavigates Stinchcombe Hill – and the golf course – before coming almost full circle. The **more direct route** (just **4½ miles/7.2km, 2¼-2¾hrs**) cuts straight across what looks on the map like the stem of a leaf. Which you choose should depend on time and the weather.

Just west of – and above – Dursley you cross **Stinchcombe Hill Golf Club** where you can get drinks and snacks or a meal at the *clubhouse* (☎ 01453-542015, food: Mon-Fri 11am-3pm, Sat & Sun 9am-3pm).

On a clear day, the views from **Stinchcombe Hill** (Map 28) more than justify the detour, but if the weather's bad, going straight across may be the better option. Either way, you'll have the opportunity to climb the **Tyndale Monument** (Map 29), perhaps to see those views from on high.

NORTH NIBLEY   [MAP 29, p143]
This little village sits below the Tyndale Monument, visible for miles around. Usually very quiet, in July the place comes alive with the North Nibley Music Festival (see p16), non-profit and community run.

After the steep climb through the woods from North Nibley, the additional ascent of the stone **Tyndale Monument** (entry £1) on Nibley Knoll may seem 121 steps too far. It's worth it, though, for some splendid views in every direction. The monument was erected in 1866 to the memory of Sir William Tyndale, who in defiance of the authorities translated the New Testament into English. He was burnt at the stake for heresy in 1536.

The village *café* (Thu-Sun 10am-5pm) on Barrs Lane is stocked with scrumptious goodies from T&C Cakes; perfect for coffee or a light lunch.

Unfortunately you may find the village pub, the **Black Horse Inn** closed, since at time of research a new tenant was being sought. It was a popular pub which also offered accommodation.

Just north of the village, *Hunts Court Huts* (☎ 01453-544632, 🖥 huntscourthuts.co.uk; 2D, en suite) offers glamping in two huts each complete with its own hot tub, kitchenette, BBQ and fire pit. Rates are from £150 per hut (sleeps 2) and there's a two-night minimum stay policy for the huts. For Cotswold Way walkers they also offer *camping* (£10pp) and there are two toilets, a shower, a kitchen and wi-fi connection.

About half a mile north of the village, *Forthay B&B* [Map 28, p142] (☎ 01453-549016, 🖥 forthaybedandbreakfast.co.uk; 2D/1T, all en suite or private facilities; 🐾), is a 17th-century farmhouse offering dog-friendly B&B. Rates are from around £50pp. With 24 hours' notice they can provide and evening meal (not Weds) and serve alcoholic drinks on request. They also run a business making their own granola and breakfast cereals so don't miss breakfast!

Stagecoach's No 60 **bus** service (see pp48-50) stops near the pub.

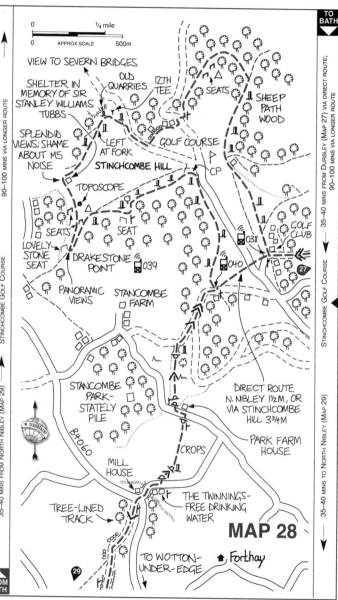

35–40 MINS FROM DURSLEY (MAP 27) VIA DIRECT ROUTE; 90–100 MINS VIA LONGER ROUTE

STINCHCOMBE GOLF COURSE

35–40 MINS FROM NORTH NIBLEY (MAP 29)

35–40 MINS FROM DURSLEY (MAP 27) VIA DIRECT ROUTE; 90–100 MINS VIA LONGER ROUTE

STINCHCOMBE GOLF COURSE

35–40 MINS TO NORTH NIBLEY (MAP 29)

TO BATH

FROM BATH

0 ¼ mile
APPROX SCALE
0 500m

VIEW TO SEVERN BRIDGES

SHELTER IN MEMORY OF SIR STANLEY WILLIAMS TUBBS

OLD QUARRIES

12TH TEE

SEATS

SHEEP PATH WOOD

SPLENDID VIEWS; SHAME ABOUT M5 NOISE

LEFT AT FORK

GOLF COURSE

STINCHCOMBE HILL

CP

TOPOSCOPE

SEATS

SEAT

LOVELY STONE SEAT

DRAKESTONE POINT 039

038

040

GOLF CLUB

27

PANORAMIC VIEWS

STANCOMBE FARM

STANCOMBE PARK– STATELY PILE

B4060

DIRECT ROUTE N. NIBLEY 1½M, OR VIA STINCHCOMBE HILL 3¾M

PARK FARM HOUSE

CROPS

MILL HOUSE

THE TWINNINGS– FREE DRINKING WATER

TREE-LINED TRACK

MAP 28

29

TO WOTTON-UNDER-EDGE

Forthay

trailblazer

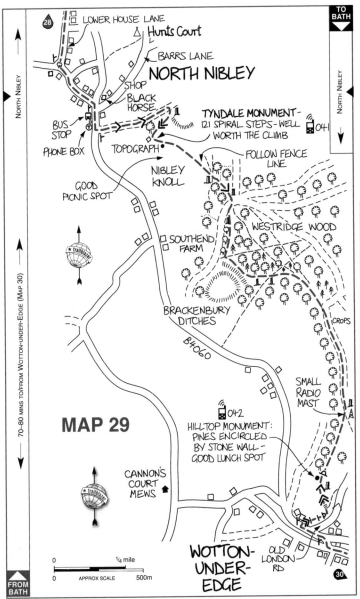

MAP 29

Hunts Court

LOWER HOUSE LANE

BARRS LANE

NORTH NIBLEY

SHOP

BLACK HORSE

TYNDALE MONUMENT –
121 SPIRAL STEPS – WELL
WORTH THE CLIMB

☎ 041

BUS STOP

PHONE BOX

TOPOGRAPH

FOLLOW FENCE LINE

NIBLEY KNOLL

GOOD PICNIC SPOT

★ trailblazer

WESTRIDGE WOOD

SOUTHEND FARM

BRACKENBURY DITCHES

B4060

CROPS

SMALL RADIO MAST

☎ 042

HILLTOP MONUMENT:
PINES ENCIRCLED
BY STONE WALL –
GOOD LUNCH SPOT

★ trailblazer

CANNON'S COURT MEWS

WOTTON-
UNDER-
EDGE

OLD LONDON RD

28

TO BATH

NORTH NIBLEY

NORTH NIBLEY

70–80 MINS TO/FROM WOTTON-UNDER-EDGE (MAP 30)

0   ¼ mile
0   APPROX SCALE   500m

FROM BATH

30

WOTTON-UNDER-EDGE
[MAP 30a, p147]

It's a friendly place, Wotton-under-Edge, and very community spirited. Almost everything happens on the appropriately named Long St, which morphs from the High St, extending downhill the length of the town. The Cotswold Way runs along this street, passing most of the shops and many pubs and cafés. The trail also takes you past some **almshouses** on Church St and near some on Culverhay; there are also almshouses on Tabernacle Pitch.

The trail continues past the 13th-century parish church of **St Mary the Virgin** before rejoining open countryside. More visible than any of these from above the town is the former **Tabernacle Church**, now an auction room.

East of the town, the Cotswold Way passes through the grounds of **Newark Park** (Map 30; ☎ 01453-842644, 🖳 national trust.org.uk; Mar-Oct Wed-Mon 11am-5pm; Feb Wed-Mon 11am-4pm, Nov & Dec Sat & Sun only 11am-4pm; £12), with almost direct footpath access from the trail. Built as a Tudor hunting lodge, it has commanding views to the south-west from its ridge-top location. Following a chequered history, during which it was converted to a fashionable house, it was finally abandoned during the war years and was given to the National Trust in 1949. Since then, both house and garden have been restored and the place is once again inhabited, with an eclectic collection of art on view to the public.

See box on p15 for details of Wotton's Arts Festival (Apr/May) and p16 for the Walking Festival (June).

Transport

Stagecoach's No 60, The Big Lemon's Nos 84 & 85 **bus** services call here as do Cotswold Green's No 40; see pp48-50.

For a **taxi**, try AK Taxis (☎ 01453-842673.

Services

For **tourist information**, find your way to the **Heritage Centre** (☎ 01453-521541, 🖳 wottonheritage.com; **fb**; Apr-end Oct Sun-Tue, Thur & Fri 10.30am-4pm, Sat 10am-3pm, Nov-end Mar Mon-Tue & Thur-Sat 10.30am-3.30pm), on the corner of Market St and The Chipping. Run entirely by volunteers, it has good displays relating to the town's history as well as offering all the normal information services.

There's an **ATM** at the Co-op **supermarket** (Mon-Sat 7am-10pm, Sun 10am-4pm), which also now houses the local **post office** (Mon-Fri 9am-5.30pm, Sat 9am-1pm). A few steps further down the road is a second supermarket, Tesco Express (daily 7am-10pm).

More personal than either of these are the excellent **delis**: Relish Deli (with paninis, salads, pizza and pies for lunch on the way – and space to eat in), Good Food (Mon-Sat 8am-6pm, Sun 10am-2pm) which is also a greengrocer, and Parson's **bakery**, with a second bakery – Walkers – further down the road.

There's a **farmers' market** (Feb-Dec first Sat of month 9am-1pm) in the Town Hall on Market St. Teas (summer Sun 2-5pm) are also served in the town hall; each week they are run by a different charity.

For **waterproofs** and other outdoor clothing, make your way to WH Thomas & Son (closed Wed & Sun), at the bottom of Long St; 'gentleman's outfitters' since 1896, they also have women's sizes. The **pharmacy** (Mon-Fri 8.30am-6.30pm, Sat 9am-5pm), is here, too, with two **medical surgeries** relatively close by: Chipping Surgery (☎ 01453-842214, 🖳 thechipping-surgery.co.uk; Mon-Fri 8am-6.30pm), on Symn Lane, and Culverhay (☎ 01453-843893, 🖳 culverhaysurgery.com; Mon 8am-8pm, Tue-Fri 8am-6.30pm), on Culverhay.

The town scores on the entertainment stakes, run at least in part by volunteers. Electric Picture House **cinema** (☎ 01453-844601, 🖳 wottoncinema.com), on Market St, has several screenings a week. Close to the car park, **Under the Edge Arts** (🖳 utea .org.uk), a community venture in Chipping Hall, hosts regular displays and a programme of events throughout the year. There's even a week-long Arts Festival (see box p15) at the end of April/early May.

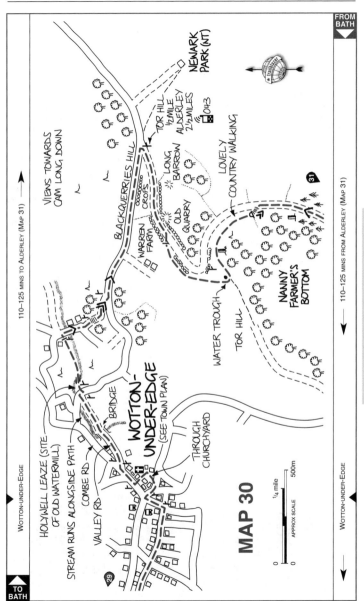

For a reviving dip at the end of a day's walking, check out the open-air **swimming pool** (☎ 01453-842086, 🖳 wottonpool.co.uk; end Apr-mid Sep, Mon-Fri 3.30-5pm & 6.30-8pm, Sat/Sun 2-4pm; times slightly different in school holidays), on Symn Lane.

Where to stay

Accommodation options in Wotton have diminished in recent years, but there are several listings on AirBnb if none of the places below can help.

Number Eleven (☎ 01453-843576, or ☎ 07966-729741, 🖳 g.ellis.bankside @gmail.com; 1T with private facilities; mid Mar to end Oct), at 11 Merlin Haven, charges from £65pp for B&B; they use the eggs from the hens at the bottom of the garden and smoked salmon and avocado can be served as an alternative if requested. Merlin Haven can be reached along a footpath to the west of the swimming pool, or by following Westfields into Dryleaze, then turning left and left again into Merlin Haven.

Back in town, the helpful and welcoming *Swan Hotel* (☎ 01453-843004, 🖳 swan hotelwotton.com; 4D/7D or T/3Tr, all en suite; 🛎; Ⓛ; 🐾), on Market St, gets good reviews. Recently refurbished, it has attractive rooms and rates, including a light breakfast (full cooked also available), are from £52.50pp.

Another option is about ¾ mile (1km) west of the town on Stumpwell Lane in **Bradley Green**, where there are several holiday cottages at *Canon's Court Mews*; you can sometimes book rooms from £105 per room for just one night. You currently need to do so through booking companies such as booking.com.

Where to eat and drink

Cafés and takeaways dominate the foody outlets in Wotton-under-Edge, and those on Long St will serve you well, with breakfast, light lunches and tea served in various styles. With some tables outside, there's *The Edge Coffee Shop* (☎ 01453-844108; 🖳 edge-coffee-wotton.co.uk; **fb**; Mon-Fri 9am-4.30pm; Sat 9am-3pm; 🐾), whose offerings include a range of sandwiches (including their fish-finger sandwich), pancakes and a decent take on the Full English.

The Ark Coffee Shop (☎ 01453-521838; Mon-Wed 9am-noon, Thu-Fri

WOTTON-UNDER-EDGE

Where to stay
1 Canon's Court Mews
2 Number Eleven
11 Swan Hotel

Where to eat and drink
4 Royal Oak Inn
6 Bunter's Café
7 Wotton British Takeaway
9 The Star Inn
10 Delight's Pizza & Kebab House
11 Swan Hotel
15 The Ark Coffee Shop
18 The Wotton Coffee Shop
21 Wine Shack at No 7
22 The Edge Coffee Shop
28 The Falcon Steakhouse
29 Hong Kong Kitchen
30 India Palace

Other
3 Chipping Surgery
12 Cinema (Electric Picture House)
13 Heritage Centre & Tourist Information
14 Under the Edge Arts
16 Pharmacy
17 Parson's Bakery
19 Good Food
20 Walkers Bakery
23 Co-op, post office & ATM
24 Relish Deli
25 Tesco Express
26 Cotswold Book Room
27 WH Thomas & Son
31 Culverhay Surgery

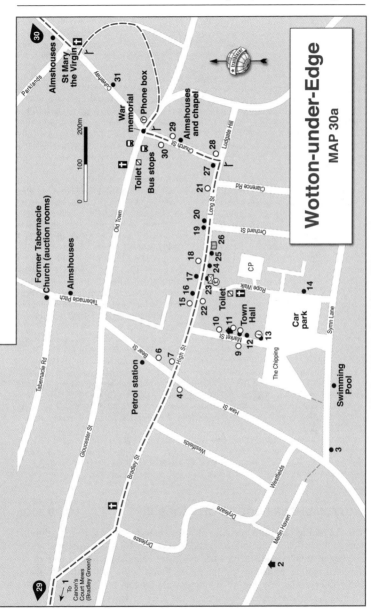

9am-noon & 2-4.30pm, Sat 9.30am-12.30pm), where a team of Christian volunteers serves up good value coffee and cakes.

A few doors further down is *The Wotton Coffee Shop* (☎ 01453-520448; **fb**; Mon-Sat 9am-5pm), with plenty of choice on the menu and a lovely garden in which to eat. It's a great place for a cream tea.

Near the petrol station there's *Bunter's Café* (Mon-Fri 7am-2pm, Sat 9am-1.30pm), where the full English is £8.50. They also have a range of sandwiches, paninis, jacket potatoes and salad boxes (from £6.50) to take away.

There are some good **pubs** too. Smartest is *Swan Hotel* (see Where to stay; food Mon-Sat noon-9pm, Sun noon-8pm) – 'no muddy boots', please – whose extensive menus include a range of British tapas (3 dishes for £15), 'gourmet' burgers from £13, and their signature jam jar sundaes (£7.50) to finish – try the five chocolate treat for a chocolate overdose. There's also rather more formal dining here.

The Star Inn (☎ 01453-844651, 🖳 starinnwotton.co .uk; **fb**; food daily noon-2pm; 🐾) gets good reviews for its food and offers a daily homemade special alongside the normal (and very cheap) pub basics, with mains around £7.95 and baguettes £4.50. Walkers (mud and all) are very welcome here and, outside of their food-serving hours, you can bring in food from outside. There's live music some weekends. The pub dates back to the 1570s and was the inspiration for the name of the White Star Shipping Line of Titanic fame.

There's also the *Royal Oak Inn* (☎ 01453-521969, 🖳 theroyaloakwottonunderedge.co.uk; food Mon-Sat noon-9pm, Sun noon-3pm; 🐾 bar area only), on Haw

St, you can eat inside or in their large garden. There are pizzas and good-value pub grub and specials each evening – eg Wednesdays is curry and a pint night.

Right at the bottom of Long St, on the corner of Church St, *The Falcon Steakhouse* (☎ 01453-521894, 🖳 falcon steakhouse.com; **fb**; Mon-Fri noon-2pm & 5-9pm, Sat noon-3pm & 5-9.30pm, Sun noon-3pm & 5-9pm) is a very popular venture, run by a local farm, and you usually need to book in advance. Their menu is heavy with meat from their own farm, such as an 8oz sirloin steak (£28.95), or you could treat yourself to the 18oz Chateaubriand sharing joint set meal: fillet tenderloin with starters, sides and desserts for two people £99.95.

Open limited times but getting rave reviews is *The Wine Shack at No 7* (☎ 01453-299693, 🖳 thewineshackatno7.co .uk; food Thur-Sat 6-9.15pm, also 1st Sat of the month noon-3pm). There's a tempting range of tapas from £4.95 as well as four sharing platters: Spanish, cheese & charcuterie, fish or vegan. As well as a good selections of wines there are jugs of Sangria or Pimms.

For Indian and Bangladeshi cuisine, there's *India Palace* (☎ 01453-843628, 🖳 theindiapalace.co.uk; daily 5-11pm), 13 Church St, which has a restaurant as well as a busy takeaway service. Nearby is *Hong Kong Kitchen* (Tue-Sun 5-10pm), which also serves fish & chips, but is takeaway only. There's also *Wotton British Takeaway* (**fb**; Tue-Sat 11.30am-2pm & 5-9pm), on High St, for fish, chicken and pies, or perhaps *Delight's Pizza & Kebab House* (Sun-Thur 3-11pm, Fri-Sat 3pm-midnight) on Market St.

WOTTON-UNDER-EDGE TO OLD SODBURY   MAPS 30-35

This **12½-mile (20.4km)** section will take about **6-7 hours**, passing through open, rolling fields, interspersed with the occasional tract of woodland, and a number of small villages with attractive stone churches. Of these, one of the most intriguing, primarily for its cubed yews, is **St Mary the Virgin** at Hawkesbury (Map 33), but it's a long downhill detour off the Cotswold Way. Similarly, tantalising glimpses through the trees of **Horton Court** (Map 34)

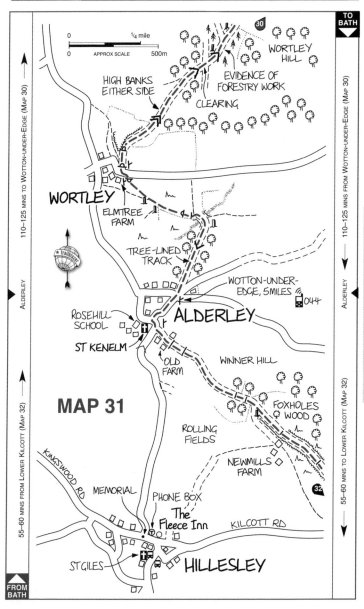

TO BATH

0 ¼ mile
APPROX SCALE
0 500m

30

WORTLEY HILL

HIGH BANKS EITHER SIDE

EVIDENCE OF FORESTRY WORK

CLEARING

WORTLEY

ELMTREE FARM

TREE-LINED TRACK

WOTTON-UNDER-EDGE, 5MILES 044

ALDERLEY

ROSEHILL SCHOOL

ST KENELM

OLD FARM

WINNER HILL

MAP 31

FOXHOLES WOOD

ROLLING FIELDS

NEWMILLS FARM

32

KINGSWOOD RD

MEMORIAL

PHONE BOX

The Fleece Inn

KILCOTT RD

ST GILES

HILLESLEY

trailblazer

110–125 MINS TO WOTTON-UNDER-EDGE (MAP 30)

ALDERLEY

55–60 MINS FROM LOWER KILCOTT (MAP 32)

110–125 MINS FROM WOTTON-UNDER-EDGE (MAP 30)

ALDERLEY

55–60 MINS TO LOWER KILCOTT (MAP 32)

ROUTE GUIDE AND MAPS

FROM BATH

might tempt the walker to tackle the very steep path down for closer inspection but see p152 before contemplating this; most will be happy to stick to the trail and the lovely drovers' road south of Hawkesbury. If the walk lacks drama, it certainly makes up for it in nomenclature: who could resist the appeal of a dip that glories in the name of **Nanny Farmer's Bottom** (Map 30)? And if you find yourself tiring, there's always the prospect of a sandwich or dinner at the Dog Inn in Old Sodbury to act as a spur.

ALDERLEY [MAP 31, p149]

There's an air of exclusivity about Alderley, from the timeless solidity of the **Church of St Kenelm** to the old stone houses which are surrounded by well-maintained gardens. The Big Lemon's Nos 84 & 85 **buses** (see pp48-50) stop by the church.

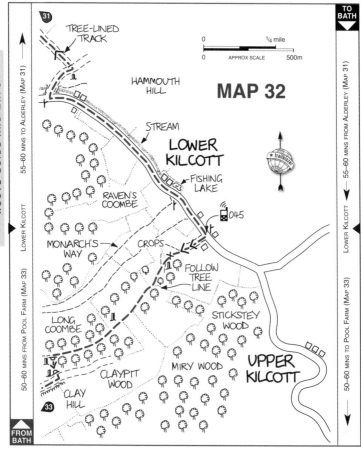

MAP 32

TO BATH

31

TREE-LINED TRACK

0 — ¼ mile
0 — APPROX SCALE — 500m

HAMMOUTH HILL

STREAM

LOWER KILCOTT

FISHING LAKE

RAVEN'S COOMBE

★ trailblazer

045

MONARCH'S WAY

CROPS

FOLLOW TREE LINE

LONG COOMBE

STICKSTEY WOOD

CLAYPIT WOOD

MIRY WOOD

UPPER KILCOTT

CLAY HILL

33

FROM BATH

55-60 MINS TO ALDERLEY (MAP 31)

LOWER KILCOTT

50-60 MINS FROM POOL FARM (MAP 33)

ROUTE GUIDE AND MAPS

55-60 MINS FROM ALDERLEY (MAP 31)

LOWER KILCOTT

50-60 MINS TO POOL FARM (MAP 33)

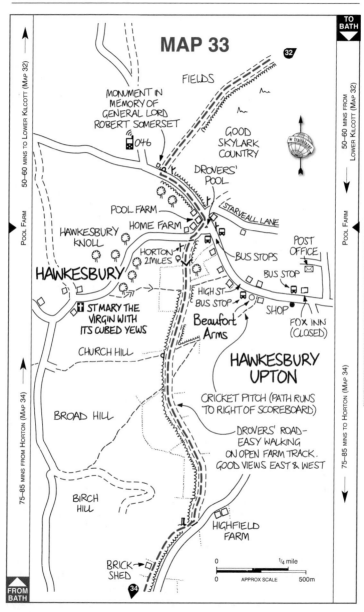

MAP 33

TO BATH

32

FROM BATH

34

FIELDS

MONUMENT IN MEMORY OF GENERAL LORD ROBERT SOMERSET

046

GOOD SKYLARK COUNTRY

DROVERS' POOL

POOL FARM

HOME FARM

STARVEALL LANE

HAWKESBURY KNOLL

HORTON 2 MILES

BUS STOPS

POST OFFICE

BUS STOP

HAWKESBURY

HIGH ST BUS STOP

SHOP

BUS STOP

FOX INN (CLOSED)

ST MARY THE VIRGIN WITH ITS CUBED YEWS

Beaufort Arms

CHURCH HILL

HAWKESBURY UPTON

CRICKET PITCH (PATH RUNS TO RIGHT OF SCOREBOARD)

BROAD HILL

DROVERS' ROAD - EASY WALKING ON OPEN FARM TRACK. GOOD VIEWS EAST & WEST

BIRCH HILL

HIGHFIELD FARM

BRICK SHED

0   ¼ mile

0   APPROX SCALE   500m

50-60 MINS TO LOWER KILCOTT (MAP 32)

POOL FARM

75-85 MINS FROM HORTON (MAP 34)

50-60 MINS FROM LOWER KILCOTT (MAP 32)

POOL FARM

75-85 MINS TO HORTON (MAP 34)

ROUTE GUIDE AND MAPS

HILLESLEY [MAP 31, p149]

Little more than a cluster of individual stone cottages with a church and a pub, Hillesley is another attractive village around half a mile (1km) from the trail.

The local watering hole, *The Fleece Inn* (☎ 01453-520003, 🖳 thefleecehillesley.com; **fb**; **food** Mon-Sat noon-2.30pm & 6-8.30pm, Sun noon-3pm; 🐾 bar only), is a haven for those who love their real ales (it was a recent winner of CAMRA's regional pub of the year) and there's live music occasionally. Good place for a lunch stop (soup and a sandwich, £8.50) and even better in the evening for good-value food, friendly staff and great beer.

The Big Lemon's Nos 84 & 85 (see pp48-50) **buses** stop by the Church of St Giles.

HAWKESBURY UPTON
[MAP 33, p151]

Is there no end to the attractive villages in this area? The heart of this one lies about quarter of a mile (0.4km) off the Cotswold Way, but with a good pub and a range of other facilities, it has plenty to offer the walker. Sadly, The Fox Inn, which did offer accommodation, is currently closed.

Beaufort Arms (☎ 01454-238217, 🖳 beaufortarms.com; **fb**; food daily noon-2.30pm & 6.30-9.30pm except Sun evening; 🐾 bar only) is very much a village hub, with plenty of real ales and scarcely a nod to the 21st century. There are pub classics such as chilli con carne and faggots, peas & chips all well priced and available in small (from £8.95) or large (from £11) portions.

At the far end of the village is the excellent village shop, **Hawkesbury Stores** (☎ 01454-238639, 🖳 hawkesburystores.co.uk; **fb**; Mon-Sat 7am-7pm, Sun 8am-1pm), community-run and with almost everything you might need including fruit and veg, filled rolls, a good range of pastries and local beers.

The **post office** (Mon, Tue & Thur-Sat 9am-1pm, Wed to noon) is located a short way beyond the pub.

The Big Lemon's Nos 84 & 85 **buses** (see pp48-50) stop by The Fox Inn.

HORTON [MAP 34]

While the village of Horton is on the Cotswold Way, most walkers will bypass its main attraction, the National Trust property of **Horton Court** (🖳 nationaltrust.org.uk), which lies at the bottom of a steep footpath off the Cotswold Way (or you could walk back along the road from the village school). It's a rather grand name for the seemingly modest but picturesque property that sits in a cottage-style garden close to the **church of St James the Elder**. At its heart is a 12th-century Norman hall, all that remains of what may be the oldest rectory in England. Other parts of the building date to Tudor times, with significant expansion and the addition of an Italianate loggia during the 16th century, and further changes in the 1920s. Though the main house is closed to visitors, the hall, Tudor Ambulatory and parts of the garden are sometimes open to the public; however, you'll need to book in advance if you wish to visit and the opening times are limited (late July to end Sep Wed & Sat 2-5pm only). However, if you have a spare £2000-£3000 to spare you could simply rent the place for a night.

The Big Lemon's Nos 84 & 85 **buses** (see pp48-50) stop by the school.

❏ **Important note – walking times**
All times in this book refer only to the time spent walking. You will need to add 20-30% to allow for rests, photography, checking the map, drinking water etc.

ROUTE GUIDE AND MAPS

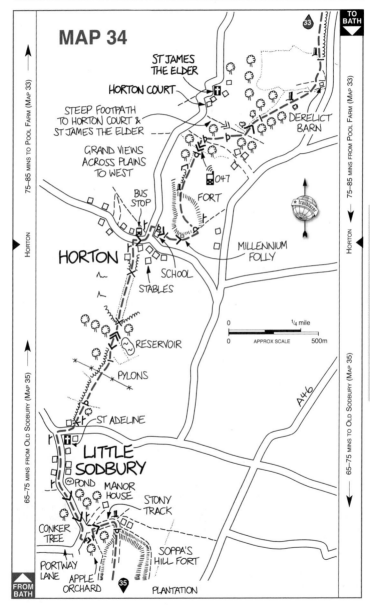

MAP 34

ST JAMES THE ELDER

HORTON COURT

STEEP FOOTPATH TO HORTON COURT & ST JAMES THE ELDER

GRAND VIEWS ACROSS PLAINS TO WEST

DERELICT BARN

BUS STOP

047

FORT

HORTON

MILLENNIUM FOLLY

SCHOOL

STABLES

RESERVOIR

0   1/4 mile

0   APPROX SCALE   500m

PYLONS

A46

ST ADELINE

LITTLE SODBURY

POND

MANOR HOUSE

STONY TRACK

CONKER TREE

SOPPA'S HILL FORT

PORTWAY LANE

APPLE ORCHARD

PLANTATION

33

TO BATH

FROM BATH

75–85 MINS TO POOL FARM (MAP 33)

HORTON

65–75 MINS FROM OLD SODBURY (MAP 35)

75–85 MINS FROM POOL FARM (MAP 33)

HORTON

65–75 MINS TO OLD SODBURY (MAP 35)

ROUTE GUIDE AND MAPS

LITTLE SODBURY [MAP 34, p153]

This pretty village is set apart by the hilltop **church of St Adeline**, offering a perfect vantage point from which to survey the landscape unrolling ahead. The churchyard is a fine place to rest your feet for a few minutes.

OLD SODBURY [MAP 35]

The trail passes through the grounds of the beautiful **St John the Baptist Church**, up on the hill, before dropping down to the village itself. In the shadow of its larger neighbour to the west, Chipping Sodbury, the village nevertheless has a lot to recommend it to the walker. Badminton Horse Trials (see box p15) in early May is likely to make accommodation hard to find.

Coachstyle's No 41 and Stagecoach's 69 & 620 **buses** (see pp48-50 for details) stop by the Dog Inn and also near the Bell Inn. For a **taxi** try Grab-a-Cab (☎ 01454-313883, 🖳 grab-a-cab-online.co.uk) which is based in Chipping Sodbury.

Cotswold Service Station (Mon-Fri 6.30am-8pm, Sat 8am-6pm), on the other side of the crossroads, is handy for stocking up on drinks and snacks for your walk.

In the centre of the village, and right on the trail, the popular ***Dog Inn*** (☎ 01454-312006, 🖳 the-dog-inn.co.uk; **fb**; 3D or T/1Tr, all en suite; ▼; Ⓛ; 🐕) offers a welcome respite. **B&B** costs from £50pp (sgl occ £80). In the bar, real ales (including Butcombe Original and Wye Valley HPA; see box on p23) and an extensive menu (**food** Mon-Fri noon-2.30pm & 6-9pm, Sat noon-9pm, Sun to 8pm) are the order of the day. The food's good value and includes sharing platters, steaks, plenty of fish, pasta and jacket potatoes, with varied vegetarian, vegan and gluten-free options as well.

Right across the road, so convenient for both pub and path, ***Rock Cottage*** (☎ 01454-314688; 2D/1Tr, all en suite; ▼; Ⓛ; 🐕) has some lovely rooms, a guests' sitting room as well as a pleasant garden that you can enjoy on a sunny day. Rates are from £42.50pp, (sgl occ £65).

Some 300m from the trail is the upmarket ***Sodbury House*** (☎ 01454-312847, 🖳 sodburyhouse.co.uk; 3S/3D or T, all en suite; ▼; Ⓛ), which offers B&B from £51pp (sgl £82), with super-kingsize beds in the doubles. In the evening, most guests gravitate towards The Dog Inn for dinner or – in the other direction – The Bell.

Just over half a mile west of Sodbury house on the road into Chipping Sodbury is ***The Bell Inn*** (☎ 01454-325582, 🖳 thebellatoldsodbury.co.uk; **fb**; 4D en suite; Ⓛ). B&B is from £62.50pp including an excellent cooked breakfast – eg Posh Poached Eggs Benedict with Parma Ham. In the pub restaurant (**food** Tue & Wed noon-2.30pm & 6-8.30pm, Thu-Sun 9am-8.30pm; pub is closed on Mon and 3-5pm on Tue & Wed) main dishes range from £16.95 to £22.95). The Sunday lunches here are popular.

Rather over half a mile (1km) in the other direction, on the main A46, the 14th-century ***Cross Hands Hotel*** (☎ 01454-313000, 🖳 greeneking.co.uk; 6S/2T/12D/1Qd, all en suite; ▼; 🐕) is just by the bus stop. Rates for accommodation vary daily and are usually best for online bookings but expect to pay from £42.50pp (sgl from £75) plus about £12pp for breakfast. They also have a **restaurant** (daily noon-10pm) with a varied menu of good-value dishes ranging from crispy chicken in a basket (£12.49) to slow-cooked lamb shank (£20.49).

Windylands (☎ 01454-323653, 🖳 windylands.co.uk; **fb**; 2D/1T, all en suite or private facilities; 🐕) is about a mile from the centre of Old Sodbury, south of Cross Hands Hotel and off the A46 down the Tormarton Rd. It's a friendly family-run place offering B&B from around £45pp. For the best prices use the online booking system on their website.

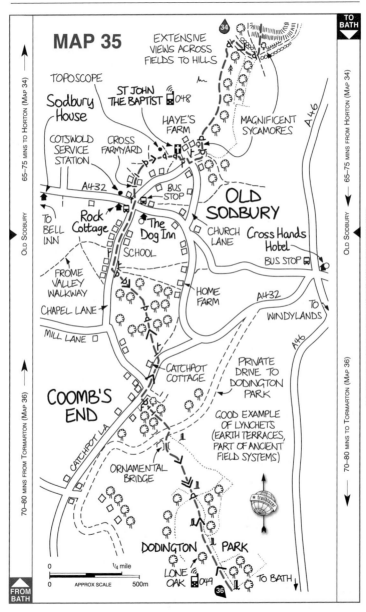

MAP 35

EXTENSIVE VIEWS ACROSS FIELDS TO HILLS

34

TO BATH

TOPOSCOPE

ST JOHN THE BAPTIST 📵 048

Sodbury House

HAYE'S FARM

MAGNIFICENT SYCAMORES

A46

COTSWOLD SERVICE STATION

CROSS FARMYARD

A432

BUS STOP

OLD SODBURY

TO BELL INN

Rock Cottage

The Dog Inn

CHURCH LANE

Cross Hands Hotel

SCHOOL

BUS STOP 🚌

FROME VALLEY WALKWAY

HOME FARM

A432

TO WINDYLANDS

CHAPEL LANE

MILL LANE

A46

CATCHPOT COTTAGE

PRIVATE DRIVE TO DODINGTON PARK

COOMB'S END

GOOD EXAMPLE OF LYNCHETS (EARTH TERRACES, PART OF ANCIENT FIELD SYSTEMS)

CATCHPOT LA.

ORNAMENTAL BRIDGE

DODINGTON PARK

LONE OAK 📵 049

36

TO BATH

0   ¼ mile
0   APPROX SCALE   500m

FROM BATH

65–75 MINS TO HORTON (MAP 34)

OLD SODBURY

70–80 MINS FROM TORMARTON (MAP 36)

65–75 MINS FROM HORTON (MAP 34)

OLD SODBURY

70–80 MINS TO TORMARTON (MAP 36)

ROUTE GUIDE AND MAPS

OLD SODBURY TO COLD ASHTON

MAPS 35-39

Despite being divided by the M4, this **9-mile (14.2km, 4¼-5hrs)** part of the walk has much to recommend it. In place of many (but not all!) of the ups and downs further north there are broad expanses of farmland. There's an unexpectedly rewarding walk across **Dodington Park**, the vast country seat of businessman James Dyson, of Dyson vacuum cleaner fame. Then there's the glimpsed glory of **Dyrham Park** (Map 37; see p158), which most certainly merits a visit.

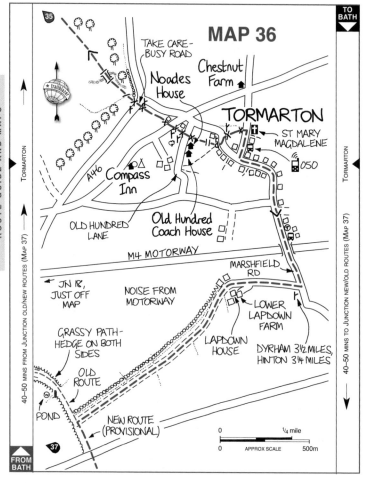

ROUTE GUIDE AND MAPS

TO BATH

35

MAP 36

TAKE CARE –
BUSY ROAD

Chestnut
Farm

Noades
House

★ trailblazer

TORMARTON

ST MARY
MAGDALENE

050

A46

Compass
Inn

Old Hundred
Coach House

OLD HUNDRED
LANE

M4 MOTORWAY

MARSHFIELD
RD

JN 18,
JUST OFF
MAP

NOISE FROM
MOTORWAY

LOWER
LAPDOWN
FARM

GRASSY PATH –
HEDGE ON BOTH
SIDES

LAPDOWN
HOUSE

DYRHAM 3½ MILES,
HINTON 3¼ MILES

OLD
ROUTE

POND

NEW ROUTE
(PROVISIONAL)

TORMARTON (MAP 37) →

40–50 MINS FROM JUNCTION OLD/NEW ROUTES (MAP 37)

TORMARTON

40–50 MINS TO JUNCTION NEW/OLD ROUTES (MAP 37)

0   ¼ mile
0   APPROX SCALE   500m

37

FROM
BATH

Note that there's a diversion in place to avoid the Beacon Lane Plantation (occasionally frequented by nudists among others) but as yet the new route is only temporary. Signs primly tell you this diversion is 'due to ongoing safety concerns' but if you're not fazed by such sights you can still follow the original route, though we'd advise you to keep your clothes on, if only to protect against the nettles!

TORMARTON [MAP 36]

In spite of its proximity to the busy M4, the village of Tormarton remains relatively unscathed by noise, or even by the 21st century, so it's an unexpectedly good place to stop for the night. With a welcoming hotel, a choice of B&Bs and even a place to camp, there are plenty of options, too. Sadly, The Major's Retreat, the pub in the centre of the village, has now closed.

The village is served by the No 41 **bus**, run by Coachstyle; see pp48-50.

Rather unexpectedly, **campers** (🐾) can pitch a tent at *Compass Inn* (☎ 01454-218242, 🖳 compass-inn.co.uk) for £10pp. There are no outdoor facilities, but they do provide a keycard so you can use the public toilets inside (available 24hrs). The hotel itself is something of a rabbit warren, independently owned but marketed under the Best Western umbrella, and with extensive gardens. It's about 500m from the village, quite close to the motorway and within sight of the A46, so noise is a factor, but it's not too bad. **Rooms** (7T/13D/4Tr/2Qd, all en suite; 🛏; Ⓛ; 🐾) have all the accoutrements of a business hotel, costing from

around £37.50pp (sgl occ room rate) though the rates can vary. It's generally very good value, though. **Breakfast** and packed lunches are available for all. Service is friendly and the **food** (daily 9-11.30am, noon-2.30pm & 5.30-8.45pm, served in the bar, restaurant or garden, is a pleasant surprise; good sandwiches at lunchtime, from £8.95, come with a proper salad.

With the Cotswold Way at the bottom of the garden, *Noades House* (☎ 01454-218278, 🖳 noadesstudio.co.uk; 1T/1D both en suite, 1T private bathroom; 🛏; Ⓛ; Mar-end Oct), on the quiet Old Hundred Lane, is exceptionally well placed. Rates for B&B are from £47.50pp.

Right next door, *Old Hundred Coach House* (☎ 01454-218420, 🖳 deedaveb @yahoo.co.uk; 1T, private bathroom; 🛏; Ⓛ; 🐾) charges from £35pp (sgl occ £40) for B&B. The beds are comfortable and the bathroom is huge! It's a lovely place run by friendly owners who can also offer lifts if you stay more than one night.

ROUTE GUIDE AND MAPS

TOLLDOWN (South of the M4) [MAP 37, p158]

South of Tormarton, on the main A46 about 500 yards from the trail, **B&B** is available at newly-refurbished *The Crown Inn* (☎ 01225-891166, 🖳 butcombe.com/the-crown-gloucestershire; **fb**; 3D/6D or T, all en suite; 🛏; Ⓛ; 🐾), where rooms are in a separate building behind the pub. Rooms generally cost from £60pp to £100pp, but rates do vary considerably – particularly during Badminton Horse Trials. Note there's a £20 charge for a dog in a bedroom.

Their **food** (Mon-Sat noon-3pm & 6-9pm, Sun noon-8pm) is highly regarded and

includes a very good Sunday roast (£19.50). Interesting sandwiches for a quick lunch include a fish finger bun with watercress and pickled fennel (£11.95) or wild mushrooms, truffled ricotta and fried egg served on sourdough toast (£8.95). It's all certainly more than your usual pub grub.

At the entrance to Dyrham Park, *Gatekeepers Lodge* (🖳 gatekeepers lodge.co.uk; 1D) is a bijou holiday cottage that is available for short stays of as little as one night but only in the quieter seasons. Charges are from £165 per night.

70–80 MINS FROM DYRHAM (MAP 38) →

JUNCTION OLD/NEW ROUTES

BEACON LANE PLANTATION

GOOD SPOT FOR SKYLARKS

CAR PARK

GRASSY PATH, HEDGE ON BOTH SIDES

ARABLE OPEN FIELDS

ARABLE OPEN FIELDS

TRAFFIC ISLAND

OLD ROUTE

WIND TURBINE

HEDGE & WALL

POND

PYLONS

MOTO CROSS TRACK

36

WATCH OUT FOR GLIDERS HERE

OLD ROUTE

NEW ROUTE (PROVISIONAL)

The Crown TOLLDOWN

A46

FIELD LANE

TAKE CARE – BUSY ROAD

WALLSEND LANE

38

BADMINTON PLANTATION

MAP 37

DYRHAM PARK

MAIN ENTRANCE TO DYRHAM PARK

trailblazer

0 ¼ mile

0 APPROX SCALE 500m

A46 ↙ TO BATH

← 70–80 MINS TO DYRHAM (MAP 38)

JUNCTION NEW/OLD ROUTES

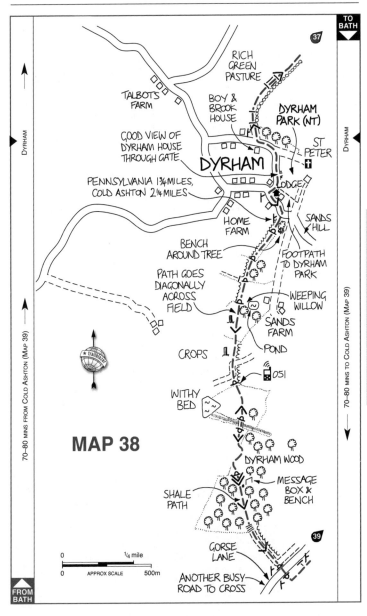

TO BATH

37

Dyrham

RICH GREEN PASTURE

TALBOT'S FARM

BOY & BROOK HOUSE

DYRHAM PARK (NT)

ST PETER

GOOD VIEW OF DYRHAM HOUSE THROUGH GATE

DYRHAM

PENNSYLVANIA 1¾ MILES, COLD ASHTON 2¼ MILES

LODGE

SANDS HILL

HOME FARM

FOOTPATH TO DYRHAM PARK

BENCH AROUND TREE

PATH GOES DIAGONALLY ACROSS FIELD

WEEPING WILLOW

SANDS FARM

CROPS

POND

051

WITHY BED

DYRHAM WOOD

MESSAGE BOX & BENCH

SHALE PATH

MAP 38

GORSE LANE

ANOTHER BUSY ROAD TO CROSS

39

70–80 MINS FROM COLD ASHTON (MAP 39)

70–80 MINS TO COLD ASHTON (MAP 39)

0   ¼ mile
0   APPROX SCALE   500m

FROM BATH

❏ **DYRHAM PARK** [Map 37, p158 & Map 38, p159]

As the Cotswold Way wends through the tiny village of Dyrham, it passes the ornamental gates of Dyrham Park (☎ 0117-937 2501, 🖳 nationaltrust.org.uk; park daily 10am-5pm or dusk; garden mid Feb-Dec daily 10am-5pm, Jan-early Feb 10am-4pm; house Mar-Oct daily 11am-5pm, Nov-Dec 10am-4pm; house, garden & park £17, NT members free), affording a splendid vista up the long drive to the house and church. If you're not pushed for time it's well worth getting sidetracked.

Familiar to many film buffs as the set location for *Remains of the Day*, the Baroque-style house nestling at the bottom of a steep valley was built at the end of the 17th century. A strong Dutch influence pervades the original décor and furnishings, and the Victorian kitchens give an indication of how life must have been for those below stairs.

The church alongside, however, is medieval and the estate itself dates back to Saxon times. Visitors can explore both the house and the formal gardens as well as 274 acres (110 hectares) of rolling parkland.

PENNSYLVANIA [MAP 39]

Now that the two B&Bs here have closed, one becoming a holiday cottage, there's only the **petrol station** (daily 6am-10pm) on the main road that could be useful to walkers. There's a branch of Londis here and they sell drinks, ice creams, sandwiches and other snacks.

COLD ASHTON
[MAP 39; MAP 40, p162]

With its location between the busy A420 and the even busier A46, Cold Ashton might seem to be blighted, but the reality is entirely different. Most of the village lies along a quiet lane to the south, beyond the church, and its cluster of small stone houses stands peacefully against a backdrop of rolling fields.

First's 35 bus (Kingswood to Marshfield) calls at both Wick and Cold Ashton Mon-Sat 9/day plus 3/day from Bristol).

Ells Kitchen Café & Takeaway (Map 39; mobile ☎ 07759 141032; **fb**; Mon-Sat 8am-2.30pm; 🐕), at **Folly End Farm,** is a great 'old school' café offering breakfast rolls and full breakfasts, lunch, tea and home-made cakes. Their opening hours can vary so check their Facebook page before going. The road is busy so if you can walk along the edge of the field it's safer.

Toghill House Farm (Map 40; ☎ 01225-891261, 🖳 toghillhousefarm.co.uk; 3D/1T/2Tr/1Q, all en suite; 🛁; 🐕) is a working farm offering B&B. In the house, rates are from £62.50pp (£85 sgl occ) including a very good breakfast. Also here is a **shepherd's hut** (☎ 07866-714395; 1D en suite) fully equipped with bathroom, loo and kitchen. It's even got underfloor heating. Rates start at £90 for one night.

Symbols used in text (see also p74)
🐕 Dogs allowed subject to prior arrangement (see pp184-6)
🛁 Bathtub in, or for, at least one room   **fb** indicates a Facebook page
Ⓛ packed lunch available if requested in advance

Sheltered at the bottom of the steep Greenway Lane, *Hill Farm* (Map 40; ☎ 01225-891952, mob ☎ 07870-358627, 🖥 hillfarmbath.com; 2D or T; (Ⓛ); Apr-Oct) is a real find. Up to four guests stay either in the **Snug Room** (1D or T; from £65pp, sgl occ full room rate) in the main house but with separate access or in the **Trough** (1D or T; from £65pp, sgl occ full room rate), a converted barn with en suite facilities and a private kitchen/dining area. Either way, everything is set up for near-effortless self-catering with the makings for breakfast and – with advance notice – dinner (£20pp for two courses and a glass of wine or beer). Best of all is the stunning view from the terrace, where guests are free to enjoy a drink or dinner.

❑ **Important note – walking times**
All times in this book refer only to the time spent walking. You will need to add 20-30% to allow for rests, photography, checking the map, drinking water etc.

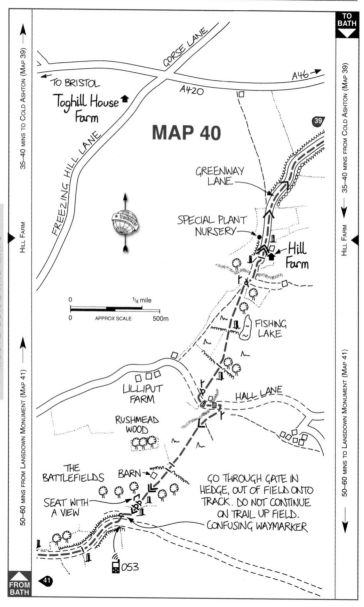

35–40 MINS TO COLD ASHTON (MAP 39) →

HILL FARM

ROUTE GUIDE AND MAPS

50–60 MINS FROM LANSDOWN MONUMENT (MAP 41) →

CORSE LANE

TO BATH

TO BRISTOL ←

Toghill House Farm

A420

A46 →

MAP 40

39

GREENWAY LANE

SPECIAL PLANT NURSERY

Hill Farm

FREEZING HILL LANE

0 ¼ mile

0 APPROX SCALE 500m

FISHING LAKE

LILLIPUT FARM

HALL LANE

RUSHMEAD WOOD

THE BATTLEFIELDS

BARN

SEAT WITH A VIEW

GO THROUGH GATE IN HEDGE, OUT OF FIELD ONTO TRACK. DO NOT CONTINUE ON TRAIL UP FIELD. CONFUSING WAYMARKER

053

FROM BATH

41

← 35–40 MINS FROM COLD ASHTON (MAP 39)

HILL FARM

50–60 MINS TO LANSDOWN MONUMENT (MAP 41) ↓

YOU CAN SEE BOTH
SEVERN BRIDGES
FROM HERE

BEACH FARM

MONUMENT TO BATTLE OF LANSDOWN

FREEZING HILL

DISPLAY BOARD BATTLE OF LANSDOWN, 1643

BEACH WOOD

STONE STILE

HANGING HILL 📟054

AVON FIRE & RESCUE

RADIO MAST

LUSH GRASS

CAR PARK

40

MAP 41

GOLF GREEN

DISPLAY BOARD - BATTLE OF LANSDOWN 1643

📟055

★ trailblazer

PIPLEY WOOD

42

GOLF COURSE

SCULPTURES BY DAVID MICHAEL MORSE

TO BATH

TO BECKFORD'S TOWER (ABOUT TWO MILES, HALF ALONG PAVEMENT BY BUSY ROAD)

0   ¼ mile

0   APPROX SCALE   500m

LANSDOWN MONUMENT

LANSDOWN MONUMENT

85–100 MINS FROM PROSPECT STILE (MAP 42)

85–100 MINS TO PROSPECT STILE (MAP 42)

TO BATH

FROM BATH

ROUTE GUIDE AND MAPS

❑ BATTLE OF LANSDOWN   [Map 40 & Map 41]

If it were not for the signboards and the monument to Sir Bevil Grenville, the walker on the Cotswold Way might cross the field at the top of **Freezing Hill** (Map 41) without a second glance. Yet little has changed since the night of 5 July 1643 when the final stages of the Battle of Lansdown were played out between two almost equally matched armies of the Royalists and the Parliamentarians.

In command of the opposing forces were two friends of long standing: Sir William Waller in charge of the Parliamentarian defence of Bath against Sir Ralph Hopton leading a Royalist attack. It was a bloody affair, with 'legs and arms flying all over the place', during which the Royalist Grenville was mortally wounded, having led the Cornish infantry in the charge up Lansdown Hill. While the battle itself was indecisive, casualties were severe. The Parliamentarians withdrew under cover of darkness, and the Royalists were thwarted in their pursuit of capturing Bath and moving on to the richer prize of Bristol.

❑ BECKFORD'S TOWER   [off Map 41, p163]

Although the Cotswold Way passes a couple of miles to the west of Beckford's Tower (🖥 beckfordstower.org.uk), you can't miss its distinctive outline and no trip to Bath would be complete without a brief nod towards William Beckford (1760-1844). Beckford's grandfather was a 17th-century plantation owner and his father three times Lord Mayor of London; Beckford himself inherited a cool £2 million, no mean fortune in the 18th century. Having built Fonthill Abbey near Salisbury, he retired to Lansdown Crescent in Bath, where he set about building the tower as a personal retreat. It was completed in 1827 and the land around it was consecrated as a cemetery in 1848 and is where Beckford was laid to rest.

The tower is now owned by Bath Preservation Trust and is **currently closed for restoration**. No date has been given for its reopening but when you are able to visit, the views from the top are worth the climb if the weather's on your side. There's an interesting museum (also currently closed) focusing on Beckford's colourful life. Note that it's nearly two miles (3km) from the Cotswold Way – you could walk from the golf course to the main road, then downhill along the pavement to the tower.

COLD ASHTON TO BATH   MAPS 39-43

After Cold Ashton comes the final **10¼-mile (16.7km, 5-6hrs)** stretch to Bath. Leaving the busy A46, the Cotswold Way returns to rolling hills dotted with cattle and sheep, the noise of traffic replaced with birdsong. It's a gradual climb to the top of the slope near Lansdown Hill, where the trail crosses the very field where the **Battle of Lansdown** (see box on p163) took place in 1643. The area is clearly demarcated with orange 'flags' and informative signboards, as well as a memorial; it doesn't take much to conjure up the chaos that must have ensued that summer evening.

As you pass **Bath racecourse** (Map 42), do make time to stop at **Prospect Stile** (now a kissing gate!), which at 230m (755ft) affords superb views across Bath (albeit marred by the gasworks) and over the Severn estuary.

The last couple of miles of the trail beyond **Weston** (Map 43) see some unexpected ups and downs as the route twists to make the most of open terrain, before the final descent past Lansdown Crescent to the grandeur of Bath Abbey.

If you'd rather stay on the downward slope, you could cut across the golf course (Map 41) to Lansdown Rd and follow this straight into Bath, taking in **Beckford's Tower** (see box above) as you go and ending up with Lansdown Crescent on your right.

WESTON   [MAP 43, p167]

Heading south, the walk down to Weston culminates in a return to a more urban world, but there are bonuses in practical terms. Well-placed for walkers is *Western Bistro* (☎ 01225-443017, 🖥 thewestern bistro.com; Mon-Sat 9am-4pm). There's a **pharmacy** (Mon-Sat 9am-6pm, Sat to 1pm) next door; a little further in the other direction is a small **supermarket**, Tesco Express (Mon-Sat 7am-11pm, Sun 11am-5pm).

First's No 4/4a **bus** (see pp48-50) operates between here and Bath, so if you can't face the steep climbs there is an alternative.

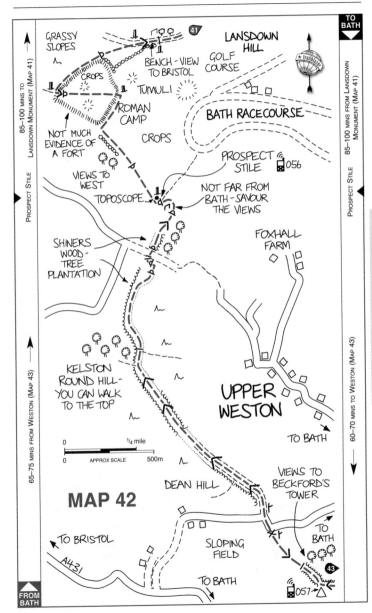

BATH [MAP 43a, pp172-3]

'Oh, who can ever be tired of Bath?'
   Catherine Morland in **Jane Austen's**
   Northanger Abbey, published in 1817

Not so long ago, as the train drew into the station at Bath, the announcer would intone in measured voice, 'Bath Spa'. It's that word 'spa' that has brought fortune to this western town, attracting 18th-century royalty to take the waters and serving as the catalyst for the construction of what we know today as Georgian Bath.

The city predates Roman times, when it was known as Aquae Sulis, but it is the Georgian buildings that are today revered and which have been protected as a World Heritage Site since 1987. Although George III (1738-1820) moved his allegiance to Cheltenham, sparking another building frenzy, Bath has never really fallen out of favour.

Today's visitors come not just to bathe in the waters at the smart Thermae Spa, but to explore the city's history at the Roman Baths, and to marvel at the soaring roof of Bath Abbey. They come, too, to investigate its museums, and – rather more prosaically – to try out any number of restaurants, hotels and bars that are around every corner. All that against a background of architecture that cannot fail to attract even the least-interested observer.

For the walker, the focal point of the city is the culmination of the trail, Bath Abbey, where you'll be greeted by an engraved limestone circle, sibling to the one in Chipping Campden (see p80).

See box p16 for details of festivals.

What to see and do

For most walkers on the Cotswold Way, the first sense of the city comes from the glimpse of Lansdown Crescent as you descend Lansdown Hill. Royal Crescent follows, leading to the smart gates of **Royal Victoria Park**, which in themselves represent a symbolic entrance to the city.

Although it is primarily Georgian Bath that draws the crowds, there are hints of medieval times in the ruins of the **city walls** along Upper Borough Walls and Barton St, north of the abbey, while no trip to Bath would be complete without visiting the **Roman Baths** (see p169).

To get a real feel for the city, join one of the two-hour **walking tours** that are run by volunteers from outside the Pump Room [65], right next to the Roman Baths. Tours depart at 10.30am and 2pm Sunday to Friday, and just at 10.30am on Saturday; between May and September, there's an additional evening walk at 6pm on Tuesday and Thursday. There's no charge – and tips are not accepted. Is this one of Bath's best-kept secrets? More info at (🖳 bathguides .org.uk).

A city with this sort of heritage must have the odd ghost hovering in the shadows. If you fancy being scared out of your wits, join a guided **ghost walk** (🖳 bathghosttours.com; daily May-Oct, Thur-Sun Mar & Apr, 8pm; £16pp), lasting just short of two hours. Tours leave from the Abbey.

For those who prefer to guide themselves, there's a **city trail** beneath your feet – quite literally: it's marked out with plaques on the pavements. There's no accompanying map but for an upbeat interpretation see 🖳 bath.co.uk/city-trail. Broadly, the trail starts near the abbey, taking in the Roman Baths and the Pump Room, before moving on to Queen Square, The Circus and the Assembly Rooms, then back towards Pulteney Bridge and Parade Gardens, finishing at Abbey Green.

❏ **COTSWOLD WAY SIGNS IN BATH**

Those unfamiliar with the city will need to keep a sharp eye out for the Cotswold Way signs, which have been reduced to discreet roundels featuring the National Trail acorn in a stylish gold metallic paint on black. Look out for these on lamp posts and bollards; nothing so rustic as a wooden fingerpost here!

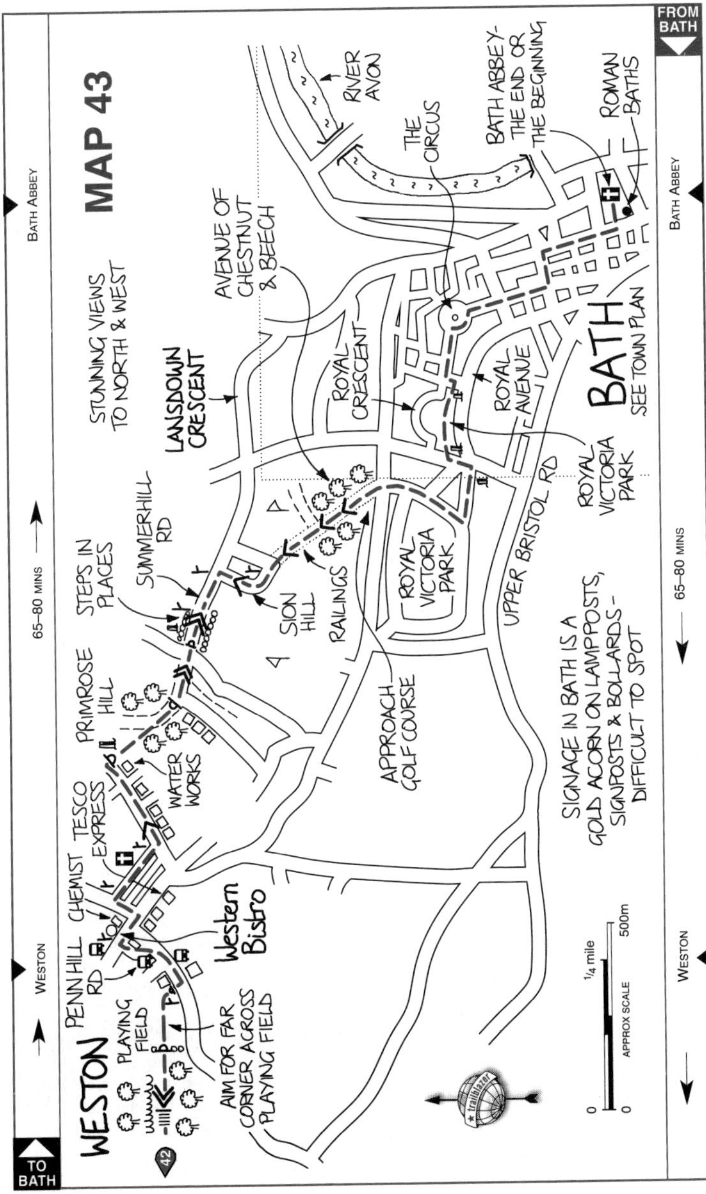

MAP 43

FROM BATH

BATH ABBEY

65–80 MINS

RIVER AVON

THE CIRCUS

BATH ABBEY – THE END OR THE BEGINNING

ROMAN BATHS

STUNNING VIEWS TO NORTH & WEST

AVENUE OF CHESTNUT & BEECH

LANSDOWN CRESCENT

ROYAL CRESCENT

BATH
SEE TOWN PLAN

BATH ABBEY

WESTON

STEPS IN PLACES

SUMMERHILL RD

PRIMROSE HILL

PENNHILL RD

CHEMIST

TESCO EXPRESS

WATER WORKS

Western Bistro

PLAYING FIELD

AIM FOR FAR CORNER ACROSS PLAYING FIELD

42

TO BATH

SION HILL

RAILINGS

ROYAL AVENUE

ROYAL VICTORIA PARK

ROYAL VICTORIA PARK

UPPER BRISTOL RD

APPROACH GOLF COURSE

SIGNAGE IN BATH IS A GOLD ACORN ON LAMPPOSTS, SIGNPOSTS & BOLLARDS – DIFFICULT TO SPOT

WESTON

65–80 MINS

WESTON

¼ mile

500m

APPROX SCALE

0

0

Further afield, the National Trust (🖥 nationaltrust.org.uk/bath-skyline) have devised a 6-mile (10km) **Bath Skyline walk** and a shorter version, **Walk to the View!**; the routes for both can be downloaded from the website. Those who would like to complete the **Cotswold Way in stages** should consider signing up for the walks led by Cotswold Voluntary Wardens, some of them based from Bath; for details, see p29.

If you've had enough of walking, there are always the double-decker **sightseeing buses** (🖥 city-sightseeing.com/en/84/bath) which operate hop-on, hop-off tours with a commentary from £22.50 a head; tickets are valid for 24 hours.

For more tour ideas see 🖥 riveradventures.co.uk who offer a Prosecco Boat Trip (£30), Discover Bath & Bridgerton with Music (£15) and Ghost Hunters Silent Disco Tour (from £15).

● **Bath Abbey** One of England's most glorious churches, Bath Abbey (🖥 bath abbey.org; Mon 9.30am-5.30pm, Tue-Fri 9am-5.30pm, Sat 9am-6pm, Sun 1-2.30pm & 4.30-6pm; £6.50) is the third church to occupy this site. Visitors are welcome to tour the building, with its magnificent flying buttresses and fan-vaulted rafters, but it is during a service, or a concert, that you can best appreciate the architecture as the sound of choral music soars skywards. Tower tours (10am-4pm; Mon-Fri 1/hr, Sat 2/hr; £15) are offered, except in bad weather and on certain days.

Over the years, three separate buildings have occupied the site of the abbey. The first, an Anglo-Saxon church, was replaced by the Normans at the end of the 11th century. When this fell into ruin at the end of the 15th century, the present abbey church was founded, but was abandoned in 1539 at the time of Henry VIII's order for the dissolution of the monasteries. The Gothic church here now was rebuilt during the reign of Elizabeth I and completed in 1616.

Take a look at the abbey doors and you'll see the sacred heart and crown of thorns that proclaim its earlier foundation as a Catholic church. To each side of the doors are statues of St Peter and St Paul, to whom the Norman church was dedicated. The statue to the left was decapitated by

---

❑ **THERMAE BATH SPA**

A wonderful way to end your walk and a great place to ease all those post-walk aches and pains, **Thermae Bath Spa** (☎ 01225-331234, 🖥 www.thermaebathspa.com; daily 9am-9.30pm; pools closed 9pm; no children under 16 in main spa, 12 in Cross Bath) is on the gloriously named Hot Bath St. At £40 a head (£45 at weekends) for the 2hr Thermae Welcome package it's expensive but at least the price includes a towel and robe, though you need to take a swimming costume. You get access to the roof-top open-air bath, the Minerva Bath, the Wellness Suite and the Springs Café.

Rather more exclusive and unlike the main baths which are modern, the **Cross Bath** is within the original Georgian walled enclosure. It's a small pool for up to 10 people, open air but without the view. The Romans built the original bath house here in the 1st century AD, fed from the Cross Spring which still flows from directly below. The current building dates from 1798 and contained the 'Tuppeny Hot', a small swimming pool that finally closed in 1978. A 1½-hour session here costs £40 but it's open only Mon-Weds & Fri 10-11.30am and Thur 6-7.30pm; book within 48 hours of your visit. At other times it's available for exclusive use (£800-1000 for 10 people).

The Cross Spring
feeding the Cross Bath

Roundheads during the reign of Charles I, with the face recarved at a later date to restore the balance – at least in part. The abbey church itself is dedicated to St Peter.

● **Roman Baths and Pump Room** Probably the greatest attraction for visitors are the **Roman Baths** (🖳 romanbaths .co.uk; daily Jan-Feb & Nov-Feb 10am-6pm, Mar-mid Jun & Sep-Oct 9am-6pm, mid Jun-Aug 9am-9pm; £20.50-23.50), on Stall St. Dating from between the 1st and 5th centuries AD, and constructed of stone, the colonnaded great bath was built to take advantage of a natural spring from which waters rise at a constant temperature of around 46°C. If the changing rooms, saunas and plunge pools are reminiscent of a modern-day spa, the temple dedicated to the goddess Sulis Minerva puts the whole thing firmly back into context. Included in the admission price is entry to the Georgian **Pump Room**, where the spring water may be sampled. For details of afternoon tea at the Pump Room, see p181.

● **Bath Assembly Rooms** Built in 1771, the lavishly designed Assembly Rooms (🖳 nationaltrust.org.uk/bath-assembly-rooms; £9 for guided tours), on Bennett St, were the creation of John Wood the Younger, and *the* place to be seen in fashionable Georgian society. Note that from 2023 for up to two years the building may be partially or even completely closed for major restoration. For many years this was also the home of the **Fashion Museum** (🖳 fashionmuseum.co uk) but this has now closed and will eventually reopen in the refurbished GPO building.

● **Herschel Museum of Astronomy** Dedicated to five generations of the Herschel family, this museum (🖳 herschel museum.org.uk; Feb-Dec Tue-Sun 10am-5pm, closed 1-2pm at weekends; £12), 19 New King St, is as much about the interior of an 18th-century townhouse as about astronomy. Already established as a musician, William Herschel moved here in 1777 with his sister, the astronomer Caroline Herschel. As a form of relaxation, he took

❑ **OPENING HOURS**
When planning your trip, note that several establishments, including the Roman Baths, stop selling tickets up to an hour before closing time, so do be sure to give yourself plenty of time.

up astronomy himself, building his own telescope and going on to discover the planet Uranus from this garden in 1781. Among the exhibits relating to everyday life is a 7ft (210cm) scale model of his 40ft (12m) telescope. Herschel went on to be appointed Astronomer Royal, forcing a move to Datchet in 1782. He died in 1823 and is buried in Berkshire, in the churchyard of St Lawrence, Upton.

● **The Holburne Museum** Fans of the Netflix series *Bridgerton* will recognise this as Lady Danbury's Mansion. Established in 1893 to showcase the collection of Sir William Holburne, this museum (☎ 01225-388569, 🖳 holburne.org; Mon-Sat 10am-5pm, to 9pm on last Fri of month, Sun/bank hols 11am-5pm; £11, Art Fund members £5.50; free Wed 3-5pm and 5-9pm on last Fri of month) lies at the end of Great Pulteney St. It is a major provincial gallery with a particularly strong emphasis on Georgian portraiture. To miss the rest of the collection would be a shame, however. Do take a look at the smaller exhibits tucked away in drawers – and allow time for a breather in the contemporary *café* (food till 4.30pm).

● **The Old Theatre Royal & Masonic Museum** (🖳 oldtheatreroyal.com, 12 Old Orchard St) is well worth visiting if you've ever wondered what went on in a Masonic Lodge. Dating from the mid 18th century, this was the first purpose-built theatre in Bath. Between 1809 and 1863 the building was a Catholic chapel and since 1865 it has been a Masonic Lodge, one of the oldest in the country. There are one-hour tours (Tue-Thur, 11am & 2.30pm, Sat 2.30pm only; £8) given by a mason, taking in the grand

Masonic Hall, the scenery loft dating back to the original theatre, the chapel and the masonic Museum. It's highly recommended.

● **Museum of Bath Architecture** (🖳 museumofbatharchitecture.org.uk; The Vineyards, The Paragon) is another excellent museum that is currently closed and without a definite reopening date.

● **Museum of East Asian Art** This museum (🖳 meaa.org.uk; Wed-Fri 11am-5pm, Sat 10.30am-5pm; £5), 12 Bennett St, based on the personal collection of a Hong Kong lawyer, offers more of an introduction to Asian art than any great insight. Among the exhibits are ceramics, bamboo carvings and an extensive collection of Chinese jade. Find it off The Circus, just a stone's throw from the Cotswold Way as it enters Bath.

● **Parade Gardens** Right in the centre of Bath, Parade Gardens (Easter-end Sep; £2) is a peaceful place to enjoy the colour of an English formal garden. Bands play here regularly in summer.

● **Royal Crescent and Lansdown Crescent** At the far right of **Royal Crescent, No 1** (🖳 no1royalcrescent.org .uk; Feb-Dec Tue-Sun 10am-5.30pm; £15) was the first house to be constructed and it was built in the Palladian style following designs by John Wood the Younger. The attraction now encompasses the servants' quarters in the neighbouring No 1A. Today's visitor will gain an insight into life both upstairs and downstairs in fashionable Georgian society; don't miss the kitchens or the cabinet of curiosities.

Royal Crescent may get all the accolades, but it is **Lansdown Crescent** (see Map 43, p167) that is first seen by those heading south on the Cotswold Way. With sheep grazing on the grassy hill in front, and fine views over the city, it arguably runs its more famous neighbour very close.

● **Victoria Art Gallery** Facing Pulteney Bridge (designed by Robert Adam and one of only three river bridges in Europe with shops that are integral to the bridge) is **Victoria Art Gallery** (🖳 victoriagal.org.uk; Tue-Sun 10.30am-5pm; Upper Gallery is free – though closed for renovations at time of research – but special exhibitions in the Victoria Gallery cost £7), built at a time of civic pride to show off the city's attributes. While the name suggests it focuses on Victorian art, the reality is a far broader mix, from the 17th century to the contemporary, and including a couple of Gainsborough paintings and Rex Whistler's glorious incarnation of British insularity, *The Foreign Bloke*. Some are linked to the city, but most were donated by wealthy Bath residents, or formed part of their collections. Displays also include sculpture, ceramics, glass, porcelain and pottery.

Entertainment
Bath does culture very well, but there's light relief on the agenda too.

Bath's **Theatre Royal** (🖳 theatreroyal .org.uk), on Saw Close, stages a wide range of high-quality productions, and – for theatre buffs – shouldn't be missed. If you've a preference for the silver screen, try the multi-screen **Odeon cinema** (🖳 odeon.co .uk) on James St, or – for more offbeat offerings – **Little Theatre Cinema** (🖳 pic turehouses.com/cinema/The_Little), on St Michael's Place. There's also the cinema-café **Tivoli Bath** (🖳 tivolicinemas.com) in the Southgate Centre at 6-8 Dorchester St.

Boat trips can be organised with the companies leaving from Pulteney Weir, with up to eight trips a day. Hour-long cruises to Bathampton Mill and back cost £12 with Pulteney Cruisers (🖳 pulteney cruisers.co .uk). There's also the *Pulteney Princess* which is a little cheaper. If you'd rather set off under your own steam, rowing boats, canoes and punts can be hired from Bath Boating Station (off Map 43a; 🖳 bathboating.co.uk; early Apr-late Sep Wed-Sun & bank hol Mon 10am-5.30pm), whose base is at the end of Forester Rd, north-east of Great Pulteney St. Boats cost £10pp for one hour or £15pp for 2 hours.

Spectators rather than participants can check out what's on at **The Rec** (🖳 bath rugby.com), home to Bath Rugby Club –

though it's a small ground by today's standards, and tickets can be hard to come by. The Rec is also used for concerts.

Arrival and departure

Whether Bath is the grand finale of your walk, or an historic starting point, there is no shortage of ways to get to and from the city.

● **By train** Bath Spa railway station is at the end of Manvers St, near the river. Services operated by GWR stop here; for details see box p46.

● **By coach** The coach/bus station is located on Dorchester St, close to both the railway station and SouthGate shopping centre which dominates the southern part of the city. National Express's No 403 service (see box p47) calls here.

● **By bus** Stagecoach's No 620 from Old Sodbury and First's No 4/4A services (see pp48-50) call at the bus station.

● **By car** Bath is about half-an-hour's drive from junction 18 of the M4. Note that Bath is in a low emissions zone so you may have to pay a £9 daily fee if you have an older car (⌨ www.gov.uk/clean-air-zones).

● **By air** The nearest airport with both domestic and international flights is Bristol; see box p45. The Airdecker bus (⌨ www.airdecker.com; daily 1-2/hr) operates between the airport and Bath.

If you want to abandon your luggage so you can explore the city, you can leave it with Bath Backpackers (£5 a bag per day, free for guests); see p174.

Getting around Bath

The centre of Bath is sufficiently compact that most visitors are happy to wander the streets on foot.

If you'd like to rent a **bike** try Bath Ebike Hire (⌨ www.bathebikehire.co.uk) and/or Bath Bike Hire (⌨ www.bathbike hire.com).

At the other end of the energy spectrum, open-top **buses** encircle the tourist areas of the city, anathema to some but a great relief from blistered feet for others. For details of both these and horse-drawn carriages, see p168.

Registered **taxis**, easily spotted by the light on the roof, can be hailed on the streets. There's also a **taxi rank** in front of the railway station. Other taxis, such as those run by *V-Cars* (☎ 01225-464646, ⌨ www.veezu.co.uk/bath) must be pre-booked).

Services

Tourist information The Visitor Information Centre has now closed, relying only on its website – ⌨ visitbath.co.uk – and some volunteer 'ambassadors' (⌨ bath bid.co.uk), who wander round the centre of Bath in blue blazers, to answer visitors' questions.

The **Bath World Heritage Centre** (⌨ bathworldheritage.org.uk, 10 York St) has to some extent replaced it with interactive displays about the city and some leaflets.

● **Money matters** All the main high street **banks** have branches with **ATMs** across the city. The most central are on Milsom St, where there are branches of Lloyds [38] or south on Southgate, where you'll find branches of Metro Bank [82], Barclays [84] and HSBC [83]. The post office (Mon-Fri 8.30am-9pm, Sat 8.30am-5.30pm, Sun 11am-3pm) is on Union St [50].

● **Shopping** Arguably the most central of the **supermarkets** for those seeking supplies is Waitrose [46] (Mon-Fri 7.30am-9pm, Sat to 8pm, Sun 11am-5pm), which is in The Podium on Northgate St. There's a large branch of Sainsbury's [61] (Mon-Sat 7am-10pm, Sun 11am-5pm) behind the old Green Park Station, and smaller Sainsbury's Locals (daily 7am-11pm) on Monmouth St [58] and opposite the bus station [87].

More interesting by far are some of the smaller, **independent shops**, where you can taste the cheese to go in your lunch before buying. Two to tempt your palate are The Fine Cheese Co [41] (☎ 01225-483407, ⌨ finecheeseshops.co.uk/bath; Mon-Sat 9am-5pm), on Walcot St across from the Podium, and Chandos Deli [11] (☎ 01225-314418; **fb**; Mon-Sat 9am-4.30pm, Sun 10am-4pm), on George St and with another branch at the station. They have their own licensed *cafés* serving sandwiches made to order and lots of other goodies.

(cont'd on p174)

ROUTE GUIDE AND MAPS

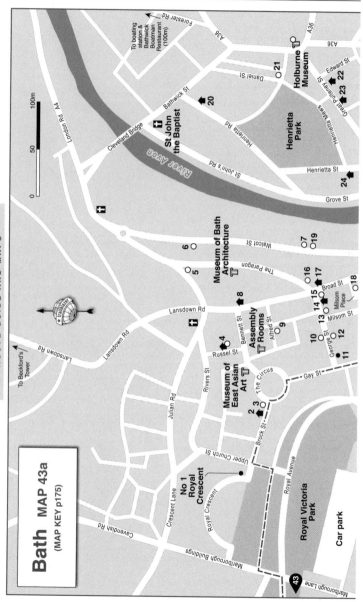

ROUTE GUIDE AND MAPS

Bath MAP 43a
(MAP KEY p175)

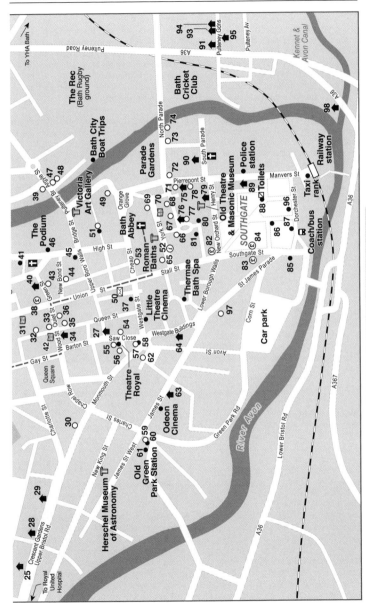

There are also several food outlets in the **Guildhall Market** [51] **(fb**; Mon-Sat 8am-5.30pm but stalls have their own hours) and an excellent **farmers' market** [60] (🖳 bathfarmersmarket.co.uk; Sat 9am-1.30pm) in the old Green Park Station (🖳 greenpark station.co.uk) in front of Sainsbury's.

For **outdoor supplies**, such as walking boots, poles and clothing, there are several outlets: BCH Camping & Leisure [85] on Southgate St; Blacks [80] and Cotswold Outdoor [81] on Abbey Gate; Millets [45] on High St; and The North Face [88] in SouthGate shopping centre.

With some excellent independent **bookshops**, Bath is an easy place to lose a bibliophile. Topping & Company [70] (🖳 toppingbooks.co.uk; daily 8.30am-9pm), has now moved into the grand former Friends' Meeting House on York St. They have a good range of maps and guides, as does the large branch of Waterstones [31] (Mon-Sat 9am-6pm, Sun 11am-5pm) on Milsom St. Also well worth a visit is the wonderfully-named Mr B's Emporium of Reading Delights [42] (🖳 mrbsemporium .com; Mon-Sat 9.30am-5.30pm, Sun 11am-5pm) at 13-15 John St.

● **Health** Royal United **Hospital** (off Map 43a; ☎ 01225-428331, 🖳 ruh.nhs.uk) is at Combe Park, about 1½ miles (2.4km) west of the city centre. **Pharmacies** include Boots in SouthGate [86] and Westgate [37].

Where to stay

While there's plenty of accommodation close to the end of the trail, by the abbey, much of it is on the expensive side. The suggestions given here and on pp176-8 include some more reasonable options, many of them grouped together in one or two areas to the south-east and west of the city, and all within easy reach of the trail.

Although seemingly limitless, Bath's accommodation can get booked up very early during Bath Festival (end May-June) and in the summer. Prices almost everywhere vary considerably, taking into account the time of year, the day of the week, the length of stay, and what is going on in the city; those given below are for

guidance, but are for a single-night stay in the main season. At weekends, usually defined as Friday and Saturday night, and bank holidays, many places also insist on a **minimum two-night stay**, especially for advance bookings.

AirBnb (🖳 airbnb.com) has numerous listings for the city.

● **Hostels** Hostel accommodation that is also central comes in various guises (though campers will be out of luck). The largest option, sleeping over 200 people, is the **YMCA** [17] (☎ 01225-325900, 🖳 ymcabath.org.uk), on Broad Street Place. Dorm accommodation (1 x 8 & 1 x 15-bed female only, 1 x 12-bed men only, 2 x 12- & 1 x 18-bed mixed dorms, shared facilities; WI-FI) is in the original building which dates from about 1888. The newer building has the private rooms (3S/9D/29T/4Tr/4Qd, most with shared facilities but 4D are en suite; WI-FI). Staying at the YMCA costs £22-25pp in a dormitory, private rooms cost £34-8 for a single and £30-42pp for two sharing. All rates include a continental breakfast at the weekend. There's a laundry for guests' use, a left-luggage facility (£2 per bag), and a gym (free for residents who have booked direct) – though that's unlikely to be of interest at the beginning or end of a 102-mile hike!

Bath Backpackers [75] (☎ 07462 791235, 🖳 bathbackpackers.com; 1 x 8- & 1 x 10-bed female dorm, 1 x 8- & 2 x 12-bed mixed dorm, 1 x 8- 10- & 12-bed private rooms, shared facilities; WI-FI), is at 13 Pierrepont St, where there's a self-catering kitchen. A dorm bed costs £18-26.40pp and private rooms are from £168.

A further option is the hostel at **St Christopher's Inn** [40] (☎ 01225-481444, 🖳 st-christophers.co.uk/bath/central-hos tel; 2 x 6- & 3 x 12-bed dorms/2D shared facilities, 1D en suite; WI-FI), at 9 Green St. A dorm bed costs from £18.50pp (one 6-bed dorm is female only); their double rooms start from £60pp (sgl occ room rate). For the best rates book online and direct. There may be a two-night minimum stay requirement at weekends but subject to availability a single-night stay may be

BATH – MAP KEY (see map pp172-3)

Where to stay

2 Brocks
4 The Queensberry
8 The Belmont
14 Travelodge Bath Central
17 YMCA
20 Chestnuts House
22 Dukes Bath
23 Edgar Townhouse
24 Kennard
25 Bay Tree House
27 Z Hotels Bath
29 The Bath House
34 Harington's Hotel
40 St Christopher's Inn
63 Premier Inn Bath City Centre
64 Travelodge Bath City Ctr
75 Bath Backpackers
76 Eight
79 The Henry Guest House
89 Anabelle's
90 Hotel Indigo Bath
91 Avon Guesthouse
93 Apple Tree
94 Brindleys
95 White Guest House
98 Travelodge Bath Waterside

Where to eat and drink

3 The Circus
4 The Olive Tree
5 The Star Inn
6 The Bell
7 Schwartz Bros
9 Woods
10 Clayton's Kitchen
15 Wagamama
16 Mantra Progressive Indian
18 Côte Brasserie
19 The Walcot, Bread & Jam
21 The Pulteney Arms
30 Scallop Shell
32 Salamander
33 Olé Tapas
35 The Raven
36 The Eastern Eye
39 Antica
43 The Old Green Tree
44 Volunteer Rifleman's Arms
47 The Bridge Coffee Shop
48 Ponte Vecchio
49 Browns
53 The Roman Baths Kitchen
54 Schwartz Bros

Where to eat & drink (cont'd)

55 Amarone
56 Garrick's Head
57 Thai Balcony
59 Green Park Brasserie & Bath Pizza Co
62 Swoon Gelato
65 Pump Room
66 Crystal Palace
67 Oak Restaurant
68 Sally Lunn's
69 The Real Italian Pizza Co
71 Salathai
72 The Green Rocket Café
73 Sotto Sotto
74 OPA
77 The Bath Bun
78 Yak Yeti Yak
96 Tivoli Cinema & Café
97 Noya's Kitchen

Other

11 Chandos Deli
31 Waterstones
37 Boots
38 Lloyds Bank & ATM
41 Fine Cheese Co
42 Mr B's Emporium
45 Millets

Other (cont'd)

46 Waitrose (in The Podium)
50 Post Office
51 Guildhall Market
52 Bath World Heritage Centre
58 Sainsbury's Local
60 Farmers' Market
61 Sainsbury's
70 Topping & Co
80 Blacks
81 Cotswold Outdoor
82 Metro Bank
83 HSBC & ATM
84 Barclays Bank & ATM
85 BCH Camping & Leisure
86 Boots
87 Sainsbury's Local
88 The North Face
96 Tivoli Cinema & Café

possible for walk-ins. A continental breakfast costs £5 if booked in advance and £6 in house. On the down side, it's above the noisy Belushi's bar and restaurant. The plus? You get 25% off food and there are some drink offers at Belushi's.

The city's YHA hostel, *YHA Bath* (off Map 43a; ☎ 0345-371 9303, 🖳 yha.org.uk/hostel/yha-bath; 1 x 2-, 5 x 3-, 1 x 4-, 6 x 5- & 6 x 6-bed rooms with en suite facilities; 2 x 2-, 2 x 4- & 3 x 6-bed rooms, plus an 8-bed male dorm and 10-bed female dorm, all with shared facilities; WI-FI in communal areas; (L), is over a mile (1.6km) east of the centre on Bathwick Hill. If you don't mind the walk, and fancy staying in an Italianate mansion, it could be worth considering. Pricing is dynamic and fluctuates widely, but members can expect to pay in the range of £20-45pp for a dorm bed, or £60-145 for two sharing a room. Some rooms have a double bed. Laundry facilities and meals are available and the hostel is licensed. There are limited self-catering facilities (no hobs or oven, just a microwave, toaster and kettle. An unlimited continental/cooked breakfast costs £5.95/£9.95pp.

● Guesthouses and B&Bs
Central Right on the Cotswold Way as you walk into Bath, near The Circus, is *Brocks* [2] (☎ 01225-338374, 🖳 brocksguesthouse.co.uk; 2D or T/4D/1Qd, all en suite; ✆; WI-FI), 32 Brock St, where a room (they no longer offer breakfast) costs around £44-80pp (sgl occ room rate).

Not far from here, at 7 Belmont, a pedestrian walkway that runs parallel to but above Lansdown Rd, you'll find *The Belmont* [8] (☎ 01225-423082, 🖳 belmontbath.co.uk; 2T/3D, all en suite; ✆; WI-FI), a traditional B&B run by Archie Watson. Charges are from £47.50pp (sgl occ £75).

At the other end of town, close to the railway station, *The Henry Guest House* [79] (☎ 01225-424052, 🖳 thehenry.com; 1S private facilities, 3D/2D or T/1Qd, all en suite; ✆; WI-FI) offers contemporary rooms in a Georgian townhouse. B&B costs £50-62.50pp (sgl/sgl occ from £105/150).

Similarly convenient for the railway

station, albeit rather noisy, is *Anabelle's* [89] (☎ 01225-330133, 🖳 anabellesguesthouse.co.uk; 1S/3D all en suite, 1D/1T private facilities, 3T shared facilities; ✆; WI-FI), where you'll pay £45-50pp for B&B (sgl occ rates on request).

Across Pulteney Bridge on Henrietta Rd is *Chestnuts House* [20] (☎ 01225-334279, 🖳 chestnutshouse.co.uk; 4D/1Tr, all en suite; WI-FI) – a stone-built house with rooms for £55-97.50pp (sgl occ £95-145).

East of the city Outside the immediate centre, there are two gluts of predominantly terraced B&Bs in residential areas that are within easy walking distance of the trail. The first, about 10 minutes' walk east of the abbey across the railway and a short stroll from the Kennet and Avon Canal, runs along **Pulteney Rd** and up **Pulteney Gardens**. On the corner of Pulteney Gardens, *Avon Guesthouse* [91] (☎ 01225-313009, 🖳 avonguesthousebath.co.uk; 1T/4D/1Tr, all en suite; ✆; Feb-Dec) charges £47.50-65pp (sgl occ from £88).

Pulteney Gardens itself harbours several Victorian homes offering B&B. At No 23, B&B at *White Guest House* [95] (☎ 01225-426075, 🖳 www.whiteguesthouse.co.uk; 1S/1T/2D, all en suite; WI-FI) will set you back from £40pp (sgl £55-60, sgl occ from £65). Cooked breakfasts are no longer available – all rooms have a fridge, coffee machine and the ingredients for a continental breakfast in the room.

At No 7, *Apple Tree* [93] (☎ 01225-337642, 🖳 appletreeguesthouse.co.uk; 5D, all en suite; WI-FI) charges £52.50-85pp (sgl occ room rate). At the end on the corner is the self-styled 'boutique B&B' *Brindleys* [94] (☎ 01225-310444, 🖳 brindleysbath.co.uk; 1D or T/5D, all en suite; WI-FI). With French-inspired décor, its rooms – some with king-sized beds – cost £70-115pp (sgl occ room rate). Note that they don't accommodate children under 12.

To the east of the abbey, over the river, are two more options. *Edgar Townhouse* [23] (☎ 01225-420619, 🖳 edgar-townhouse.co.uk; 2S/3T/12D/1Qd, all en suite; WI-FI), at 64 Great Pulteney St, offers B&B

❑ **TWO-NIGHT MINIMUM STAY**

Virtually all B&B-style accommodation options in Bath require a minimum stay of two nights at weekends and also at peak periods. But if there is availability at short notice most would consider a one-night stay.

for £50-87pp (sgl £81-90, sgl occ rates on request). Room only rates are also available. They now have a bar (daily 6-8pm).

Round the corner at ***Kennard*** [24] (☎ 01225-310472, 🖳 kennard.co.uk; 1S private facilities, 1T/8D/1Tr all en suite), 11 Henrietta St, you'll pay from £72.50pp (sgl/sgl occ £100/130) for B&B. They actually have two single rooms but usually only let one at a time unless the people booking are a group of friends.

West of the city A second clutch of guesthouses and B&Bs is at **Crescent Gardens**, an elevated section of **Upper Bristol Rd** that's just a few minutes' walk from the trail – and the centre of Bath. Closest of these is ***The Bath House*** [29] (mob ☎ 07711-119847, 🖳 thebathhouse.org; 1T or D/4D, all en suite; ▼), at No 40, another self-styled 'boutique B&B' where most rooms have king-sized four-poster beds; they cost £49.50-79.50pp (sgl occ £89-149). They also have two self-catering **apartments**, about 100 yards away on James St. One sleeps up to three people (1T or D plus a sofa bed; £49.50-89.50pp, sgl occ £89-169); the other up to five (1T or D/1Tr; £159-289 for up to five people sharing). In both apartments a complimentary continental breakfast is provided for the first morning.

Last up is ***Bay Tree House*** [25] (☎ 07780-901718, 🖳 baytreehousebath.co.uk; 1D/1Tr, both en suite), No 12, with rooms for £45-50pp (sgl occ from £81). They no longer provide a cooked breakfast but put ingredients for a 'light/takeaway' breakfast for each room into a communal fridge.

Comprising two elegant Georgian townhouses on Great Pulteney St, ***Dukes Bath*** [22] (☎ 01225-787960, 🖳 dukesbath.co.uk; 17D including some suites, all en suite; ▼; **fb**) is at Nos 52-3 and gets excellent reviews. Best rates are off their website and pricing is dynamic, ranging from around £55pp-£105pp.

• **Hotels** With B&Bs climbing steadily up the price ladder, it's not unreasonable to shop around for one of the cheaper hotels. Relatively new on the scene is ***Premier Inn Bath City Centre*** [63] (☎ 0333 321 9326, 🖳 premierinn.com; 23D/31Tr/44Qd, all en suite; ▼), 4 James St West. Rates can vary hugely from day to day, though the best are online. Standard rates (non refundable and pay at time of booking) start at around £42 for a room sleeping up to two adults, Advance (pay when you book but fully refundable up to 28 days before arrival) from £69 and Flex rates from £86 (cancel up to 1pm on the day and pay on arrival).

In a similar mould are three branches of **Travelodge** (🖳 travelodge.co.uk); all have a good number of double, twin and triple rooms and all rooms are en suite with baths. The older ***Bath Central*** [14] (☎ 0871-984 6219) is indeed central, at 1 York Buildings on George St, though has now been upstaged by the even more central ***Bath City Centre*** [64] (Bath Spa; ☎ 0871-984 6523), at 6-10 Westgate Buildings, very close to the Roman baths. There's also ***Bath Waterside*** [98] (☎ 0871-984 6407) on Rossiter Rd and in more tranquil surroundings to the south, on the Kennet and Avon Canal though rooms facing the road can be a bit noisy. Once again rates can vary hugely from day to day, though are best online: Saver rates (non-refundable and paid at time of booking) can come in as low as £48 per room and Flexible rates (can cancel up to noon on arrival date) are more likely to be from £66. Wi-fi (£3 for 24hrs) and an unlimited breakfast (£9.50pp) are extra.

Billing itself as 'compact luxury', ***Z Hotels Bath*** [27] (☎ 01225 613160, 🖳 www.thezhotels.com/hotels/bath/; 149D all en suite; **fb**), is centrally-located at 7 Saw Close, opposite the Theatre Royal. Accommodation here can be exceptionally good value – from £50 for a small internal room (ie £25pp) without a window in low season. There are also larger rooms with windows from £60 and a few family rooms from £87.50, with extra beds for children.

A rather more personal option is *Harington's Hotel* [34] (☎ 01225-461728, 🖳 haringtonshotel.co.uk; 9D/1D or T/3Tr, all en suite; ✆; ✖), 8-10 Queen St, just off the square, where B&B costs £50-111.50pp (no discount for sgl occ).

The more central *Eight* [76] (☎ 01225-724111, 🖳 www.eightinbath.co.uk; 1S/2T/15D/2Tr, all en suite; ✆) is an independent boutique hotel occupying a listed townhouse just behind the abbey, though some of the rooms are in a sister property around the corner at 3 North Parade Passage. It opened in 2021 and they welcome walkers. B&B costs £102.50-165pp (sgl £190-205, sgl occ room rate).

Hotel Indigo Bath [90] (☎ 01225-460441, 🖳 bath.hotelindigo.com; 50D or T / 110D, all en suite; ✆), at 2-8 South Parade in another beautiful Georgian terrace, is part of the IHG group. Rooms are very comfortable ranging from standard doubles and twins to premium doubles and suites. Prices range from £60-180pp (sgl occ room rate); There's a smart restaurant, The Elder, here.

At the top end of the scale, one boutique hotel stands out: *The Queensberry* [4] (☎ 01225-447928, 🖳 thequeensberry .co.uk; 15D/14D or T, all en suite; ✆) on Russel St. Stylish and contemporary, its rooms come in at £50-225pp (sgl occ room rate); the rate includes a £20 allocation towards items off the à la carte breakfast menu. The hotel has a Michelin-starred restaurant, The Olive Tree (see p179).

Where to eat and drink

Eating out in Bath is easy. The problem lies in choosing where to go from the broad array of pubs, restaurants, cafés and fast-food joints whose menus demand attention at every turn. The following, then, is no more than a selection of options within easy reach of the centre. Others abound, especially around Kingsmead Square, so you'll be spoiled for choice.

● **Traditional and contemporary** As you walk into (or out of) Bath along the Cotswold Way, you'll pass *The Circus* [3] (🖳 thecircusrestaurant.co.uk; lunch Mon-Fri noon-2.30pm Sat to 2pm, dinner from 5pm and snacks served in between), on Brock St, aptly located near The Circus. You can have breakfast, elevenses, lunch or tea here, or dine in style. Whatever your choice, the décor is pleasantly informal and the menus are both seasonal and appetising; pheasant Kyiv filled with a confit garlic compound butter, with colcannon potatoes and a porcini mushroom sauce (£26.90) for example.

❏ BATH SPECIALITIES

● **Bath bun** Created in the 17th century by Sally Lunn, the original Bath bun is a light bread roll, akin to a large French brioche and still served at the eponymous Sally Lunn's (see pp181-2) in Bath. Later, though, the term 'Bath bun' became associated with a sweetened roll sprinkled with sugar and this is now the more widely known of the two.

● **Bath Oliver** The plain savoury biscuit served as an accompaniment to cheese was the creation of one Dr Oliver, who practised in Bath during the 18th century. It's widely available in supermarkets and delicatessens.

● **Bath chap** The breadcrumbed boiled cheek of a pig, these normally come in a cone shape. Find them at the Guildhall Market in Bath.

● **Bath soft cheese** An old Bath recipe is said to lie behind the creation of this cheese, which is available at the city's Saturday morning farmers' market.

● **Bath asparagus** Not so much a culinary speciality as a rare summer delicacy, Bath asparagus grows wild in the hills around the city, the locations a closely guarded secret. As you might expect, it is strictly protected.

In a prime location right in front of the abbey, and hugely popular with tourists, is *The Roman Baths Kitchen* [53] (🖥 roman bathkitchen.co.uk; Sun-Thur 9am-6pm, Fri-Sat 9am-9pm). Separate daytime and dinner menus have a fairly broad range of dishes, from small and large and sharing plates to grills and salads.

Long a local favourite is *Green Park Brasserie* [59] (☎ 01225-338565, 🖥 green parkbrasserie.com; daily 11-late, food Wed-Sat noon-10pm, Sun noon-4 but pizza available daily), 6 Green Park Station, where there's the added buzz of live jazz in the evening (Wed-Sat). Rather grandly located in the old booking hall of the restored Green Park Station, it spills over on to the old station concourse, now the home of the Bath Pizza Co (see below). Good-value specials noon-6pm (weekdays) include a burger & beer or pasta & prosecco (£14.95), or bottomless brunches, Fri/Sat 11-3pm with two courses and all you can drink for £37. Note that they sometimes close for private functions. Also here and open daily *Bath Pizza Co* [59] (☎ 01225-588886, 🖥 bathpizzaco.com; daily noon-late) does great pizza and deals such as pizza and a pint/proseocco for £12.95. Eat in or take away.

Clayton's Kitchen [10] (☎ 01225-724386 🖥 claytons-kitchen.com; Wed & Thur noon-2.30pm & 6-9.30pm, Fri noon-2.30pm & 6-10pm, Sat noon-3pm & 6-10pm, Sun noon-3pm & 6-9pm), on George St, has been run by Michelin-starred chef Robert Clayton since he opened it in 2012. Main dishes include roasted Cotswold chicken with risotto of porchini and shitake mushrooms, truffle oil and parsnips (£28) and roast loin of venison with port wine sauce (£46).

By the boating station, a 10-minute walk from the centre and at the top of Forester Rd, is an excellent riverside restaurant, *The Bathwick Boatman* [off Bath map, p172] (☎ 01225-428844 🖥 bathwick boatman.com; food Thu-Sat noon-2pm & 5-8.30pm, Sun noon-5pm). Family-run, they claim to serve 'good honest food' and they do that perfectly! Note that they operate a reservation-only policy: phone or go online.

On Orange Grove, *Browns* [49] (🖥 browns-restaurants.co.uk; Mon-Sat 9am-11pm, Sun to 10.30pm) is part of an upmarket but good-value chain. The atmosphere in this former police station and magistrate's court is buzzing, the menu broad and prices reasonable. Open for breakfast, brunch, lunch, afternoon tea and dinner.

Racing paraphernalia adorns the walls of the established *Woods* [9] (🖥 woods restaurant.com; Wed-Sat noon-2.30pm & 5-8.30pm, Sun noon-2.30pm), a family-run place on Alfred St, opposite the Assembly Rooms. Come for their bar menu with goodies such as Provençal fish soup (£11.95); a two-course fixed-price menu at lunch or early dinner (£30); or select from dishes that might include pan-fried fillet of hake on potato hummus with chick pea, lemon and coriander salsa (£23.95). There's also a deli here, open Wed-Sat 11am-3pm.

For a celebration, a classy venue could be appropriate. Round the corner from Woods, on Russell St, *The Olive Tree* [4] (🖥 olivetreebath.co.uk; Tue-Sun 6.30-8.30pm, Fri-Sun 12.30-1.30pm) is the exclusive and top-quality restaurant at The Queensberry Hotel (see Where to stay), exuding calm and contemporary style. Boasting a Michelin star, there's a six-course tasting menu for £130 or if that's out of your budget the three-course lunch menu is £60.

Also with a Michelin star is *Menu Gordon Jones* [off Bath map, p173] (☎ 01225-480871 🖥 menugordonjones.co.uk; Wed-Sat 12.30-9pm) but you'll need a taxi to get there as it's in Bear Flat (2 Wellsway BA2 3AQ), just to the south of the city centre. Offering dishes that are not for anyone with any kind of dietary requirements other than the best food, Gordon Jones states on his website: 'We are eager to make our dishes as good as they can be so we are unable to offer vegan and vegetarian options.' The lunch or dinner tasting menu is £90 or £175 paired with wines. Pre-booking required.

● **Mediterranean** There's more than a passing nod to French café culture at *Côte Brasserie* [18] (🖥 cote-restaurants.co.uk;

ROUTE GUIDE AND MAPS

Mon-Thur 11.30am-10pm, Fri & Sat 9am-10pm, Sun 9am-9.30pm) in Milsom Place, too, where *moules frites* at £14.95 jostle for space on the menu with *poulet breton* (£16.75).

For Italian cuisine in many guises, you'll be spoiled for choice. Combine your meal with a touch of history at the stylish Italian *Amarone* [55] (🖳 amaroneristorante.co.uk; Mon-Thur 5.30-10pm, Fri noon-2.30pm & 5.30-10pm, Sat noon-2.30pm), which occupies part of the house where Beau Nash lived and died, next to the theatre on Barton St. Pasta is £16-21, main dishes £18-25 and steak £32.

At the riverside *Ponte Vecchio* [48] (🖳 pontevecchiobath.com; Mon-Fri noon-3pm & 6-10pm, Sat & Sun noon-10pm) in a prime position overlooking the weir, next to The Rec, it's all about the setting. Dine inside or out in their wood and stainless-steel take on a traditional boathouse from an Italian menu with pizzas from £11.95 and pasta from £16.95.

Alternatively, make your way down to the grotto-like setting of *Sotto Sotto* [73] (🖳 sottosotto.co.uk; Tue-Sat noon-2pm & 5-10pm), on North Parade. Come for the (slightly noisy) atmosphere and for dishes such as *pollo e salsiccia* (chicken in white wine, £19.75) or *scamone de agnello* (rump of lamb with a pistachio crust, £31.50).

Near Pulteney Bridge there's more excellent Italian food at *Antica* [39] (🖳 anticabath.co.uk; daily noon-10pm), at 5 Argyle St. Good-value set lunches are £22/25 for 2/3 courses.

At 90 Walcot St, *The Walcot* [19] (🖳 walcothousebath.com; Sun-Thur 9-11pm & Fri/Sat 9am-3am), is a busy restaurant and bar open long hours. The menu includes half a dozen oysters for £20, whole grilled plaice with caper and lemon butter (£22) and a 600g bavette for two (£60) plus vegetarian options. In the same building is a table service cocktail bar *Bread & Jam*, and a dance club.

If you're just after a pizza, there's the aforementioned *Bath Pizza Co* [59] (see p179) or the unpretentious but popular *Real Italian Pizza Co* [69] (🖳 realitalianpizza.co.uk; daily 11am-11pm), on York St,

where busy chefs do wonders with a wood-fired pizza oven.

Tapas are on hand at *Olé Tapas* [33] (🖳 oletapas.co.uk; Mon-Fri noon-3 & 5-10pm, Sat noon-11pm, Sun noon-10pm), 1 John St, a buzzing little place with offerings of fish, chorizo, aubergine and more, at £6.95-16.95 per dish. And then there's Greek cuisine and meze dishes at *OPA* [74] (🖳 opabath.com; Mon-Sat noon-2am), on North Parade.

● **World cuisines**

There are several restaurants serving Indian cuisine and one of the more interesting is *Mantra Progressive Indian* [16] (🖳 mantraofbath.co.uk; daily noon-2.30pm & 5-10.30pm) at 5 Bladud Buildings, The Paragon. Dishes include delicious South Indian *dosas* (rice pancakes) and other dishes from around the subcontinent – Hyderabadi biriyanis, Goan fish dishes and Kashmiri lamb.

A must for the setting alone is *The Eastern Eye* [36] (☎ 01225-422323, 🖳 easterneye.com; daily noon-2.30pm & 6-11.30pm), 8a Quiet St, even if you're not a huge fan of Indian cuisine – though it's good. Occupying the first floor of a 19th-century building adorned with sculptures of 'Commerce' and 'Genius', it sits beneath a magnificent three-domed ceiling.

Rather less smart is the irresistibly named *Yak Yeti Yak* [78] (🖳 yakyetiyak.co.uk; Tue-Fri 5-10pm, Sat & Sun noon-2pm & 5-10pm), on Pierrepont St, run by a couple who know Nepal intimately. There are pork or vegetable filled momos, chicken with ginger and garlic, and saffron-infused yoghurt. It's reasonably-priced, authentic Nepalese cuisine.

Just a few steps up the road is the popular Thai restaurant *Salathai* [71] (🖳 salathai-bath.co.uk; daily noon-2pm & 6-9pm), where set menus cost from £24.95, or £22.95 for vegetarian.

There's also the tranquil setting of *Thai Balcony* [57] (☎ 01225-444450, 🖳 thaibalcony.co.uk; daily noon-2.30pm, & 6-10.30pm), at 1 Seven Dials above the Sainsbury's Local on Saw Close. It has been here since 1990 and is usually busy so reserving a table is recommended. The staff are friendly and it is a relaxing place to eat. The menu is extensive and includes *gaeng ped yang* (duck red curry) for £15.95 and a good selection of vegetarian dishes with *pad Thai jay* for £13.95.

Noya's Kitchen [91] (🖥 noyaskitchen .co.uk; Tue-Sat noon-3.30pm, plus Friday supper club from 7pm) is an excellent Vietnamese restaurant at 7 St James's Parade. The light authentic dishes include *pho*, delicious noodle soup (£15) and a good range of vegan and vegetarian choices.

For a reliable source of good, inexpensive food with plenty of noodles, you can't beat the relaxed *Wagamama* [15] (🖥 waga mama.com/restaurants/bath; daily 11am-10pm, Fri & Sat to 11pm) next to the Travelodge on the corner of George and Broad streets; it's great for vegetarians, too.

● **Vegetarian and fish** Vegetarians and vegans beat a path to *Oak Restaurant* [67] (🖥 oakrestaurant.co.uk; daily noon-2.30pm & 5.30-9.30pm), 2 North Parade Passage, close to the abbey, and go no further. Formerly the popular Acorn, it has gone up a notch: an Evening Five Course Feast is £49. It's probably better value to order dishes singly.

Simpler is *The Green Rocket Café* [72] (🖥 thegreenrocket.co.uk; Mon-Thur 9am-4.30pm, Fri-Sat 9am-9pm, Sun 9.30am-4.30pm), on the corner of North Parade & Pierrepont St. A regularly changing lunch and dinner menu is served from noon – sandwiches to noodles, burgers (a mushroom, sundried tomato & basil rice burger for £13.50), salads (tempeh Caesar salad for £13.50) and pasta. They also offer a takeaway service.

For top class fish dishes that are ethically-sourced, there's the *Scallop Shell* [30] (🖥 thescallopshell.co.uk; Mon-Sat noon-2.30pm, & 4.30-9.30pm, Sun noon-3pm), at 22 Monmouth Place. Main dishes are £15.95-£24. You'll usually have to book in advance to get a table.

● **Bars, pubs and pub grub** For the most part, opening hours quoted in this section relate to when **food** is served; almost all venues serve drinks outside these hours.

Just behind the theatre, the *Garrick's Head* [56] (🖥 garricksheadpub.com; daily noon-3.30pm & 5.30-9pm) retains the atmosphere of a pub, with a good bar menu and more. They even brew their own eponymous house ale. The building was the former home of Beau Nash.

Despite the onslaught of modernisation, plenty of pubs remain unscathed. For a quiet drink and well-prepared food, *Crystal Palace* [66] (🖥 crystalpalacepub .co.uk; Mon-Sat noon-9pm, Sun noon-8pm), on Abbey Green, is absolutely central; the walled garden behind is an added bonus for lunch in the summer months. Rather less peaceful is *The Pulteney Arms* [21] (🖥 thepulteneyarms.co.uk; Mon-Fri noon-2.30pm & 6-9pm, Sat noon-3pm & 6-9pm, Sun noon-3pm), on the corner of Daniel St and Sutton St. This is the 'rugby' pub, frequented by players and spectators, and heaving when Bath are playing just across the river at The Rec.

There's simple, no-nonsense fare at *The Raven* [35] (🖥 theravenofbath.co.uk; Mon-Sat 11am-9pm, Sun 11am-8.30pm), on Queen St, a no-frills, CAMRA award-winning pub which concentrates on pies – pork pies, steak pies, vegetarian pies, plus imaginative creations such as Heidi pies (goat's cheese) and Mooless Moo (jackfruit) pies – all £11.20 and washed down with real ale.

If you're after nothing more complicated than a good pint, you'll be spoiled for choice (hours given here are **pub hours**, not those for food). Claiming to be the smallest pub in Bath, the *Volunteer Rifleman's Arms* [44] (☎ 01225-425210; daily 11am-11pm) is centrally located on New Bond Street Place; they do serve food here, but for many it's all about the beer. Close by there's *The Old Green Tree* [43] (☎ 01225-448259; Mon-Sat noon-10.30pm, Sun to 4.30pm), Green St, then you could move on to *Salamander* [32] (🖥 salamanderbath.co.uk; Mon-Sat noon-9pm, Sun noon to 6pm), on John St, for a more Victorian atmosphere, or the CAMRA Pub of the Year 2022: the 16th-century *The Star Inn* [5] (☎ 01225-425072; noon-2.30pm &

5.30pm-midnight, Fri & Sat noon-1am, Sun noon-midnight), with its four small bars, where real ale is drawn straight from the barrel. They don't serve meals but filled rolls may be available. See box on p23 for more details of the beers.

You could round off the evening at *The Bell* [6] (⌨ thebellinnbath.co.uk; Mon-Tue 4-11pm, Wed-Sat 1-11pm, Sun noon-10.30pm) at 103 Walcot St. It's community-run and has live music three evenings a week – see the website for details – and pizza Wed-Fri 4-9pm and at weekends.

● **Teahouses and cafés** Walking the Cotswold Way throws up its fair share of trials, from steep hills to unpredictable rain and cold, when a cup of tea is rarely more welcome. Bath doesn't disappoint. Perhaps this is the time to treat yourself to afternoon tea at the *Pump Room* [65] (☎ 01225-444477, ⌨ romanbaths.co.uk/pump- room-restaurant; daily Mar-Dec 9.30am-5pm, Jan & Feb from 10am but note that they may close an hour or so earlier if there is a festival or special occasion), one of the great institutions of Bath. Built between 1795 and 1797, the Pump Room exudes the elegance of the era, with its grand chandeliers and classical music played by the Pump Room Trio. Although you can take morning coffee or lunch here, it's at teatime that it comes into its own. You don't have to have the full works of sandwiches, scones, cakes and pastries (£37.50pp) – but it's certainly tempting. Tables may be reserved during the week and for breakfast and lunch (noon-2.30pm) on Sunday, but not at other times; at busy periods expect to queue for 30-40 minutes. If you just want to marvel at the building, you can combine it with a visit to the Roman Baths (see p169).

Old-fashioned tea doesn't have to be quite so posh, though. The oldest house in Bath, at 4 North Parade Passage, dates back to around 1482 and houses *Sally Lunn's* [68] (☎ 01225-461634, ⌨ sallylunns.co.uk; daily 10am-9pm; dinner from 5pm, advance booking advised). This is the home of the Bath bun (see box on p178), which was created by Ms Lunn when she lived here in the 17th century.

Just round the corner (with another entrance on North Parade Passage), the name has been taken up at *The Bath Bun* [77] (⌨ thebathbun.com; Tue-Sat 9.30am-5pm, Sun & Mon 11am-5pm), where there is pretty china and the colourful cup cakes are very popular.

The Bridge Coffee Shop [47] is a small café and takeaway perfectly located by Pulteney Bridge overlooking the weir. It's open for breakfast, lunch and tea, closing around 5.30pm.

● **Cheap eats and fast food** It's not difficult to find some form of fast food among the many outlets around the city, not to mention the occasional 'greasy spoon' joint where you can get a standard fry up, and any number of sandwich bars.

One of the best proponents of the burger is *Schwartz Bros* (⌨ schwartzbros.co.uk), with a branch on **Saw Close** [54] (Sun-Tue noon-11pm, Wed & Thur to midnight, Fri & Sat to 1am) and another on **Walcot St** [7] Wed & Thur 5-10pm, Fri & Sat to midnight, Sun to 9pm).

For slow-churned top class ice-cream join the queue outside *Swoon Gelato* [62] (⌨ swoononaspoon.com; daily noon-9pm), at 15 Kingsmead Sq.

APPENDIX A: GPS & WHAT3WORDS WAYPOINT REFERENCES

Each waypoint below was taken on the route at the reference number marked on the map as below. **GPS references** are given below. **What3words references** that correspond to these waypoints are also shown here and may be particularly useful in an emergency (see p57). Gpx files for waypoints can be downloaded from ⬜ trailblazer-guides.com.

MAP	WAYPT	MAP REFERENCE	DESCRIPTION	WHAT3WORDS
1	001	N52° 03.018' W01° 46.913'	start of Cotswold Way, Chipping Campden	boggles.skim.hindered
1	002	N52° 03.525' W01° 47.752'	kissing gate on Dover's Hill	udder.sport.commander
2	003	N52° 01.862' W01° 49.687'	toposcope – Fish Hill	diets.tend.notebook
3	004	N52° 01.458' W01° 50.165'	Broadway Tower	marble.goal.galloped
3	005	N52° 02.197' W01° 51.172'	junction of road, Broadway	templates.doghouse.code
3	006	N52° 01.678' W01° 52.427'	guidepost, Broadway Coppice	text.resort.partly
4	007	N52° 00.332' W01° 52.842'	cattle grid – Shenberrow	sometime.swatting.dabble
4	008	N52° 00.003' W01° 53.040'	Shenberrow Hill	bogus.spring.sounds
5	009	N52° 00.403' W01° 54.146'	corner of road by The Vine, Stanton	suppose.became.strictest
5	010	N51° 59.377' W01° 54.748'	gate to Stanway House	rags.scenes.icon
6	011	N51° 58.322' W01° 53.473'	Stumps Cross	vies.mows.pounding
6	012	N51° 58.070' W01° 54.563'	monument – Beckbury Camp	letter.thuds.should
7	013	N51° 58.157' W01° 55.655'	leave road by Hailes Abbey	falters.refer.fever
8	014	N51° 57.218' W01° 57.825'	corner of North St, Winchcombe	reporter.whistle.directors
9	015	N51° 55.690' W01° 58.255'	kissing gate by Belas Knap	profited.readers.trials
10	016	N51° 56.542' W02° 01.018'	Cleeve Hill car park	villager.crucially.clean
10	017	N51° 56.160' W02° 01.328'	Cleeve Hill toposcope	zinc.circle.vans
11	018	N51° 55.600' W02° 01.325'	Cleeve Hill fort, marking track by path junction to Southam	suitcase.exhale.accented
13	019	N51° 52.606' W02° 01.227'	bridge over spill by Dowdeswell Reservoir	jumpy.jars.thing
14	020	N51° 51.827' W02° 02.207'	guidepost, Wistley Hill	twisty.alleyway.prepared
14	021	N51° 51.193' W02° 02.865'	junction with Hartley Lane, Seven Springs	giggle.sprinkler.vowel
15	022	N51° 51.822' W02° 04.550'	Leckhampton Hill trig point	tape.outbound.reclined
15	023	N51° 50.987' W02° 04.925'	track meets road	hatch.president.unpacked
16	024	N51° 50.598' W02° 05.783'	A417 crossing (roadworks here until 2027)	inert.arrives.cones
16	025	N51° 50.073' W02° 06.893'	The Peak	snoozing.awkward.bulbs

MAP	WAYPT	MAP REFERENCE		DESCRIPTION	WHAT3WORDS
18	026	N51° 49.922'	W02° 09.312'	Cooper's Hill	octagonal.advances.stiff
19	027	N51° 48.358'	W02° 11.518'	steps to trig point, Painswick Hill	drill.congratulations.relay
20	028	N51° 47.205'	W02° 11.592'	junction with A46, Painswick	daring.playful.mows
20	029	N51° 46.808'	W02° 13.120'	The Edgemoor Inn	quietly.boggles.mistaking
21	030	N51° 47.008'	W02° 14.685'	Way leaves road by disused well (Cliff Wood)	slimming.pixel.typhoon
21	031	N51° 46.697'	W02° 15.745'	Haresfield Beacon	snatched.skate.worms
22	032	N51° 45.325'	W02° 15.522'	gate on Maiden Hill	rewarding.urge.scavenger
23	033	N51° 44.395'	W02° 15.192'	Oil Mills Bridge	stalemate.dragonfly.exposing
25	034	N51° 42.702'	W02° 18.037'	Nympsfield display boards	stoops.skins.vessel
26	035	N51° 41.908'	W02° 18.355'	Uley Long Barrow (Hetty Pegler's Tump)	walkway.snippets.scan
26	036	N51° 41.527'	W02° 18.610'	Uley Bury	snipe.unusually.shepherdess
27	037	N51° 41.617'	W02° 19.482'	Cam Long Down	masterpiece.vision.canoe
28	038	N51° 40.818'	W02° 22.037'	routes divide by Stinchcombe Hill Golf Club	edgy.adventure.defender
28	039	N51° 40.803'	W02° 22.938'	Drakestone Point (scenic route)	blatantly.chained.hides
28	040	N51° 40.725'	W02° 22.247'	convergence of paths, Stinchcombe Hill	stealthier.pokers.fussy
29	041	N51° 39.528'	W02° 22.353'	Tyndale Monument	reviews.primary.increases
29	042	N51° 38.492'	W02° 21.555'	hilltop monument above Wotton-under-Edge	fixtures.redeemed.treaty
30	043	N51° 38.347'	W02° 19.310'	Tor Hill & Alderley signpost	cards.driftwood.kebabs
31	044	N51° 37.033'	W02° 19.995'	Wotton-under-Edge 5-mile sign, Alderley	buckling.kitten.frosted
32	045	N51° 35.975'	W02° 18.482'	track meets road	grows.ranged.bind
33	046	N51° 35.220'	W02° 19.780'	monument to General Lord Somerset	jolly.forwarded.crawled
34	047	N51° 33.663'	W02° 20.453'	wood near Horton Court	woof.rate.clasping
35	048	N51° 32.070'	W02° 21.275'	St John the Baptist, Old Sodbury	bronzer.convinced.dean
35	049	N51° 30.906'	W02° 21.032'	lone oak, Dodington Park	boots.eating.likely
36	050	N51° 30.427'	W02° 20.087'	Tormarton bus stop	movie.split.frosted
38	051	N51° 28.200'	W02° 22.735'	kissing gate above withy bed	shows.wedge.scale
39	052	N51° 27.182'	W02° 21.584'	Cold Ashton church	shadows.bogus.lakes
40	053	N51° 25.875'	W02° 23.392'	kissing gate at top of hill	titles.firepower.woodstove
41	054	N51° 25.787'	W02° 24.892'	Hanging Hill	gurgling.speedily.limbs
41	055	N51° 25.405'	W02° 24.317'	turn by Lansdown Golf Course	think.ounce.slimming
42	056	N51° 24.782'	W02° 24.832'	Prospect Stile	fact.unwound.chained
42	057	N51° 23.720'	W02° 24.062'	Weston trig point	stones.aware.income
43	058	N51° 22.883'	W02° 21.563'	Bath Abbey (end/start of Cotswold Way)	shock.gossip.smart

APPENDIX B – WALKING WITH A DOG

WALKING THE COTSWOLD WAY WITH A DOG

Many are the rewards that await those prepared to make the extra effort required to bring their best friend along the Cotswold Way. You shouldn't underestimate the amount of work involved, though. Indeed, just about every decision you make will be influenced by the fact that you've got a dog: how you plan to travel to the start of the trail, where you're going to stay, how far you're going to walk each day, where you're going to rest and where you're going to eat in the evening etc.

If you're also sure your dog can cope with (and will enjoy) walking, say, 10-14 miles or more a day for several days in a row, you need to start preparing accordingly. Extra thought also needs to go into your itinerary. The best starting point is to study the village and town facilities table on pp34-7 (and the advice below), and plan where to stop and where to buy food.

Looking after your dog

To begin with, you need to make sure that your own dog is fully **inoculated** against the usual doggy illnesses, and also up to date with regard to **worm pills** (eg Drontal) and **flea preventatives** such as Frontline – they are, after all, following in the pawprints of many a dog before them, some of whom may well have left fleas or other parasites on the trail that now lie in wait for their next meal to arrive. **Pet insurance** is also a very good idea; if you've already got insurance, do check that it will cover a trip such as this.

On the subject of looking after your dog's health, perhaps the most important implement you can take with you is a **plastic tick remover**, available from vets for a couple of quid. These removers, while fiddly, help you to remove ticks safely (ie without leaving the head behind buried under the dog's skin).

Being in unfamiliar territory also makes it more likely that you and your dog could become separated. All dogs now have to be microchipped but make sure yours also has a tag with your contact details on it (a mobile phone number would be best if you have one).

When to keep your dog on a lead

● **On the edge of the escarpment** It's a sad fact that, every year, a few dogs lose their lives falling over the edge of steep slopes.

● **When crossing farmland** This is particularly important in the lambing season (around February to May) when your dog can scare the sheep, causing them to lose their young. During this time, most farmers would prefer it if you didn't bring your dog at all. Farmers are allowed by law to shoot at and kill any dogs that they consider are worrying their sheep. Dogs running free in standing crops can also cause damage, so do take care to prevent this. The exception to the 'dogs on leads' rule is if your dog is being attacked by cows. A few years ago there were three deaths in the UK caused by walkers being trampled as they tried to rescue their dogs from the attentions of cattle. The advice in this instance is to let go of the lead, head speedily to a position of safety (usually the other side of the field gate or stile) and call your dog to you.

● **Around ground-nesting birds** It's important to keep your dog under control when crossing an area inhabited by ground-nesting birds, which are usually active between March and June; a dog on the loose at this time could inadvertently destroy the nest, or frighten the adult birds away. Most dogs love foraging around in the woods but make sure you have permission to do so; some woods are used as 'nurseries' for game birds and dogs are only allowed through them if they are on a lead.

● **By roads etc** For obvious reasons.

What to pack

You've probably already got a good idea of what to bring to keep your dog alive and happy, but the following is a checklist:

● **Food/water bowl** Foldable cloth bowls are popular with walkers, being light and taking up little room in a rucksack. You can get also get a water-bottle-and-bowl combination, where the bottle folds into a 'trough' from which the dog can drink.

● **Lead and collar** An extendable one is probably preferable for this sort of trip. Make sure both lead and collar are in good condition – you don't want either to snap on the trail, or you may end up carrying your dog through sheep fields until a replacement can be found.

● **Medication** You'll know if you need to bring any lotions or potions.

● **Bedding** A simple blanket may suffice, or you can opt for something more elaborate if you aren't carrying your own luggage.

● **Poo bags** Essential.

● **Hygiene wipes** For cleaning your dog after it's rolled in, errm, stuff.

● **A favourite toy** Helps prevent your dog from pining for the entire walk.

● **Food/water** Remember to bring treats as well as regular food to keep up the mutt's morale. That said, if your dog is anything like mine the chances are they'll spend most of the walk dining on rabbit droppings and sheep poo anyway.

● **Corkscrew stake** Available from camping or pet shops, this will help you to keep your dog secure in one place while you set up camp/doze.

● **Tick remover** See p185.   ● **Raingear** It can rain!   ● **Old towels** For drying your dog.

When it comes to packing, I always leave an exterior pocket of my rucksack empty so I can put used poo bags in there (for deposit at the first bin I come to). I always like to keep all the dog's kit together and separate from the other luggage (usually inside a plastic bag inside my rucksack). I have also seen several dogs sporting their own 'doggy rucksack', so they can carry their own food, water, poo etc – which certainly reduces the burden on their owner!

Cleaning up after your dog

It is extremely important that dog owners behave in a responsible way when walking the path. Dog excrement should be cleaned up. In towns, villages and fields where animals graze or which will be cut for silage, hay etc, you need to pick up and bag the excrement.

Staying with your dog

In this guide we have used the symbol 🐕 to denote where a hotel, pub, B&B or campsite allows dogs to stay, although this always needs to be arranged in advance; many places have only one or two rooms that they deem suitable, and in some dogs need to sleep in a separate building. Some places make an additional charge (usually per night but occasionally per stay), while others may require a deposit, which is refundable if the dog doesn't make a mess. Hostels (both YHA and independent) do not permit dogs unless they are an assistance (guide) dog.

When it comes to **eating**, most landlords allow dogs in at least a section of their pubs, though very few restaurants do. Make sure you always ask first, then ensure that your dog doesn't run around the pub but is secured to your table or a radiator.

Henry Stedman

INDEX

Page references in **red** type refer to maps

Map key

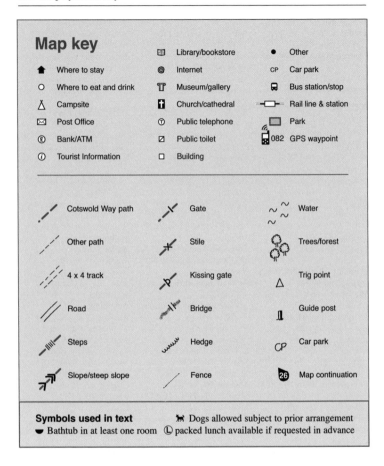

♠ Where to stay	📖 Library/bookstore	● Other
○ Where to eat and drink	@ Internet	CP Car park
⚠ Campsite	🏛 Museum/gallery	🚌 Bus station/stop
⊠ Post Office	🏛 Church/cathedral	Rail line & station
ⓔ Bank/ATM	☏ Public telephone	Park
ⓘ Tourist Information	☑ Public toilet	082 GPS waypoint
	□ Building	

Cotswold Way path	Gate	Water
Other path	Stile	Trees/forest
4 x 4 track	Kissing gate	Trig point
Road	Bridge	Guide post
Steps	Hedge	CP Car park
Slope/steep slope	Fence	26 Map continuation

Symbols used in text   🐕 Dogs allowed subject to prior arrangement
🛁 Bathtub in at least one room   Ⓛ packed lunch available if requested in advance

Kilimanjaro – the trekking guide Henry Stedman, 6th edn, £16.99
ISBN 978-1-912716-48-7, 368pp, 40 maps, 50 colour photos

At 5895m (19,340ft) Kilimanjaro is the world's tallest freestanding mountain and one of the most popular destinations for hikers visiting Africa. Route guides & maps – the 6 major routes. City guides – Nairobi, Dar-es-Salaam, Arusha, Moshi & Marangu.

Peru's Cordilleras Blanca & Huayhuash
The Hiking & Biking Guide Neil & Harriet Pike, 2nd edn, £17.99
ISBN 978-1-912716-17-3, 242pp, 50 maps, 40 colour photos

This region, in northern Peru, boasts some of the most spectacular scenery in the Andes, and most accessible high mountain trekking and biking in the world. This practical guide contains 60 detailed route maps and descriptions covering 20 hiking trails and more than 30 days of paved and dirt road cycling.

Tour du Mont Blanc Jim Manthorpe, 3rd edn, £16.99
ISBN 978-1-912716-15-9, 256pp, 60 maps, 50 colour photos

At 4807m (15,771ft), Mont Blanc is the highest mountain in western Europe. The trail (105 miles, 168km) that circumnavigates the massif, passing through France, Italy and Switzerland, is the most popular long-distance walk in Europe. Includes day walks. Plus – Climbing guide to Mont Blanc

Moroccan Atlas – the trekking guide
Alan Palmer, 2nd edn, £14.99
ISBN 978-1-905864-59-1, 420pp, 86 maps, 40 colour photos

The High Atlas in central Morocco is the most dramatic and beautiful section of the entire Atlas range. Towering peaks, deep gorges and huddled Berber villages enchant all who visit. With 73 detailed maps, 13 town and village guides including Marrakech.

Iceland Hiking with Reykjavik city guide
Jim Manthorpe, 1st edn, £15.99
ISBN 978-1-912716-15-1, 204pp, 41maps, 50 colour photos

Iceland offers a world of hiking opportunities like no other place on earth. The famous 55km Laugavegur trek takes you past glaciers, volcanoes, steaming fumaroles and hot springs all set in a landscape of yellow rhyolite and black ash. This guide gives you plenty of other options from hiking below the largest ice-cap in Europe at Skaftafell, to Reykjavik day hikes.

The Inca Trail, Cusco & Machu Picchu
Alex Stewart & Henry Stedman, 6th edn, £14.99
ISBN 978-1-905864-88-1, 370pp, 70 maps, 30 colour photos

The Inca Trail from Cusco to Machu Picchu is South America's most popular trek. This guide includes hiking options from two days to three weeks. Plus plans of Inca sites, guides to Lima, Cusco and Machu Picchu. Includes the High Inca Trail, Salkantay Trek and the Choquequirao Trail. Plus two Sacred Valley treks: Lares Trail and Ausangate Circuit.

Trekking in the Everest Region Jamie McGuinness 6th edn, £15.99
ISBN 978-1-905864-81-2, 320pp, 95 maps, 30 colour photos

Sixth edition of this popular guide to the world's most famous trekking region. Covers not only the classic treks but also the wild routes. Written by a Nepal-based trek and mountaineering leader. Includes: 27 detailed route maps and 52 village plans. Plus: Kathmandu city guide

TRAILBLAZER'S BRITISH WALKING GUIDES

We've applied to destinations which are closer to home Trailblazer's proven formula for publishing definitive practical route guides for adventurous travellers. Britain's network of long-distance trails enables the walker to explore some of the finest landscapes in the country's best walking areas. These are guides that are user-friendly, practical, informative and environmentally sensitive.

● **Unique mapping features** In many walking guidebooks the reader has to read a route description then try to relate it to the map. Our guides are much easier to use because walking directions, tricky junctions, places to stay and eat, points of interest and walking times are all written onto the maps themselves in the places to which they apply. With their uncluttered clarity, these are not general-purpose maps but fully edited maps drawn by walkers for walkers.

'The same attention to detail that distinguishes its other guides has been brought to bear here'.

THE
SUNDAY TIMES

● **Largest-scale walking maps** At a scale of just under 1:20,000 (8cm or 3¹/₈ inches to one mile) the maps in these guides are bigger than even the most detailed British walking maps currently available in the shops.

● **Not just a trail guide – includes where to stay, where to eat and public transport** Our guidebooks cover the complete walking experience, not just the route. Accommodation options for all budgets are provided (pubs, hotels, B&Bs, campsites, bunkhouses, hostels) as well as places to eat. Detailed public transport information for all access points to each trail means that there are itineraries for all walkers, for hiking the entire route as well as for day or weekend walks.

Cleveland Way *Henry Stedman*, 1st edn, ISBN 978-1-905864-91-1, 240pp, 98 maps

Coast to Coast *Henry Stedman*, 10th edn, ISBN 978-1-912716-25-8, 268pp, 109 maps

Cornwall Coast Path (SW Coast Path Pt 2) *Stedman & Newton*, 7th edn,
ISBN 978-1-912716-26-5, 352pp, 142 maps

Cotswold Way *Tricia & Bob Hayne,* 5th edn, ISBN 978-1-912716-41-8, 204pp, 53 maps

Dales Way *Henry Stedman*, 2nd edn, ISBN 978-1-912716-30-2, 192pp, 50 maps

Dorset & South Devon (SW Coast Path Pt 3) *Stedman & Newton*, 3rd edn,
ISBN 978-1-912716-34-0, 340pp, 97 maps

Exmoor & North Devon (SW Coast Path Pt I) *Stedman & Newton*, 3rd edn,
ISBN 978-1-9912716-24-1, 224pp, 68 maps

Glyndŵr's Way *Chris Scott,* 1st edn, ISBN 978-1-912716-32-6, 220pp, 70 maps **(Feb 2024)**

Great Glen Way *Jim Manthorpe,* 2nd edn, ISBN 978-1-912716-10-4, 184pp, 50 maps

Hadrian's Wall Path *Henry Stedman*, 7th edn, ISBN 978-1-912716-37-1, 250pp, 60 maps

London LOOP *Henry Stedman,* 1st edn, ISBN 978-1-912716-21-0, 236pp, 60 maps

Norfolk Coast Path & Peddars Way *Alexander Stewart*, 2nd edn,
ISBN 978-1-912716-39-5, 224pp, 75 maps

North Downs Way *Henry Stedman*, 2nd edn, ISBN 978-1-905864-90-4, 240pp, 98 maps

Offa's Dyke Path *Keith Carter*, 6th edn, ISBN 978-1-912716-42-5, 268pp, 98 maps

Pembrokeshire Coast Path *Jim Manthorpe*, 6th edn, 978-1-912716-13-5, 236pp, 96 maps

Pennine Way *Stuart Greig*, 6th edn, ISBN 978-1-912716-33-3, 272pp, 138 maps

The Ridgeway *Nick Hill*, 5th edn, ISBN 978-1-912716-20-3, 208pp, 53 maps

South Downs Way *Jim Manthorpe*, 8th edn, ISBN 978-1-912716-47-0, 204pp, 60 maps

Thames Path *Joel Newton*, 3rd edn, ISBN 978-1-912716-27-2, 256pp, 99 maps

West Highland Way *Charlie Loram*, 8th edn, ISBN 978-1-912716-29-6, 224pp, 60 maps

'The Trailblazer series stands head, shoulders, waist and ankles above the rest.
They are particularly strong on mapping ...'
THE SUNDAY TIMES

TRAILBLAZER
British Walking Guides
SEE p196 FOR FULL TITLE LIST

Orkney

Thurso

Stornoway

Skye

Scottish Highlands Hillwalking Guide

Inverness

Great Glen Way

Aberdeen

Fort William

SCOTLAND

Mull

West Highland Way

Arran

Milngavie

Glasgow

Edinburgh

Berwick upon Tweed

Kirk Yetholm

Pennine Way

N. IRELAND

Belfast

Bowness-on-Solway

Carlisle

Wallsend

Newcastle upon Tyne

Hadrian's Wall Path

Coast to Coast

St Bees

Bowness-on-Windermere

Robin Hood's Bay

Filey

REP. OF IRELAND

Isle of Man

Dales Way

Helmsley

Cleveland Way

Dublin

Ilkley

York

Pennine Way

Leeds

Hull

Liverpool

Manchester

Prestatyn

Edale

Bangor

Anglesey

Offa's Dyke Path

Lincoln

Nottingham

ENGLAND

Glyndŵr's Way

Welshpool

Knighton

Birmingham

Knettishall Heath

Norfolk Coast Path & Peddars Way

Cromer

Norwich

Great Yarmouth

Cardigan

WALES

Cotswold Way

Chipping Campden

The Ridgeway

Ivinghoe Beacon

London LOOP

Pembrokeshire Coast Path

Amroth

Kemble

London

Thames Path

Chepstow

Cardiff

Bristol

Bath

Overton Hill

Canterbury

Exmoor & N Devon Coast Path

Minehead

Winchester

Salisbury

Farnham

Dover

North Downs Way

Bude

Exeter

Poole

Portsmouth

Brighton

Eastbourne

South Downs Way

Cornwall Coast Path

Plymouth

Dorset & S Devon Coast Path

Isle of Wight

Isles of Scilly

ENGLISH CHANNEL

IRISH SEA

| 0 | 50 | 100km |
| 0 | 25 | 50 miles |

	Chipping Campden	Broadway	Stanton	Wood Stanway	Hailes	Winchcombe	Cleeve Hill	Dowdeswell Reservoir	Seven Springs	Crickley Hill	Birdlip
Broadway	6										
	9.5										
Stanton	10.5	4.5									
	17	*7.5*									
Wood Stanway	12.5	6.5	2								
	20	*10.5*	*3*								
Hailes	16	10	5.5	3.5							
	25.5	*16*	*8.5*	*5.5*							
Winchcombe	18	12	7.5	5.5	2						
	29	*19.5*	*12*	*9*	*3.5*						
Cleeve Hill	24	18	13.5	11.5	8	6					
	38.5	*29*	*21.5*	*18.5*	*13*	*9.5*					
Dowdeswell Res'voir	29	23	18.5	16.5	13	11	5				
	46.5	*37*	*29.5*	*26.5*	*21*	*17.5*	*8*				
Seven Springs	32	26	21.5	19.5	16	14	8	3			
	51	*41.5*	*34*	*31*	*25.5*	*22*	*12.5*	*4.5*			
Crickley Hill	37	31	26.5	24.5	21	19	13	8	5		
	59	*49.5*	*42*	*39*	*33.5*	*30*	*20.5*	*12.5*	*8*		
Birdlip	39.5	33.5	29	27	23.5	21.5	15.5	10.5	7.5	2.5	
	63	*53.5*	*46*	*43*	*37.5*	*34*	*24.5*	*16.5*	*12*	*4*	
Cranham Cnr	43.5	37.5	33	31	27.5	25.5	19.5	14.5	11.5	6.5	4
	69.5	*60*	*52.5*	*49.5*	*44*	*40.5*	*31*	*23*	*18.5*	*10.5*	*6.5*
Painswick	46	40	35.5	33.5	30	28	22	17	14	9	6.5
	73.5	*64*	*56.5*	*53.5*	*48*	*44.5*	*35*	*27*	*22.5*	*14.5*	*10.5*
Stonehouse	54.5	48.5	44	42	38.5	36.5	30.5	25.5	22.5	17.5	15
	87	*77.5*	*70*	*67*	*61.5*	*58*	*48.5*	*40.5*	*36*	*28*	*24*
Selsley Common	56	50	45.5	43.5	40	38	32	27	24	19	16.5
	89.5	*80*	*72.5*	*69.5*	*64*	*60.5*	*51*	*43*	*38.5*	*30.5*	*26.5*
Dursley	63.5	57.5	53	51	47.5	45.5	39.5	34.5	31.5	26.5	24
	101.5	*92*	*84.5*	*81.5*	*76*	*72.5*	*63*	*55*	*50.5*	*42.5*	*38.5*
North Nibley	68.5	62.5	58	56	52.5	50.5	44.5	39.5	36.5	31.5	29
	109.5	*100*	*92.5*	*89.5*	*84*	*80.5*	*71*	*63*	*58.5*	*50.5*	*46.5*
Wotton-u-Edge	70.5	64.5	60	58	54.5	52.5	46.5	41.5	38.5	33.5	31
	113	*103.5*	*96*	*93*	*87.5*	*84*	*74.5*	*66.5*	*62*	*54*	*50*
Hawkesbury Upton	78	72	67.5	65.5	62	60	54	49	46	41	38.5
	125	*115.5*	*108*	*105*	*99.5*	*96*	*86.5*	*78.5*	*74*	*66*	*62*
Little Sodbury	81.5	75.5	71	69	65.5	63.5	57.5	52.5	49.5	44.5	42
	130.5	*121*	*113.5*	*110.5*	*105*	*101.5*	*92*	*84*	*79.5*	*71.5*	*67.5*
Old Sodbury	83.5	77.5	73	71	67.5	65.5	59.5	54.5	51.5	46.5	44
	133.5	*124*	*116.5*	*113.5*	*108*	*104.5*	*95*	*87*	*82.5*	*74.5*	*70.5*
Coomb's End	84	78	73.5	71.5	68	66	60	55	52	47	44.5
	134.5	*125*	*117.5*	*114.5*	*109*	*105.5*	*96*	*88*	*83.5*	*75.5*	*71.5*
Tormarton	85.5	79.5	75	73	69.5	67.5	61.5	56.5	53.5	48.5	46
	137	*127.5*	*120*	*117*	*111.5*	*108*	*98.5*	*90.5*	*86*	*78*	*74*
Pennsylvania	91.5	85.5	81	79	75.5	73.5	67.5	62.5	59.5	54.5	52
	146.5	*137*	*129.5*	*126.5*	*121*	*117.5*	*108*	*100*	*95.5*	*87.5*	*83.5*
Cold Ashton	92	86	81.5	79.5	76	74	68	63	60	55	52.5
	147	*137.5*	*130*	*127*	*121.5*	*118*	*108.5*	*100.5*	*96*	*88*	*84*
Bath	102	96	91.5	89.5	86	84	78	73	70	65	62.5
	163	*153.5*	*146*	*143*	*137.5*	*134*	*124.5*	*116.5*	*112*	*104*	*100*

Cotswold Way
DISTANCE CHART

(route via Selsley Common and Stinchcombe Hill)

miles/*kilometres* (approx)

	Cranham Corner	Painswick	Stonehouse	Selsley Common	Dursley	North Nibley	Wotton-under-Edge	Hawkesbury Upton	Little Sodbury	Old Sodbury	Coomb's End	Tormarton	Pennsylvania	Cold Ashton	Bath
Painswick	2.5														
	4														
Stonehouse	11	8.5													
	17.5	*13.5*													
Selsley Common	12.5	10	1.5												
	20	*16*	*2.5*												
Dursley	20	17.5	9	7.5											
	32	*28*	*14.5*	*12*											
North Nibley	25	22.5	14	12.5	5										
	40	*36*	*22.5*	*20*	*8*										
Wotton-under-Edge	27	24.5	16	14.5	7	2									
	43.5	*39.5*	*26*	*23.5*	*11.5*	*3.5*									
Hawkesbury Upton	34.5	32	23.5	22	14.5	9.5	7.5								
	55.5	*51.5*	*38*	*35.5*	*23.5*	*15.5*	*12*								
Little Sodbury	38	35.5	27	25.5	18	13	11	3.5							
	61	*57*	*43.5*	*41*	*29*	*21*	*17.5*	*5.5*							
Old Sodbury	40	37.5	29	27.5	20	15	13	5.5	2						
	64	*60*	*46.5*	*44*	*32*	*24*	*20.5*	*8.5*	*3*						
Coomb's End	40.5	38	29.5	28	20.5	15.5	13.5	6	2.5	0.5					
	65	*61*	*47.5*	*45*	*33*	*25*	*21.5*	*9.5*	*4*	*1*					
Tormarton	42	39.5	31	29.5	22	17	15	7.5	4	2	1.5				
	67.5	*63.5*	*50*	*47.5*	*35.5*	*27.5*	*24*	*12*	*6.5*	*3.5*	*2.5*				
Pennsylvania	48	45.5	37	35.5	28	23	21	13.5	10	8	7.5	6			
	77	*73*	*59.5*	*57*	*45*	*37*	*33.5*	*21.5*	*16*	*13*	*12*	*9.5*			
Cold Ashton	48.8	46	37.5	36	28.5	23.5	21.5	14	10.5	8.5	8	6.5	0.5		
	77.5	*73.5*	*60*	*57.5*	*45.5*	*37.5*	*34*	*22*	*16.5*	*13.5*	*12.5*	*10*	*0.5*		
Bath	58.5	56	47.5	46	38.5	33.5	31.5	24	20.5	18.5	18	16.5	10.5	10	
	93.5	*89.5*	*76*	*73.5*	*61.5*	*53.5*	*50*	*38*	*32.5*	*29.5*	*28.5*	*26*	*16.5*	*16*	

TRAILBLAZER TITLE LIST

Adventure Cycle-Touring Handbook
Adventure Motorcycling Handbook
Australia by Rail
Cleveland Way (British Walking Guide)
Coast to Coast (British Walking Guide)
Cornwall Coast Path (British Walking Guide)
Cotswold Way (British Walking Guide)
The Cyclist's Anthology
Dales Way (British Walking Guide)
Dorset & Sth Devon Coast Path (British Walking Gde)
Exmoor & Nth Devon Coast Path (British Walking Gde)
Glyndŵr's Way (British Walking Guide)
Great Glen Way (British Walking Guide)
Hadrian's Wall Path (British Walking Guide)
Himalaya by Bike – a route and planning guide
Iceland Hiking – with Reykjavik City Guide
Inca Trail, Cusco & Machu Picchu
Japan by Rail
Kilimanjaro – the trekking guide (includes Mt Meru)
London Loop (British Walking Guide)
London to Walsingham Camino
Madeira Walks – 37 selected day walks
Moroccan Atlas – The Trekking Guide
Morocco Overland (4x4/motorcycle/mountainbike)
Nepal Trekking & The Great Himalaya Trail
Norfolk Coast Path & Peddars Way (British Walking Gde)
North Downs Way (British Walking Guide)
Offa's Dyke Path (British Walking Guide)
Overlanders' Handbook – worldwide driving guide
Pembrokeshire Coast Path (British Walking Guide)
Pennine Way (British Walking Guide)
Peru's Cordilleras Blanca & Huayhuash – Hiking/Biking
Pilgrim Pathways: 1-2 day walks on Britain's sacred ways
The Railway Anthology
The Ridgeway (British Walking Guide)
Scottish Highlands – Hillwalking Guide
The Silk Roads – a route and planning guide
Sinai – the trekking guide
South Downs Way (British Walking Guide)
Thames Path (British Walking Guide)
Tour du Mont Blanc
Trans-Canada Rail Guide
Trans-Siberian Handbook
Trekking in the Everest Region
The Walker's Anthology
The Walker's Anthology – further tales
West Highland Way (British Walking Guide)

For more information about Trailblazer and our
expanding range of guides, for guidebook updates or
for credit card mail order sales visit our website:

trailblazer-guides.com

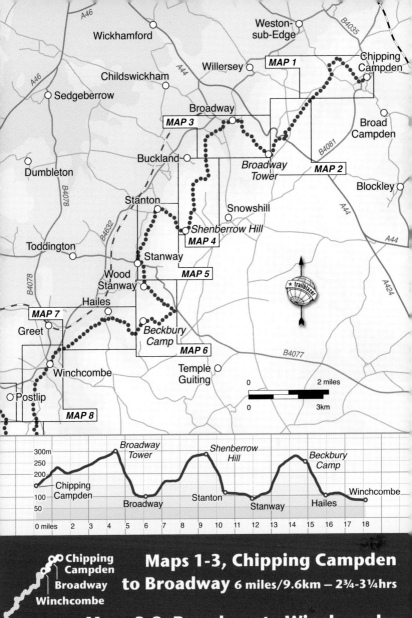

Maps 1-3, Chipping Campden to Broadway 6 miles/9.6km – 2¾-3¼hrs

Maps 3-8, Broadway to Winchcombe 12 miles/19.6km – 5½-6½hrs

NOTE: Add 20-30% to these times to allow for stops

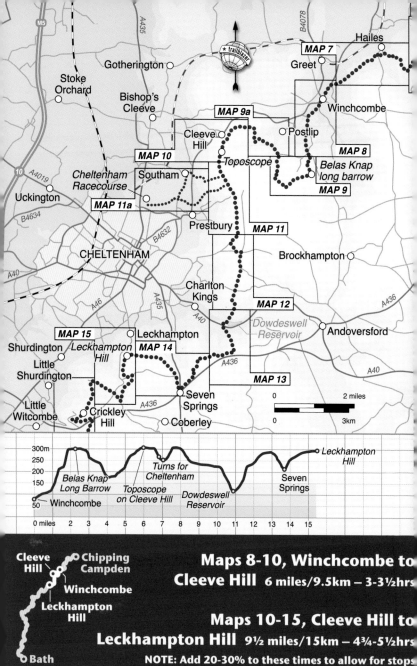

M5

A435

B4078

★ trailblazer

Hailes

MAP 7

Greet

Gotherington

Stoke
Orchard

Bishop's
Cleeve

Winchcombe

Postlip

MAP 9a

MAP 8

Cleeve
Hill

Belas Knap
long barrow

MAP 10

Toposcope

MAP 9

A4019

Cheltenham
Racecourse

Southam

10

A4019

Uckington

MAP 11a

B4634

B4632

Prestbury

MAP 11

Brockhampton

CHELTENHAM

A40

A46

A435

Charlton
Kings

A436

A40

MAP 12

*Dowdeswell
Reservoir*

Andoversford

A436

A40

MAP 15

Leckhampton

MAP 14

Shurdington

*Leckhampton
Hill*

Little
Shurdington

MAP 13

Seven
Springs

0   2 miles

Little
Witcombe

Crickley
Hill

A436

Coberley

0   3km

300m
250
200
150
50

*Belas Knap
Long Barrow*

Winchcombe

*Turns for
Cheltenham*

*Toposcope
on Cleeve Hill*

*Dowdeswell
Reservoir*

Seven
Springs

Leckhampton
Hill

0 miles   2   3   4   5   6   7   8   9   10   11   12   13   14   15

Cleeve
Hill

Chipping
Campden

Winchcombe

Leckhampton
Hill

Bath

**Maps 8-10, Winchcombe to
Cleeve Hill** 6 miles/9.5km – 3-3½hrs

**Maps 10-15, Cleeve Hill to
Leckhampton Hill** 9½ miles/15km – 4¾-5½hrs

NOTE: Add 20-30% to these times to allow for stops

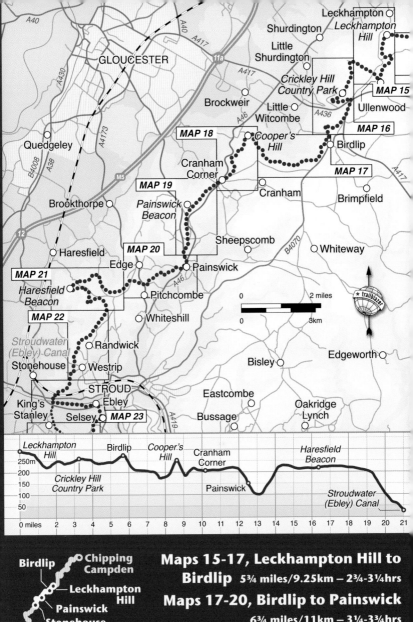

Maps 15-17, Leckhampton Hill to Birdlip 5¾ miles/9.25km – 2¾-3¼hrs

Maps 17-20, Birdlip to Painswick 6¾ miles/11km – 3¼-3¾hrs

Maps 20-23, Painswick to Stonehouse (canal) 9 miles/14.6km – 4¼-5hrs

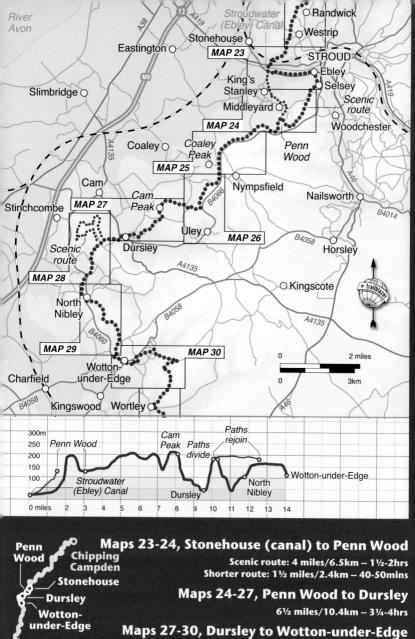

River Avon

Randwick

Westrip

Eastington

Stonehouse

MAP 23

STROUD

Stroudwater (Ebley) Canal

Slimbridge

Ebley

Selsey

King's Stanley

Middleyard

MAP 24

Scenic route

Woodchester

Penn Wood

Coaley

Coaley Peak

MAP 25

Nympsfield

Nailsworth

Cam

Cam Peak

MAP 27

B4066

Stinchcombe

Uley

MAP 26

Horsley

Dursley

B4058

Scenic route

A4135

Kingscote

MAP 28

A4135

North Nibley

B4058

MAP 29

MAP 30

Charfield

Wotton-under-Edge

Kingswood

Wortley

0   2 miles

0   3km

Elevation profile

300m
250
200
150
100

Penn Wood

Stroudwater (Ebley) Canal

Cam Peak

Paths divide

Paths rejoin

Dursley

North Nibley

Wotton-under-Edge

0 miles   2   3   4   5   6   7   8   9   10   11   12   13   14

Penn Wood

Chipping Campden

Stonehouse

Dursley

Wotton-under-Edge

Bath

Maps 23-24, Stonehouse (canal) to Penn Wood

Scenic route: 4 miles/6.5km – 1½-2hrs
Shorter route: 1½ miles/2.4km – 40-50mins

Maps 24-27, Penn Wood to Dursley

6½ miles/10.4km – 3¼-4hrs

Maps 27-30, Dursley to Wotton-under-Edge

Direct route: 4½ miles/7.2km – 2¼-2¾hrs
Scenic route: 6¾ miles/11km – 3¼-3¾hrs

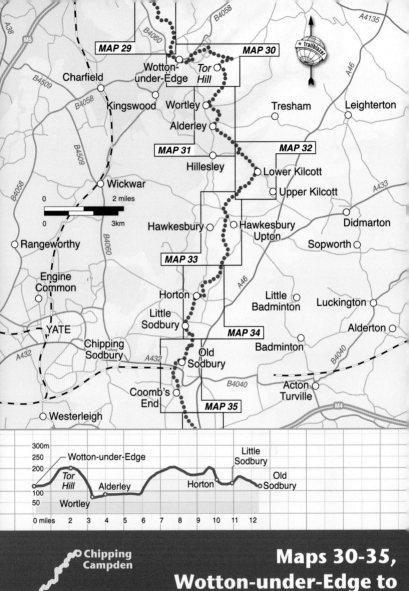

Maps 30-35, Wotton-under-Edge to Old Sodbury

12½ miles/20.4km – 6-7hrs

NOTE: Add 20-30% to these times to allow for stops

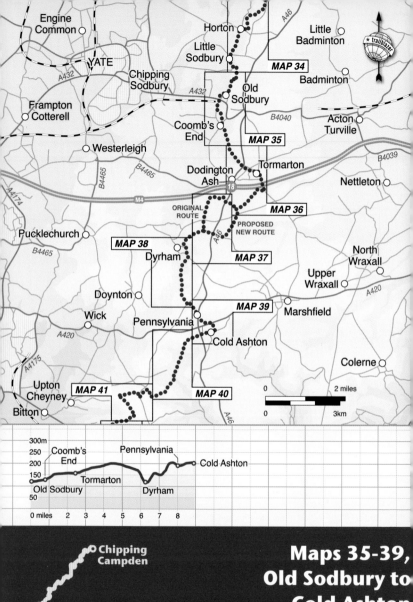

Engine Common

YATE

Chipping Sodbury

A432

Frampton Cotterell

Westerleigh

B4465

B4465

A4174

M4

Pucklechurch

B4465

Doynton

Wick

A420

Upton Cheyney

Bitton

A4175

MAP 41

Horton

Little Sodbury

MAP 34

A432

Old Sodbury

Coomb's End

MAP 35

Dodington Ash

Tormarton

18

ORIGINAL ROUTE

PROPOSED NEW ROUTE

A46

MAP 36

MAP 38

Dyrham

MAP 37

Pennsylvania

Cold Ashton

MAP 39

Marshfield

MAP 40

A46

A46

Little Badminton

Badminton

B4040

Acton Turville

B4039

Nettleton

North Wraxall

Upper Wraxall

A420

Colerne

0   2 miles

0   3km

300m
250
200
150
100
50

Coomb's End

Old Sodbury

Tormarton

Dyrham

Pennsylvania

Cold Ashton

0 miles   2   3   4   5   6   7   8

Chipping Campden

Old Sodbury
Cold Ashton
Bath

Maps 35-39,
Old Sodbury to
Cold Ashton

9 miles/14.2km – 4¼-5hrs
NOTE: Add 20-30% to these times to allow for stops

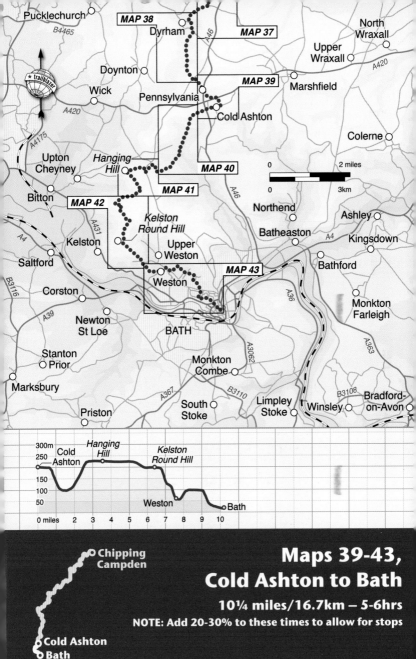

Pucklechurch
B4465

MAP 38
Dyrham
A46
MAP 37

North
Wraxall

Upper
Wraxall
A420

Doynton

Wick

Pennsylvania
MAP 39
Marshfield

Cold Ashton

A4175

Colerne

Upton
Cheyney

Hanging
Hill
MAP 40

Bitton

MAP 42
MAP 41

A46

Northend

Ashley

Kelston
Round Hill

A431

Batheaston
A4
Kingsdown

Kelston

Upper
Weston

Bathford

Saltford
A4

MAP 43

Weston

A36

Monkton
Farleigh

B3116
Corston

A39
Newton
St Loe

BATH

A363

0   2 miles
0   3km

Stanton
Prior

A367
Monkton
Combe

A3062

B3110

B3108

Limpley
Stoke

Winsley

Bradford-
on-Avon

Marksbury

Priston

South
Stoke

300m
250

Cold
Ashton

Hanging
Hill

Kelston
Round Hill

150
100
50

Weston

Bath

0 miles   2   3   4   5   6   7   8   9   10

Chipping
Campden

Maps 39-43,
Cold Ashton to Bath

10¼ miles/16.7km – 5-6hrs
NOTE: Add 20-30% to these times to allow for stops

Cold Ashton
Bath

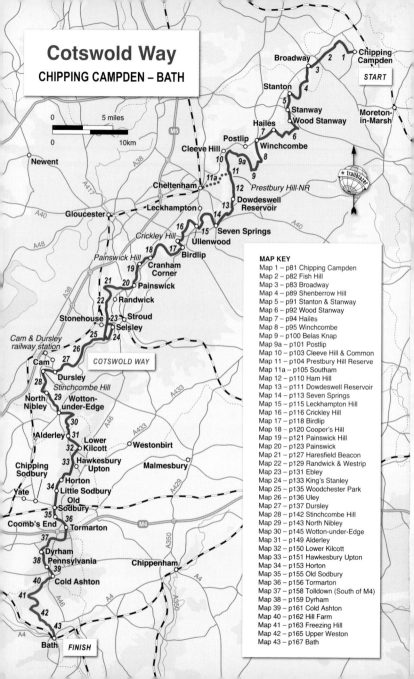

Cotswold Way

CHIPPING CAMPDEN – BATH

START

0 — 5 miles

0 — 10km

Broadway

Chipping Campden

1
2
3

Stanton

4

5

Stanway

Wood Stanway

Hailes

7

6

Postlip

Winchcombe

Cleeve Hill

10

9a

8

9

11

Newent

11a

Cheltenham

12

Prestbury Hill NR

Leckhampton

13

Dowdeswell Reservoir

14

Gloucester

16

15

Seven Springs

Crickley Hill

Ullenwood

18

17

Birdlip

Painswick Hill

19

Cranham Corner

21

20

Painswick

22

Randwick

Stonehouse

23

Stroud

25

Selsley

24

Cam & Dursley railway station

26

Cam

27

COTSWOLD WAY

Dursley

28

Stinchcombe Hill

North Nibley

29

Wotton-under-Edge

30

Alderley

31

Lower Kilcott

32

Westonbirt

33

Hawkesbury Upton

Malmesbury

Chipping Sodbury

34

Horton

Little Sodbury

Yate

Old Sodbury

35

36

Coomb's End

Tormarton

37

Dyrham

38

Pennsylvania

39

Chippenham

40

Cold Ashton

41

42

43

Bath

FINISH

trailblazer

Moreton-in-Marsh

MAP KEY

Map 1 – p81 Chipping Campden
Map 2 – p82 Fish Hill
Map 3 – p83 Broadway
Map 4 – p89 Shenberrow Hill
Map 5 – p91 Stanton & Stanway
Map 6 – p92 Wood Stanway
Map 7 – p94 Hailes
Map 8 – p95 Winchcombe
Map 9 – p100 Belas Knap
Map 9a – p101 Postlip
Map 10 – p103 Cleeve Hill & Common
Map 11 – p104 Prestbury Hill Reserve
Map 11a – p105 Southam
Map 12 – p110 Ham Hill
Map 13 – p111 Dowdeswell Reservoir
Map 14 – p113 Seven Springs
Map 15 – p115 Leckhampton Hill
Map 16 – p116 Crickley Hill
Map 17 – p118 Birdlip
Map 18 – p120 Cooper's Hill
Map 19 – p121 Painswick Hill
Map 20 – p123 Painswick
Map 21 – p127 Haresfield Beacon
Map 22 – p129 Randwick & Westrip
Map 23 – p131 Ebley
Map 24 – p133 King's Stanley
Map 25 – p135 Woodchester Park
Map 26 – p136 Uley
Map 27 – p137 Dursley
Map 28 – p142 Stinchcombe Hill
Map 29 – p143 North Nibley
Map 30 – p145 Wotton-under-Edge
Map 31 – p149 Alderley
Map 32 – p150 Lower Kilcott
Map 33 – p151 Hawkesbury Upton
Map 34 – p153 Horton
Map 35 – p155 Old Sodbury
Map 36 – p156 Tormarton
Map 37 – p158 Tolldown (South of M4)
Map 38 – p159 Dyrham
Map 39 – p161 Cold Ashton
Map 40 – p162 Hill Farm
Map 41 – p163 Freezing Hill
Map 42 – p165 Upper Weston
Map 43 – p167 Bath